# The Greys
## *a long and noble line*

## A biography of the family of Lady Jane Grey

## Anthony Squires

The Silk Press
2002

# Silk Press Books

A division of the Silk Press Limited
14a Bath Street
Hale
Cheshire WA14 2EJ
Telephone 0161 929 4884
Fax 0161 929 8656

ISBN 1 902685-10-5

**Acknowledgement of Copyright**
The publishers would like to thank the following organisations for kindly allowing the reproduction of images in this book:
The National Trust, 36 Queen Anne's Gate, London SW1H 9AS
English Heritage Photographic Library, Saville Row, London W1X 1AB
The Royal Collection, Stable Yard House, St James's Palace, London SW1A 1JR
Courtauld Institute of Art, Somerset House, Strand, London WC2R 0RN

# The Greys: a long and noble line

# *Preface*

THIS book has been written for the general reader. I have borne in mind that many, if not most citizens of Great Britain born after 1960 may well have received little, if any formal instruction in British history. Older readers, on the other hand, may wish to regard the background material included here as a helpful aide memoire.

I have consciously tried to avoid introducing any suggestion of political correctness, the different forms of which have blighted so many historical novels, motion pictures, television documentaries and much popular history. The people of the past can be judged only by the standards of their times.

Before I began research on the line of Greys which included the ill-fated Lady Jane, I wondered why no one had already attempted a serious biography. The reason soon became clear: the great lack of sources for the early years. When one considers the Greys were a wealthy and powerful force through five centuries and must have generated a vast archive of family papers, it comes as a great disappointment to discover that so little has survived.

A huge volume of material from the family's origins to about 1620 has simply disappeared. One wonders if it has not been systematically and deliberately destroyed, as was the case with the Lucy family papers at Charlecote in Warwickshire. In recent years very elderly residents of the village of Newtown Linford in Leicestershire have recalled a bonfire of old documents, which was said to have lasted three days and which probably destroyed a sizeable portion of the early Grey archive, at least that relating to Leicestershire. There is certainly a shortage of diaries, correspondence and other papers which enable the biographer to breathe life into what may otherwise remain as a dry and dusty catalogue of an individual's official activities and duties.

The ways in which individuals are identified has been decided upon in a rather arbitrary manner, but the aim throughout has been to remove any doubt as to who is under discussion at any one time. There were so many men among the Greys named Henry, Thomas, George and Harry that following the titled males through the generations can present problems. The family trees are therefore included to guide the reader.

Spellings have been modernised where this clarifies the meaning or makes for easier reading. Sources are given in abbreviated forms for those who wish to follow up points of interest. Many readers may well wish to dispense with the references and bibliography altogether.

I wish to record my gratitude to the very many people who have assisted in various ways over the years. Firstly, I give special thanks to my colleague Joan Stevenson who has been a constant source of help and encouragement during the many excursions we have shared on the trail of the Greys. Professor Leonard

Cantor read my first draft and made many helpful comments and suggestions. Peter Lee and Clive Alford have shared with me their very considerable knowledge of the Greys at Dunham and without their help any thoughts of publication by me would probably have been abandoned long ago. Margaret Stone and the staff of the National Trust at Dunham Massey and elsewhere were there with help and advice. John Hodgson, who catalogued the Grey papers from Dunham Massey Hall at the John Rylands Library and Sandy Haynes, who is performing much the same sort of task with the Grey archives at Enville, have given outstanding help and support. The Countess of Loudoun and her late husband, Mr Peter Abney-Hastings, gave generously of their time during my research into the Hastings family. David Ramsey has swapped notes and views on the Greys with me over the years and more recently John Crocker, Ernie Miller and Robin Stevenson helped with the technical side of production. My thanks also go to the staff of the many libraries and record offices I have contacted or visited over the years.

**Anthony Squires**
**Cosby, Leicester**
**November 2002**

*Arms of Harry Grey, 4th Earl of Stamford*

# Contents

# Illustrations

# The Grey Family: a long and noble line

# *Introduction*

THERE can be few more poignant and widely known episodes in English history than the life and death of Lady Jane Grey, the "Nine Day Queen". The details of her short life and the circumstances surrounding her execution have echoed down the centuries and have been the subject of at least two major motion pictures. With the benefit of hindsight, we can appreciate only too well how Jane was the victim of a deadly mix of social, economic and religious factors, compounded by her parents' greed and ambition, which together produced a national crisis in mid-16th century England.

The Lady Jane Affair was just one episode in the very varied fortunes of a family which was to prove to be a very long and noble line. From the Middle Ages to the early 18th century, but with the exception of the 50 years following Jane's execution, the leading members of every generation of Greys played prominent roles in national or local affairs. There were two queens and three marquesses before Jane – and her father was also a duke. Thereafter, and over a period of about 50 years, the family slowly regained a prominent position in society. The first Earl of Stamford was a Parliamentary general in the Civil War; his son worked vigorously for the execution of Charles I and was a rival to Cromwell. The Greys were prominent in the Restoration of 1660 and the Glorious Revolution of 1688, both of which events brought a monarch to the English throne.

When Queen Anne dismissed the second Earl of Stamford from all his offices of state in the early 18th century, the Grey family experienced a fundamental and permanent change in their fortunes. Thereafter, they never did return to national office, where the important decisions of government were made. In effect, they retired to their country estates. There, with the exception of the eighth Earl, they found themselves cast in the roles of major landowner, Lord Lieutenant, Justice of the Peace, focus of the local Anglican community, patron of arts, and local arbiter and promoter of many different aspects of good taste and fashion.

Modern historians enjoy the benefits of hindsight which allows judgements to be made with a wide perspective. Our rapidly changing modern world is largely shaped by science and technology and is one of satellites and telecommunication, frozen embryos and sperm banks, instant millionaires and dot.com billionaires, all set against a rapid decline in religious belief and "traditional" values. It requires a great deal of effort to understand the actions of the people of ages past whose circumstances were so different from our own.

A case in point is the family. One may regard one's own marital and other family relationships as sometimes complex and difficult, but they must surely pale into insignificance when seen against the circumstances surrounding aristocratic inter-marriage. Particularly during the Middle Ages, the social, economic and political relationships which might result from a single union could prove so complex that today they almost defy description and beggar belief. But again, unless an effort is made to understand the forces, motives and relationships which shaped these early lives, our ancestors may simply remain to us as characters on a distant stage, acting out unfathomable dramas.

The Grey family of this book derive their title from the village of Groby (pronounced "Grooby") which lies five miles north-west of Leicester. Over much of the period covered in these pages (circa 1450 to 1976), there were many other persons named Grey (variously Greye, Gray and Graye) in prominent social, religious or political positions. Some, such as the different lines of Greys of Shirland, of Sandiacre, of Rotherfield and of Bassett House, died out in the titled line by the reign of Elizabeth I. Only the Greys of Groby descended to the late 20th century in the unbroken titled male line.

The difficulty in determining kinship in this and other aristocratic families is compounded by the practice of members referring to even very distant relatives as "cousin". However, by the 17th century and with few exceptions, the various families called Grey shared nothing but their surname. George Harry, the fifth Earl of Stamford (1737-1819), was no discernible relative of Charles Grey, second Earl Grey (1764-1845) the Whig prime minister popularly remembered for his reforms and a blend of tea. Similarly the tenth Earl of Stamford (1896-1976) had no family ties with Edward Grey, Viscount Grey of Falloden (1862-1933), the Liberal foreign secretary and distinguished ornithologist, who metaphorically saw the lights go out all over Europe at the start of the First World War.

Very closely bound up with the history of the Greys of Groby is that of another aristocratic family, the Hastings, who also arrived in Leicestershire during the late Middle Ages. The fortunes of one cannot be adequately accounted for without reference to the activities of the other. Rivalry and conflict between the two emerged in the mid 1400s, reached a peak on the battlefields of the Civil War of the 17th century and flickered to a close on the race courses of England 200 years later. Over four centuries and longer, it seemed the two families found themselves on opposing sides in just about every national crisis. Such a long-term inter-family feud is perhaps without parallel within the English aristocracy.

In many respects the story of the Greys differs only in detail from the histories of many other aristocratic families. Unlike the Howards (Dukes of Norfolk), the Grosvenors (Dukes of Westminster) and Stanleys (Earls of Derby), the Greys of Groby did not manage to stay the course to the end of the 20th century.[1] The tenth and last Earl of Stamford led what he thought was an aristocratic lifestyle, but he committed the cardinal error of leaving no male heir. He was an old man in the 1960s and 70s and did not adapt readily to rapidly changing economic conditions and, for his class, the very hostile social forces which were sweeping the nation. With him, it seems as though his noble line had lost its way, had run out of steam and he was the one who finally called it a day.

# Chapter 1

# *Family Origins*

T he compilers of noble pedigrees like to feel a certain cachet is attached to showing that an ancestor "came over with the Conqueror". So often there is no hard evidence for such a claim, although a little juggling with the facts may produce a plausible lineage. During the Middle Ages various prominent branches of the Greys liked to believe they were descended from one such eleventh century adventurer whose ancestral home was Croy in Picardy. They would also continue the line back to the Vikings who had settled in France in the eighth century. At the time of Domesday Book (1086), compiled twenty years after the Conquest, one Anchitell Grey is recorded as holding lands in Oxfordshire, including the manor of Rotherfield, and he may well have been a member of Duke William's army.[1] Yet from that time, and for more than a hundred years, there is very little reliable evidence for the descent of that line of the Greys we are following. In the later twelfth century, a certain Henry de Grey had a grant from King Richard I of the manor of Thurrock in Essex.[2] Henry's great grandson, also Henry, married twice and from his three sons descended in turn the main medieval lines of the Greys. These included the Greys of Codnor, the Greys of Wilton, the Greys of Sandiacre, the Greys of Ruthin, the Greys of Kent and, in due course, the Greys of Groby.

It was from Henry Grey of Thurrock's second son, John, by his second wife Emma, that our line sprang (see the family tree). Their first son Reginald (?-1308), who fought in Edward I's campaigns in the wild valleys and mist-shrouded mountains of Wales, was summoned to Parliament as first Lord Grey of Wilton.[3] Reginald's son was John, second Lord Wilton, who fought at the English victory on the field of Bannockburn. Three generations later, another Reginald was the celebrated 3rd Lord Ruthin. He died in 1441 at the amazing age of about 80, and of natural causes rather than by the sword in the mud of a battlefield.[4]

This Reginald Grey, Lord of Ruthin, led a very full life. Much of his time was spent serving the King in Parliament, in ceremonies of state, in administrative positions of the realm, and fighting the King's enemies both at home and abroad. While serving in North Wales in 1402 he was taken prisoner by the notorious chieftain Owen Glendower. His release cost him 10,000 marks (£6,600), a truly ruinous sum. His capture was as much a political act by Glendower as it was a simple demand for a ransom, for about this time the early rumblings could be detected of what was later to become civil war in England. In the hidden valleys of Wales Glendower was plotting with the Yorkist Mortimers, but Reginald of Ruthin had a strong Lancastrian background. Reginald also claimed to be the heir to the arms, titles and lands of Edward Hastings, late Earl of Pembroke, but he had to wait twenty years before a decision in his favour was forthcoming. This lengthy and particularly acrimonious dispute was to mark the beginning of a deep animosity between the families

*Groby Old Hall, Leicestershire circa 1800. The ancestral home of the Greys*

of Hastings and Grey, a relationship which was destined to rumble on down through the centuries.[5]

The second wife of Reginald, 3rd Lord Ruthin, was Joan, the daughter of Sir William Astley. That family's lands lay in Warwickshire and they were to remain an important part in the rise and fall of the fortunes of many generations of the Greys. By Joan, Lord Ruthin had three sons. The youngest, Robert, married Eleanor Lowe who brought to him estates at Enville in Staffordshire, a similarly important property in the story of the Greys of Groby. The second son, John gave rise to a dynasty of Greys at Barwell and Basset House in south-west Leicestershire. But it was the marriage of oldest son Edward to Elizabeth Ferrers, the heiress of Henry, Baron Ferrers of Groby in the same county, which concerns us here.

Uncertainty concerning their origins in England also surrounded the Ferrers family. Henry Ferrers (?died 1138) was granted the castle of Tutbury in the early 12th century, although it was held at the time by a Norman, Hugh de Abrincis. It is therefore possible that Henry arrived in England after the Conquest. For his support in the governance of England, he was rewarded by King Henry I with extensive lands, particularly in Derbyshire and Leicestershire.[6] His son, Robert, was subsequently created Earl of Derby for his sterling services to the crown. Four generations later, after the death of William de Ferrers in 1254, this illustrious line divided. The senior branch descended from Robert to become the Ferrers of Chartley, the Devereux Lords Ferrers, Viscounts Hereford and Earls of Essex. It was from Sir Robert's younger brother, William, that the cadet line descended as the Ferrers of Groby.[7]

The Groby Ferrers were ennobled when William Ferrers' son, also William, was summoned repeatedly to royal service by both Edward I and Edward II. Five more generations of father and son served their monarchs well, holding many offices of state and seeing military command in France, Gascony, Scotland, Wales and in that sink of many military and political careers – Ireland. When Henry Lord Ferrers of Groby died in 1445 he left a granddaughter, Elizabeth, as his sole heir. It was she who married the dashing Sir Edward Grey, thus re-establishing a link between the two noble families of Grey and Ferrers which had first taken place a century and a half earlier.[8]

Sir Edward must have congratulated himself on making such a good marriage, at least as far as the "worldly goods" part of the contract was concerned. To his own modest lands and his £40 a year as a retainer of the Duke of Buckingham, he could now add the estates of his wife. She was the sole heiress to what in truth was one of the wealthiest baronies in England, the lands of which extended over nine counties and generated a rent roll of £606 a year. Sir Edward had seen the Ruthin title pass to his nephew but he instead gained the ancient title of Lord Ferrers of Groby, even if it was in the right of his wife. This first son of a second marriage was to found the line of Greys of Groby. Their further descent from Edward's son, Sir John, and his wife, Elizabeth Woodville, was to prove more interesting and eventful than Sir Edward could probably have ever imagined.

In the strict hierarchy of medieval times the leading nobles held the land, the basis of all wealth, position and power, direct from the King. He distributed and retrieved – at his absolute discretion – honours, rewards, grants and offices of profit. In return, the nobles were expected to attend Parliament when summoned and carry out the business of the government of the realm, all at his behest and according to his delegation. This was their duty which could not be avoided; a quiet life by the fireside was very seldom an option, even in old age. There was no organised central government since the King did no more than shield his subjects from foreign invasion, protect existing rights and allow a man and his family to live peacefully at the level at which they found themselves. The lack of a standing army meant the nobles, such as the Greys, had to be proficient in the martial arts, be able to supply fighting men from their tenants and lead them on the battlefield at the King's command. The system of primogeniture, inheritance by the first born son, ensured that estates held together so that nobles remained wealthy enough to fulfil their obligations.

Government was a constantly shifting agreement between monarch and nobles. They in their turn watched each other minutely. David Starkey has pointed out that the system of noble hierarchy and government meant that everything was, in effect, a political act, not only marrying, but praying, the enjoyment of leisure and, of course, dying. Everything in a man's life, including his friends and even members of his own family, were sacrificed to power.[9] Over-mighty subjects and the power politics they and their families generated posed an ever present danger; effective government was thus very dependent on the personal qualities of the monarch. A regal minority was a special problem as the rival noble claimants jostled and fought for the custody and upbringing of the future king, or intrigued to displace him. The mingling of personal attitudes and the considerations of kinship were mixed in the approach to public duties. The changing of sides by a family to support a victor did not necessarily mean disaster for the members concerned; pardon by the monarch for leaders vanquished in battle was a regular occurrence.

The small number, between 50 and 60, of the leading noble families in late 15th century England meant that the supply of suitable marriage partners at any one time was very limited. The production of legitimate male offspring for the transmission of titles and landed estates, was the chief concern of every high born family, especially since noble lines were apt to die out in the third or fourth generation for lack of a suitable heir. Any feelings of love or affection between the two parties brought together in matrimony was seen by them and their families as a bonus. Marriages were often between young children and betrothal was even between unconceived and unborn, but anticipated, offspring. A woman without a husband had no legal and very limited social standing unless she was the widow of a lord. The provision for dowry and dower was a perennial problem, although a bride who was a wealthy peeress in her own right might alleviate the burden. Since the fortunes of noble families were so tightly tied to national interests, permission to marry was the gift of the king. To act otherwise was a very grave offence.

To this competitive, ever-changing and usually volatile noble society of 15th century England were added the threads of the dynastic problems following the death of King Edward III. Of his four sons, the leading antagonists were Edmund, Duke of York, and John (of Gaunt), Duke of Lancaster. Throughout the late 14th and 15th centuries tensions grew and politics became polarised as the leaders, their descendants and adherents plotted and vied for the crown. Matters reached a head during the reign of the inept Lancastrian King Henry VI (1422-1461). Between 1455 and 1487 took place the extended struggle for supremacy between York and Lancaster which was to become known as the Wars of the Roses. So bitter were the conflicts that fortunes, estates, titles and not infrequently noble lives could be lost on the outcome of a single battle. Caught up and swept along in a vortex only partly of their making, the various branches of the Greys, including the Greys of Groby, played an important role in the anarchy and mayhem and in its aftermath.

# Chapter 2

# *The Rise to Power*

## Thomas Grey and the Woodvilles (to 1471)

The Ferrers of Groby had long been supporters of the Yorkist cause, but with the marriage of Sir Edward Grey and Elizabeth Ferrers the Lancastrian allegiance of the Greys had prevailed. A bride of suitable social and political background was sought for their son, the young Sir John Grey. The chosen lady was Elizabeth Woodville, eldest daughter of Sir Richard Woodville (or Widville) and Jacquetta, Duchess of Bedford. The Woodvilles, however, had no special standing. They were just a decent country family with lands in five counties who had filled offices of local government since the 14th century. Sir Richard Woodville had served Henry VI in France, was knighted at Leicester and had succeeded to the modest but ancient family estates, including that at Grafton in Northamptonshire. He had a big and athletic frame and was considered one of the most handsome men in England.

His wife Jacquetta was of different origins altogether. Her first husband had been a king's son and, as the sister of the Count of Pol, she had high aristocratic connections in Luxembourg. At seventeen she became the wife of the ageing John of Lancaster, Duke of Bedford. Then, within eighteen months of the Duke's death, she married Woodville. For him it was a stroke of good fortune for it lifted him from the lower gentry to the impoverished end of the peerage. However, they had married in secret and without the King's licence and this brought down the royal wrath and a fine of £1,000. Later in the same year they were pardoned. Elizabeth, their third child, was born in 1437 and became the sought after bride of Sir John Grey. To Sir John and Elizabeth two sons were born: Thomas (later Marquess of Dorset) and Richard. It was during the boys' formative years that the Wars of the Roses engulfed the nation and the Greys.

The need to take sides in the conflict divided the different lines of Greys, who by this time were sharing a common surname rather than any close ties of kinship. Richard, Lord Grey of Powys, fought at Ludworth in 1459 on the side of the Yorkists, only to surrender to the King and forfeit his estates. Reginald, Lord Grey of Ruthin, took the field for the same cause at the Yorkist victory of Mortimers Cross. Of the Lancastrian Greys, Sir Reginald, third son of Viscount Lisle, fell as his side triumphed at Wakefield. At Northampton in 1460, Edward Grey, Earl of Kent, was leading the King's rear guard when he went over to the Earl of Warwick, a move that decided the day in favour of the Yorkists. The following year, in the merciless slaughter in a snow storm at Towton which brought Edward of York to the throne, even Earl Rivers switched loyalties. There is a cruel irony in the fact that, in the great triumph of the Lancastrians at the second battle of St Albans (February 1461), one of the very few gentlemen of quality among the victors who were killed was Sir John Grey of Groby.

ELIƷABETH . REGINA . REGIS .
EDWARDI . ANGLIE . ✕

*Elizabeth Woodville, wife of Edward IV (R Van der Weyden)*

So it was that Dame Elizabeth Grey found herself a widow with two small sons to support and on the slenderest of means. Sir John Grey's lands had come to her by jointure but they had been confiscated by the new Yorkist administration and Elizabeth's problems were pressing. Such influence that her mother, Jacquetta, could bring to bear at court was to prove fruitless. After several months of waiting for her case to be heard, Elizabeth decided on a personal approach to the King.

At this time Elizabeth was aged 27 with looks which had hardly diminished by bearing two children and the sorrows of family loss. According to the chronicler Hall, "She was a woman more of formal countenance than of excellent beauty, but yet of such beauty and favour with her sober demeanour, lovely looking and female smiling (neither too wanton nor too humble), beside her tongue was eloquent and her wit so pregnant."[1] Above all it was her long blonde hair, sleek and shining and almost to her knees, which first attracted the King. Yet at the same time her attractive features and good carriage could be marred by a petulant drooping mouth, which rendered her shrewd and calculating rather than generous, gracious and queenly.[2]

Of Edward, all were agreed that he was generously blessed with good looks. To the writer of the *Croyland Chronicle* he was "a person of most elegant appearance and remarkable above all others for the attraction of his person". According to another, "King Edward was very tall of personage, exceeding the stature of almost all others, of comely visage, pleasant look, broad chested, the residue even to his feet proportionally correspondent".[3] A strong, athletic and virile man, he was made for the pleasures of the flesh. He was also aided by a powerful memory which enabled him to recall at an instant the names and estates of most of his subjects from the highest lord to the humblest private gentleman.[4]

The story of the couple's meeting at Grafton is well known. Elizabeth had contrived to present her case to the King when he was out hunting. Beneath an oak tree he pressed himself upon her, but neither reward nor menaces, not even his dagger at her throat, would make her submit to his passion. It was to be the crown or nothing, she told him.[5] She had no wish to become just his latest mistress, to be cast off when he tired of her. Later, on 1st May 1464, according to an anonymous chronicler, they married "in a most secret manner ... which spousals were solemnised early in the morning at a town named Grafton, near Stoney Stratford, at which marriage was no person present but the spouses, the Duchess of Bedford her mother, the priest, and two gentle women, and a young man to help the priest sing."[6]

After the ceremony they went to bed for three or four hours before the groom returned to Stoney Stratford, claiming he had been out hunting the whole day. Five months later Edward was finally obliged to reveal his secret to an astonished court and country. The deed was done and Elizabeth was Queen of England.

Even before she set about having a family with the King, Elizabeth moved to secure the future of her two sons, Thomas and Richard Grey, who now found themselves royal stepsons. A serious problem was the fact that her mother-in-law, Lady Ferrers of Groby, had remarried and her new husband, Viscount Bouchier, had a very powerful voice at court. It seemed very likely that the Ferrers inheritance might pass to the Bouchiers rather than the Grey brothers. In a bid to press her claim Elizabeth sought a powerful ally in the form of William Lord Hastings, the King's closest confidant. The deal they struck shows clearly how children were bought and sold in the cause of inheritance and how short the lives of the principals might be. The thirteen year-old Thomas Grey (or if he should die his brother Richard) was to marry the eldest daughter born to Lord Hastings within the following five or six years. If no daughter appeared, the choice would be one of the daughters of Ralph, his brother and, if that arrangement failed, to one of the daughters of Dame Anne Ferrers, their sister.[7] Following such a marriage, all the profits of the lands recovered for Thomas (or Richard) were to be divided equally between Elizabeth and Lord Hastings. The cost of the marriage to Lord Hastings' daughter was to be 500 marks (£333) with a refund of 250 marks from Elizabeth if both of the boys should die.[8]

The elaborate scheme however came to naught; but in 1466 the Queen engineered a second marriage, this time between Thomas, then aged fifteen, and Lady Anne Holland. Anne was the only child of the Duke of Exeter and his Duchess, who was Thomas' step-aunt and also sister of the King. There was a problem: Anne was already betrothed to another man and her release by the Duchess from the arrangement cost the Queen 4,000 marks. After less than a year of marriage to Thomas, Anne died leaving the usual problems of the wardship of an under-aged heiress. What had promised to be a sound investment for the Greys turned out to be a very costly failure.[9] Later, in 1483, the Queen negotiated yet another marriage, this time between her infant grandson, also called Thomas, and the deceased Anne's half sister. This Lady, who was ancestor of the House of Manners, later Earls of Rutland, had been made Exeter's heir. The arrangement, from which Richard Grey was also to benefit financially, cost the Queen 5,000 marks, payable as a sweetener to her husband, the King! In the event this marriage, too, did not take place, but the legislation to disinherit the Hollands was to inflict serious damage on the Woodvilles' reputation and standing in the country.

Against this background of social and political intrigue and family acrimony, there is no record of Thomas Grey's personal relationship with his royal stepfather. Neither is it known where the young man lived or who were the important male influences during his formative years. Over a period of a decade or so, he was in the company of men of fortune, hordes of scheming aunts, uncles, cousins and half cousins and a myriad of even more distant kin. His mother had a total of eleven brothers and sisters and she used her influence at court to set about making good marriages for as many of them as possible.

Elizabeth the Queen was very conscious that people saw her as an upstart who had seemingly inherited her mother's supposed powers of sorcery to bewitch the King into marriage. At a time when personal relationships with the monarch dominated politics, the royal court was so much the centre of patronage as to be, in the words of J R Lander, "almost the stock exchange of the day'.[10] Working from within, Elizabeth recognised and made the most of the opportunities to rebuild her family's fortunes and advance its status. The court, wrote Paul Kendall Murray, was "like a tropical garden, not altogether reclaimed from the jungle; overheated, luxuriant in blooms of pageantry and the varicoloured plumage of tilting knights, rustling with the endless whispers of faction, dense with suspicion, half truths and hatred".[11]

In retrospect Elizabeth's marriage to the King can be seen as the worst possible mix of social, political and economic factors, to say nothing of the moral and legal considerations. It was also unfortunate for the King that so many of his wife's generation had survived childhood. Prior to 1461 the Woodvilles had concluded two other good marriages: Elizabeth's sister Jacquetta to Lord Strange of Knockin and her brother, Anthony Woodville, to Lady Scales. For the Woodvilles the gates to the marriage market stood wide open.

Of Elizabeth's other brothers, John Woodville, in search of a fortune, married Catherine Neville, the three times widowed Duchess of Norfolk and the King's aunt. He was aged 20 and she was said to be about 80 but was probably nearer 65, yet she outlived him by fourteen years.[12] Another brother, Lionel Woodville, was made Bishop of Salisbury aged 29. His bishopric along with all the others in the country was in effect an

*Earl Rivers presenting Caxton to Edward IV (from a manuscript in Lambeth Palace)*

administrative position but it could be said to be quite wealthy and was probably on a par with that of Norwich which was worth £900 a year.[13] Two of Elizabeth's other sisters also achieved success in entering the peerage. In particular, Katharine was hitched to the boy Duke of Buckingham, much to that young man's disgust. Finally Richard Woodville, father of the brood, was created Earl Rivers and given the Treasurership of England, a post which allowed a corrupt man unrivalled opportunity to siphon off money to his own ends. The Woodvilles "whose arrogance shone as brightly as the newness of their fortunes" appeared to have made a clean sweep of the peerage, a fact deeply resented and long remembered by those families who felt they had been excluded.[14]

Seven Woodville marriages and two major promotions within two years only added to long standing jealousies and hatred in royal circles and added to the King's difficult social juggling act and political chess game. The hordes of Woodvilles and their dependents had become a political force at court. Ranged against them were most of the Nevilles, the King's own family, whose fractious members naturally coveted the important positions of power and authority. Edward's cousin, the Earl of Warwick, known to history as "the kingmaker", particularly resented Edward's marriage to Elizabeth and the rise of the upstart Woodvilles. This explosive situation resulted in Warwick imprisoning Edward for a time and in the deaths of the Queen's father, Rivers, and brother John. Eventually, Edward escaped to Holland, returned with an army and killed his cousin in battle at Barnet in April 1471.

If Thomas Grey, still in his teenage years, was expecting further royal preferment during these roller coaster years he was to be disappointed. He had yet to prove himself not only as a man but, as the oldest son of a Lancastrian family, also a loyal subject of a Yorkist king. Loyalty and service, rather than rank and the length of one's family tree, were the two qualities that now gathered rewards.

Thomas' opportunity came in May 1471 at Tewkesbury when he fought for his stepfather in the battle which saw the collapse of the Lancastrian cause. When, a few weeks later, he took his place at court, it was as a man eager to make the most of the opportunities this new status presented. The world, so he believed, lay at his feet.

# Chapter 3

# *Affairs of State*

## Thomas Grey and the Woodvilles (to 1483)

Thomas Grey did not have long to wait in order to make his mark in royal circles and in 1471 he was created Earl of Huntingdon. This was a title which had been held since the Conquest by members of some of the noblest families in England including the Hollands, his late wife's family.[1] His mother the Queen, secure in the defeat and death of Warwick in April of that same year and having produced a royal male heir, found her husband amenable to a certain amount of wifely influence and pillow talk. For Thomas it was a promising start.

At least for the time being the King believed there was no longer any serious danger from the Lancastrians and felt he could relax with his confidants and closest friends. Contemporary observers agreed on his lifestyle and activities. He was usually gentle in nature, cheerful in aspect and was skilled in helping strangers relax when addressing him. He was also fond of the good things in life; his royal person displayed expensive jewels, fine clothes and the latest fashions, and he furnished the many royal residences with furniture, tapestries and other comforts. At the same time, he was successful where so many men before and since have failed: he could control his wife's spending.

Dominic Mancini, a visitor to the royal court in 1483, observed that Edward also had a dark side. "He was licentious in the extreme … he pursued without discrimination the married and the unmarried, the noble and the low … however, he took none by force".[2] In his sessions of worldly excesses and merry making, he was joined by Thomas Grey, Richard Grey, his brother-in-law Sir Edward Woodville and even by his chamberlain, Lord Hastings. Into the early hours they ate, drank and wenched in the King's private chambers. As the Queen later complained of Hastings, one of the few men who could drink her husband under the table: "He was secretly familiar with the King in wanton company".[3]

Of a morning and with better control of his faculties, Thomas Grey returned to the snakes and ladders of court life. Hastings he hated because he was the King's man who had risen from a lowly background through loyalty and ability, rather than through position and birth, to become the monarch's most trusted advisor. He had shared Edward's poverty in exile and the perils of the battlefield. In 1471 Hastings had raised 3,000 men in support of his master's cause and had been rewarded with manors and estates of defeated Lancastrians in the Midlands. Much to Thomas' deep disgust, some of those lands included the manor of Ashby-de-la-Zouch, which lay adjacent to the Greys' own estates in north-west Leicestershire. With his hordes of liveried retainers, Hastings was able to bring much of the north-east Midlands under his tight personal control.

*Jane Shore – from a drawing said to be after an original portrait painted in 1484*

In his turn William Hastings viewed Thomas Grey with equal suspicion and contempt. Grey was a man who had also come from a background which, on his father's side, had been as modest as his own. But Grey, by a stroke of luck and a fit of passion on the part of his mother, had been catapulted to a position which he did not merit and into a world where he did not belong. Everywhere at court and beyond there were Grey's relatives, the Woodvilles, a pack of scheming, ambitious, grasping upstarts, quick to take offence and slow to forgive. Lord Hastings enjoyed the complete trust of his monarch who could view his chamberlain's conflict with Grey only with deep regret. Thomas Grey, the King decided, was acceptable as a drinking companion but he was shifty and scheming and was not to be trusted with the secrets of government. It was to this heady mixture of hatred and intrigue was added another potent factor: mistress Jane Shore.

Jane was the daughter of a prosperous City merchant. As a young woman she had married a mercer much older than herself and while serving in his shop had met Lord Hastings, who had fallen in love with her. In turn she came to the King's attention and on whom she had much the same effect. According to Sir Thomas More, this femme fatale, who could capture men's hearts so easily, was of medium height and of pale complexion with rich golden hair, grey eyes and a full round face, admirably proportioned but inclined to plumpness. Yet it was not so much her beauty which attracted the opposite sex "for a proper (excellent) wit had she and could both read and write, merry of company (and) ready and quick of answer, neither mute nor full of babble'.(4) At this time (1476) the King had three children by his Queen, but this did not prevent him moving Jane to court as a lady's maid. It was here, too, that Thomas Grey met her and silently joined Lord Hastings in a longing for her.

That both men were married was of little consequence. A man of high birth who was not satisfied with his arranged marriage was expected to take a mistress. Hastings had married Katherine Neville, the King's cousin and sister of Richard Neville, Earl of Warwick, "the Kingmaker". She had first been the wife of William, Lord Bonville and her dowry for that marriage had cost her father a very large sum. The Bonvilles, Lancastrians to the end, had extensive estates in the West Country. William, the first Lord Bonville, had married Elizabeth, daughter of the fourth Lord Harrington whose lands lay in the Furness district of Lancashire. Their son, also William, could therefore expect to inherit both titles and a very large fortune in due course. Unfortunately, father and son were killed at the first battle of St Albans (1460) and the sole heir to the titles and the estates was William the Younger's daughter, the six month old Cicely. By Act of Parliament the late Lord Bonville was restored in the blood which meant Cicely would inherit his estates when she reached the age of sixteen. The King at his pleasure granted the wardship of the child to her mother who was now responsible for the administration of some 30,000 Bonville acres which produced an annual income of £1,000.(5)

A struggle for the possession of the inheritance began between Hastings, who was fearing for the security of his wife's jointure, and the grasping Woodville Queen. In the summer of 1474 Hastings made a tactical move. After much bargaining, conducted in the spirit of not allowing a strained relationship to get in the way of a good profit, Thomas Grey was married to the fourteen year old Cicely, now Lady Bonville and Harrington and thus found to his disgust that he had also become his chief enemy's nephew.

The following year Thomas was awarded the Order of the Garter and resigned his Earldom of Huntingdon to become the Marquess of Dorset. The new title recognised his status at court and his connections with the West Country. A dukedom was available for royal sons by birth or marriage, but such an appointment would make an already difficult situation impossible for the King. No, Thomas would have to settle for the dignity and degree of a Marquess and be satisfied with it. From the King's point of view the death of Anne Holland was a blessing, for now the Greys could not pursue a claim to her late father's Exeter dukedom.

In the summer of that year (1475) Dorset also found himself answering the royal summons to serve the King on the invasion of France. Edward had never forgiven the French King for helping his enemies, especially his rebellious cousin Warwick. Subsequently, the King of England had negotiated an alliance with the Duke of Brittany and with his brother-in-law, Duke Charles of Burgundy. It was agreed that the forces of all three would attack France simultaneously. Edward, at the head of an army containing most of the English nobility, would be marching – as he liked to believe – in the footsteps of his warrior ancestors, Edward III and Henry V – in a bid to regain the former English lands in France. Thus it was in July Dorset set sail in an armada of boats, and surrounded by all the paraphernalia of battle: armoured knights with their horses and servants, artillery, bowmen and men-at-arms, 11,000 persons in all. Lord Grey of Codnor, Lord Grey of Ruthin together with a great assemblage of distant relatives, friends and foes were also present. Lord Hastings was present with 40 men and 300 archers.

At Calais they hung around for ten days waiting for Duke Charles and his army to join them, but he did not appear. Eventually they moved off and spent two nights on the battlefield of Agincourt. In vain they waited; Charles had changed his mind and the Duke of Brittany had scarcely stirred. Dorset noted with disgust that his pay of ten shillings a day was barely covering the cost of his expenses during the wretched affair. After a month of no action, a "peace" was negotiated. Edward's large army was bought off with French gold and there were pensions for all his senior nobles. Dorset was outraged when Hastings was given 2,000 crowns a year, the largest pension of all and much larger than his own.[6]

At home and more relaxed, Dorset concentrated his thoughts on the ever-pressing matter of keeping up a household fit for a family of his rank and standing. In June 1477 Cicely produced their third child, a boy who was called Thomas after his father. There had already been two earlier sons but both had died shortly after birth. Young Thomas was a healthy child and seemed destined to carry on the noble line. Over the years six sons and eight daughters were born. The task of finding suitable marriage partners for the offspring of a marquess and a relative of the King, to say nothing of raising money for the dowries the girls would expect of their father when they married, required careful planning. After the execution by the King of his own brother, the Duke of Clarence in February 1478, Dorset received some modest but welcome spoils of the man's estates.[7] These were the keeperships, lordships and masterships of the late Duke's manors. Dorset, of course was not expected to perform more than a supervisory role and scrutinise the accounts of the men who did the actual day-to-day work. Also, important from the financial point of view, was the opportunity to make a very handsome profit from the wardship of Clarence's infant son, the Earl of Warwick.

Of concern to Dorset were the finances of Lord Hastings. The man's extensive estates in the East Midlands, mostly granted by a grateful king for loyal service, generated an immense rent roll. His many offices of steward and constable were also very profitable and extended his influence considerably. He also drew income and the generous pension from abroad. As his wealth had grown he had enlarged and strengthened his castle at Ashby-de-la-Zouch where he added a tower with walls which were eight feet thick and which rose 90 feet to the sky. Also, in 1480, he had begun work on what was to be a magnificent moated country house at nearby Kirby Muxloe, and there were plans for even more houses.[8]

Life at court with all its inherent dangers could also be very enjoyable, especially the noisy and colourful jousting at which Dorset excelled. With his uncle, Earl Rivers, he led the challengers at the jousting following the marriage of the four-year-old Prince of Wales to the six-year-old Norfolk heiress, Anne Mowbray. The Woodvilles liked to believe themselves the dominant force at court and jousting matches and other revelries were opportunities to flaunt their colours and shout their favours so as to emphasise the fact they had the upper hand in affairs of state.

Then in April 1483 disaster struck. The King was suddenly taken ill and died two weeks later "neither worn out with old age nor yet seized with any known kind of malady" recorded the *Croyland Chronicle*.[9] Today we may reasonably suppose that pneumonia complicated by pleurisy or a coronary thrombosis are the two most likely causes.[10]

# Chapter 4

# *Flight into Exile*

## Thomas Grey and the Woodvilles (1483-84)

As the King lay on his death bed he summoned Hastings and Dorset in an effort to reconcile them from what the early Tudor historian Polydore Vergil describes as "the privy hatred" each felt for the other. In the quiet and darkened royal bedchamber the two men solemnly shook hands and vowed mutual forgiveness; but within days of their sovereign's death Hastings enraged Dorset by persuading the grieving Jane Shore to live with him in the apartments provided for her by the King.

Personal problems aside, there was no time for fighting over mistresses. The Queen was not slow to realise the need for immediate action against the dangers in which she and her family now found themselves. The Prince of Wales, aged 12, had succeeded to the crown as King Edward V and his father had appointed Richard Duke of Gloucester, the boy's uncle, as Protector. This was not good news for the Queen, for whoever held the wardship of a minor effectively made all the decisions for him until he came of age. From the Woodvilles' point of view, it was essential that the young King was by his mother's side, protected from his enemies and under her family's control. This would allow a coronation to be held at the earliest possible opportunity; after that the Protector's powers would cease and the young monarch would issue his own commands, guided in everything by his Woodville family. Dorset knew that such an arrangement would please few outsiders. First there was Hastings, the old foe; then there was the immensely rich Duke of Buckingham who had been married very much against his wishes to one of the Queen's sisters; and finally there was Protector Richard himself, a Neville with ambitions like the rest of his family.

The Woodvilles first resolved to take control of London. On 12th April, Dorset, as the newly-appointed Constable of the Tower, clattered his horse over the draw bridge and through the ancient gates to take command and to seize the royal treasure. At about the same time, Sir Edward Woodville set to fitting out the royal fleet under the same dubious authority. For a week Dorset and the Queen dominated the council. With threats, entreaties, bribes and appeals to the members' self interests they gained a majority for their proposals. "We are quite important enough," Dorset had been heard to boast, "to make laws and govern by ourselves without the King's uncle."[1] It was a game of bluff with a high price to pay for the losers.

At the time of the late King's death the persons of importance in the realm were dispersed around the kingdom. The Protector was at his castle at Middleham in Yorkshire and may not have learned of events in the capital for several days had not Lord Hastings promptly dispatched messengers to him with the news.

*Middleham Castle, Yorkshire, for many years the home of Richard, Duke of Gloucester*

Earl Rivers, Dorset's uncle, and Richard Grey, Dorset's brother, were at Ludlow with the young King. It was near Northampton that Gloucester and Buckingham caught up with the royal party en route for London. In an act of blatant treachery, Rivers, Grey and others of the party were arrested and sent north for detention.

The Queen heard the news of the incident towards midnight of the same day and at once moved out of Westminster. She took with her the young Duke of York, her five daughters, her brother bishop Lionel, and as many of her possessions that she could move, to the sanctuary of the Abbot of Westminster's lodging. The early hours of the morning saw a scene of panic and chaos. "Chests, coffers, packes, fordles, trusses all on men's backs, no man unoccupied, some lading, some going, some discharging, some coming for more, some breaking down walls to bring in the next way, and some yet drew to them that hope to carry the wrong way." The Archbishop of York found the Queen "sitting alone on the rushes all desolate and dismayed" and comforted her the best he could.[2] Her world was collapsing around her. Her secret marriage to the King all those years ago had brought a bitter reward; she was detested by the Commons, hated by most of the nobility and was believed by her Neville relatives to have supported and even encouraged the execution of her brother-in-law, the Duke of Clarence. Such, she could now reflect on, was the price of twenty years of scheming, double dealing and avarice.

On 2nd May the Woodville house of cards finally came tumbling down. The city was in panic at the prospect of invasion by Gloucester's 2,000 armed men, even if they were escorting the King. Two days later the boy and his uncle reached the city as Dorset sat in gloomy impotence in sanctuary with his family.

It was not long before his worst fears were confirmed. On the 14th the Protector showed his hand by challenging the legitimacy of the late monarch's marriage to Elizabeth. The young King and all Edward's children, he maintained, were bastards. With rising support and little opposition, Gloucester eventually felt strong enough to deal with the troublesome Lord Hastings. At a meeting of his council Richard struck. Hastings was arrested and according to Sir Thomas More, "was brought forth (from the Tower) into the green beside the chapel within the Tower and his head laid down upon a long log of timber and there stricken

*The Tower of London in the 15th century*

off".[3] It was truly a particularly grizzly and squalid end for such a nobleman but, Dorset mused, his lordship should have realised he was dealing with a tyrant and come to some agreement with the Woodvilles. Now at last he (Dorset) might see Jane Shore, who had been acting secretly as courier of his messages to the outside world, but the Protector was one step ahead of him and had put her in gaol.

In a desperate effort to secure the young King's coronation, the Queen had been persuaded to release the Duke of York to the Protector on the promise of his safe conduct and so that he could play with his brother in the Tower. Since it had been built in the days of William I, the Tower of London had been as much a residence of English monarchs as it had been a gaol. On the face of it the Protector's proposal seemed a reasonable one. It was on 26th June Richard accepted a petition from Parliament, presented to him by Buckingham, which invited him to accept the crown. Dorset was now profoundly suspicious; Buckingham too had a claim to the throne and was acutely aware of the ways of the Nevilles. Thereafter, the two Princes were never seen alive again. Neither were the Queen's father and her second son Richard, executed by order of Gloucester at Pontefract the same week.

Dorset remained angry but powerless in the gloomy, crowded and insanitary confines of the Sanctuary. It was not the place where royal children should be housed never mind brought up. Some sort of rapprochement with Richard, however temporary and insincere, was better than a life sentence behind high walls. Eventually Dorset agreed to attend the King's coronation along with 30 or so other red-robed peers and black-gowned bishops. When he looked around the gathering he noted many shades of Grey were also present: the Earl of Kent, his brother-in-law's father; Viscount Lisle, his paternal uncle; Lord Grey of Powys and the aged Reginald, Lord Grey of Wilton. How many of them, Dorset wondered, would also turn against this King to whom they were now pledging their allegiance.

The uneasy peace which followed the coronation was soon shattered. After barely two weeks Dorset saw his manors in Devon and Cornwall confiscated by royal decree. A month later his opportunity to strike back came when a revolt led by the Duke of Buckingham broke out. Not wishing to join the list of Richard's victims, Dorset slipped out of sanctuary, avoiding the troops who had the surrounding countryside cordoned off and who were searching woods and standing corn with dogs.[4] At first he headed north, then turned south and west for Exeter. There, on 18th October, he led a rising of his tenants along with Thomas St Ledger, the late King's brother-in-law and Peter, bishop of Exeter, one of Dorset's many cousins. In the unseasonal heavy rains Buckingham's rebellion failed and he was executed. Dorset's own action also came to nothing and once again he took flight.

Now the King's wrath knew no bounds. From Leicester he thundered that:

*"the traitorous Thomas, late Marquess of Dorset, which not fearing God, nor the peril of his soul, hath many and sundry maids and widows and wives, damnably and without shame, devoured, deflowered and defouled, holding the unshameful and mischievous woman called Shaw's wife in adultery".*[5]

A fine piece of character assassination indeed, and to drive the message home he put a price of 1,000 marks on Dorset's head.

With all hope of reconciliation with the new regime gone, Dorset had no choice but to flee the country. With his mother and family still in sanctuary, the Marquess and his six year-old son Thomas took a boat to Brittany. Here they joined the small band of exiles gathered around the Welshman Henry Tudor, Earl of Richmond and pretender to the English throne.

# Chapter 5

# *The King's Loyal Servant?*

**Thomas Grey (1484-1501)**

In the ancient town of Vannes in southern Brittany, Dorset found himself among the exiles, now several hundred strong, who had deserted Richard or, like himself, had been driven from the kingdom. When he looked around, Dorset saw the Woodvilles and their friends were well represented. Apart from himself and his son Thomas, there was bishop Lionel who had also escaped from sanctuary, Richard Woodville (Earl Rivers) and Sir Edward Woodville who had already been resident for several weeks.

Life in the town was pleasant enough for these men of fortune, at least as far as material comforts were concerned. There was an allowance from Duke Francis of 400 livres a month for Dorset and more than enough ale houses and stews to draw the money from his pockets. In the glittering surroundings of Vannes Cathedral he had joined Richmond in making offerings at the high altar. With the Earl now styling himself "King of England", the town was almost a court in exile; but not quite. Deprived of position, wealth, family contact and the gossip of a real court there was a strange unease, a feeling of unreality, and an urgent desire on the part of the exiles to return home victorious.

Later the following year the political climate in Brittany changed abruptly. Duke Francis had come to an understanding with the English King that the exiles would no longer be welcome in Brittany and they would receive no more shelter from him. A quick move was vital, and so it was that Richmond's followers found themselves in the bustling world of the French capital, Paris. Here, moves to mount an invasion of England quickened. Plans were drawn up and the long arm of secret diplomacy reached out to those parts of Europe from which it was thought help might be forthcoming.

It was not long before messengers brought Dorset news from England that his mother had reached an understanding with King Richard. Reading between the lines of her letters, Dorset could well believe that life in the Sanctuary had become impossible. Richard, she told him, had made a promise that she and her daughters would be allowed their freedom, would be treated with respect, and would be provided for in the future. The King had somehow persuaded Elizabeth that he had not been responsible for the disappearance of the Princes in the Tower. Rumours on the streets of London spoke of Buckingham as the culprit and that he was simply waiting for his opportunity to seize the throne. As it was, only the two young boys – if indeed they were still alive – and their so-called Protector uncle stood in his way. As far as Dorset could see, his best prospects lay in England with Richard rather than with Richmond. Even if the Earl was able to mount an invasion, Dorset, from his knowledge of the plans and preparations, may very well have decided it was far from certain to succeed.

Early the following year, Dorset with his son Thomas set off secretly by night on the long and difficult ride along muddy roads to Flanders where they would look for a boat to England. Their absence was soon noticed; Dorset knew too much about the Earl's plans for invasion and had to be stopped. Richmond's riders in pursuit eventually caught up with the fugitives near the border and Dorset was persuaded to return with them. His flight was an act of perfidy which he and his son would come to regret.

On 1st August 1485 Richmond, at the head of his tiny invading force, set out from Harfleur for England. Three weeks later he defeated Richard on Bosworth Field. The violent end of the King was seen as God's favour to the victors, for was it not true that the Almighty gave and took away kingdoms on the field of battle? Richard's death was to mark the end of the lawlessness of the Plantagenet Kings. Henry of Richmond as King Henry VII set out to mould a new regime, one dedicated to the reconciliation of the warring Houses of York and Lancaster and one which would see the dawning of a new age in English history. Dorset meanwhile had been left behind in France as surety for a debt owed by Richmond to the French King. This left the Marquess isolated in exile, out of touch and deeply troubled. If Richmond did not triumph in battle, Dorset could expect a long and even permanent exile in poverty. If the invasion was successful Richmond may well decide simply to forget about Dorset, leaving him to the mercy of the French King.

At the English court the spirit of reconciliation which had arisen for the many vanquished at Bosworth slowly moved in Dorset's favour. In his first Parliament, Henry reversed the attainder which Richard had placed on the Marquess. Without this Dorset would remain a nobody, for an act of this nature was the most solemn penalty known to the Common Law. Attainder for treason, as in Dorset's case, meant that a man forfeited to the crown all his lands and possessions and could expect imprisonment, torture or even a trip to the scaffold. If charged and found guilty under the term "corruption of the blood", he could expect legal death for himself and his family. Such acts of apparent great clemency like that now shown by Henry towards him and many others were not uncommon. A monarch on a shaky throne needed the cooperation of great regional magnates in order to help manage his realm. Dorset would probably be useful to the King, if carefully watched and supervised.

Restored to apparent favour in court circles, Dorset had time to take stock. Most, but not all of his estates were returned to him. Some of his manors of the Harrington inheritance, such as Chorley and Bolton-le Moor, were withheld. Others were now lost permanently including those which Henry had granted to Lord Stanley in recognition of that peer's contribution to the victory at Bosworth.[1] As a result of his perfidy in France, and in order to ensure his attainder was reversed, Dorset had been obliged to renounce all grants made to him by Edward IV, except those concerned with his creation of Marquess of Dorset.[2] Perhaps most vexing was the renouncing of all agreements concerning the vast estates of the Duke of Exeter, his first wife's father, and of the very profitable wardship and marriage of the Earl of Warwick. Dorset may have reached the position of Privy Councillor but there was no place for him in the King's inner circle where the most important decisions of state were made.

To add to Dorset's list of grievances was the favour shown to the 19 year-old Edward Hastings, the son of the executed Lord William Hastings. Like Dorset, Edward had also married a wealthy heiress who was a peeress in her own right. At first he supported Richard but later had a change of mind and, with men from his Midlands estates, had fought for Richmond at Bosworth. It was plain to all that his family's star was rising once again and this was a matter of great concern for a man in Dorset's circumstances.

On 14th January 1486, Henry, now by the Grace of God King of England, married Elizabeth the Queen dowager's daughter, who was also Dorset's step sister. The marriage was above all an act of statesmanship, but it also drew the monarch and the Marquess into a relationship which was only to add to the problems of both men.

The following year Dorset again came under suspicion from the King. A challenger to the throne had appeared in the person of a twelve year-old boy called Lambert Simnel. He was put forward by exiled Yorkists as Edward Plantagenet, Earl of Warwick and son of the late Duke of Clarence, who had been Dorset's step uncle. Although it was widely known that Simnel was an imposter, the son of a baker, the rebels gathered an army and mounted an invasion led by John de-la-Pole, Earl of Lincoln. At this Dorset found himself in the grim confines of the Tower, not this time as Constable but as captive and alongside the real Earl of Warwick, his former ward. There had been rumours that Dorset might have been in touch with the rebels. Lord Dorset, the King gave out, would surely not mind a spell in the Tower if he was a true friend. It was a warning which was not wasted. In a savage and most bloody clash of arms at Stoke near Newark, the invaders including Lincoln, were defeated and Simnel's cause collapsed. A few days later Dorset breathed the air of freedom once again. His spell in the Tower marked the beginning of what was later to become a monstrous game of stick and carrot by a king more cunning and wily than the entire Woodville family.

During the following three years Dorset kept his head down and did the King's bidding in various offices of state. These were the masterships of parks and forests, the stewardships of various royal manors and the responsibility for collecting customs and subsidies. At the same time he was losing members of his family. Sir Edward Woodville was killed in service abroad and three of his half sisters had died. Sir Richard Woodville, the last Earl Rivers, had died too, and lacking heirs, had left Dorset his estates including property in Calais.

It was early in 1492 that Dorset's mother, now a sick and frail woman, was granted a pension by the King and entered the Nunnery of Bermondsey, where she was to spend her last few months of life. The building stood half a mile below the Tower and on the opposite bank of the Thames in green and pleasant countryside. The King, it was whispered, had taken the opportunity to rid himself of his fractious mother-in-law. In the nunnery she was well out of sight and her wagging tongue could do him no harm. At the end of the first week in June she died with Dorset and her surviving daughters around her bed. After a simple and private funeral, hardly befitting a former Queen of England, she was laid to rest in St George's Chapel at Windsor, close to the body of her late husband.

During her final days in religious calm and contemplation this remarkable woman could reflect on the extraordinary course of her life. Her two husbands had both died suddenly, one on the battlefield and the other in bed. One of her first husband's brothers died in battle; of those of her second husband, one perished the same way and one was murdered. Her father was murdered as was her younger son Richard. Of her siblings she alone reached the age of forty. All seven sisters had died before her. Of her brothers, two were beheaded, one died in battle and one died young. She had married a king in great secrecy and had given him ten children. Two were murdered (in the Tower), and four died at the young ages of fourteen, ten, two and a few weeks. She had been forced to share her husband with numerous mistresses, notably Jane Shore. In addition, she had been highly unpopular with most of the nobles and throughout her life her personal safety had frequently been at risk. She had lost wealth, position, family and even the opportunity of a second crown. But at least she had the satisfaction of knowing that she had outlived that dreadful old dragon Lady Ferrers, her mother-in-law, who had cruelly attempted to deprive her son Thomas of his rightful Ferrers inheritance.

A few days before Elizabeth's death, the King waved a very big stick at Dorset to ensure he remained, as the royal missive had it, "loving and true".[3] In return for a pardon for unspecified offences, the Marquess was to surrender the great bulk of his estates and those of his wife Cicely to crown-nominated trustees who were to draw the profits for the King. Dorset was to receive such income as the King judged he needed. Moreover, Dorset was to supply the King in writing with any and all information he might learn about any plots or treasons against the royal person. All evil rumours, seditious whispers and disloyal mutterings were to be relayed to the monarch. Should the Marquess have the misfortune to be taken prisoner abroad, any ransom would be paid from the sale of his manors.[4] The King had not finished there. Dorset was to relinquish the wardship and marriage of his own son Thomas. The boy, then aged fifteen, was to remain in England under close royal supervision. If he was married by the age of nineteen, when the King returned him to his father, the Marquess would pay the King £10,000.[5] Finally, Dorset was to find persons willing to put up a total of £10,000 bail. In order to meet this monstrous imposition, no fewer than 55 relatives and friends were persuaded to come forward. The list was headed by John Grey, Viscount Lisle, and Henry Lord Grey of Codnor, each with £1,000. At the bottom of the list, with modest but welcome support, was Thomas Quadryng, "mercer", with £50. If the Marquess behaved himself, the King would be prepared to forgive, at least in a legal and a financial sense. The noose around the Marquess' neck would be loosed, at least a little.

It was little consolation to Dorset to know he was not alone in such a humiliating situation. Henry Percy, the Earl of Northumberland, Lord Abergavenney, Richard Grey, the Earl of Kent and Dorset's relative, together with a good many others regarded as having malcontented dispositions were treated similarly. This government "in terrorum" proved to be so successful that by 1497 Henry had performed the remarkable feat of transforming his rebellious nobles from feuding semi-regal magnates into rich landlords owing their status to a strong crown.

It had not escaped Dorset's notice that Edward Hastings had not been one of those who had come to his aid, neither had the man been subject to the royal wrath. Indeed, Hastings had done very well for himself by marrying Mary Hungerford, sole heiress of the wealthy Thomas, Baron Hungerford, Botreaux, Molyns and Moels. From this inheritance he was granted the lordship, barony and honour of Hastings. Attainted by Richard III, Hastings had fought at the battles of Bosworth and Stoke, thus demonstrating to the world his allegiance when Dorset was languishing in captivity. He had also recovered his father's lands, some of which lay in the same West Country counties as Dorset's own. Hastings had been called to Parliament in 1487 while Dorset had been overlooked. For the Marquess this was all a matter of grave concern.

Hardly had he buried his mother than Dorset was climbing into the saddle once more, this time tied politically and financially hand and foot. The King had decided to invade France, the result of the latest quarrel between monarchs the origins of which were in the usual shifting alliances and bids for another's territory. As the flotilla of boats carrying 11,000 men, 1,200 horsemen, their equipment, servants and baggage left Sandwich for Calais, Dorset hoped he would be given the opportunity to demonstrate his

*Bradgate House, Leicestershire*

*Above – building on the house was begun circa 1500 by the 1st Marquess of Dorset*

*Below – the ruins of the house circa 2000*

military prowess, dispose of many of the king's enemies and in so doing work his way back into royal favour. He was to be disappointed. The invasion which began on such a high note turned out to be a re-run of the fiasco of 1475: little action, much quarrelling among the commanders and the English King paid off handsomely to go home. An angry Marquess had failed to make his mark.

The following year Dorset was first called to serve as a commissioner of the King's peace, a brief which was to extend to over nine counties at various times.[6] In Leicestershire he occupied the bench with such local gentlemen as Geoffrey Sherrard of Stapleford, Sir Ralph Shirley of Staunton Harold and William Assheby of Lowesby.[7] These were men who had done well out of grazing sheep and cattle, had successfully set up as merchants in the towns or had otherwise benefited from a rising tide of prosperity and who now aspired to become knightly. Dorset preferred to attend in person meetings only in those shires where his estates lay; upstart local gentlemen had to be regularly reminded of their place in matters of the government of the realm.

At other times Dorset delivered prisoners to gaol and enquired into all manner of treasons, felonies and conspiracies in London. As the years went by he realised that he was not any nearer enjoying the King's trust. There was, it seemed to the Marquess, at least one man, such as the King's uncle Jasper, Earl of Pembroke, on each of the bodies on which Dorset served to keep an eye on him. As if to rub salt into his wounds, the King had insisted on paying the Marquess a week's visit at his manor house at Ottery St Mary in far away Devon, as one stop on a royal progress of the West Country in 1495.[8] Such an imposition by the king was by no means an isolated occurrence. On his visit to Lord Stanley in Lancashire, Henry had insisted on inspecting in person his lordship's entire Lathom estate. There seemed no limits to what a subject might expect from his paranoid King.

It is doubtful if Henry VII exercised all the financial options regarding the bonds for good behaviour which he placed on Dorset and other nobles. An attempt to extract the last pound would have ruined many families and driven them to rebel at the earliest opportunity. Joan, the widow of Edward Viscount Lisle, was released after only eight months from the £1,000 bond her husband had put forward against his good behaviour. Dorset was to show his compliance the following year when he was called upon to put down a rising in Cornwall by men protesting against unjust taxation. He had learnt his lesson, and as J R Lander has pointed out, the Marquess, now a loving and true servant of the King, was probably cleared from most, if not all of his financial impositions by 1499, although the debate about the precise nature of the Marquess' problems continues.[9]

Carefully watched, but no longer a serious threat, Dorset was left to re-ordering and re-assembling his damaged finances. He first looked to his estates which were scattered over thirteen counties and included land in Calais. In the farming world many changes were taking place. The markets now favoured the larger producers, especially if they abandoned ploughland in favour of flocks and herds. Many of Dorset's more humble tenants were of little profit to him and on some of his manors they effectively prevented any improvement in productivity. At Weddington in Warwickshire he had already enclosed the entire manor and went on to convert all the arable to pasture, "whereby 300 acres went out of cultivation, the houses were allowed to go to ruin and 60 persons were driven from their homes, losing their occupations."[10] He was active too at Wicken in Northamptonshire where homes were pulled down so that thirty acres of village ploughland could be converted to pasture. Dorset looked to other of his properties which might benefit from improvement. At Cotesbatch in Leicestershire, he used his wardship of Walter Devereaux, the young lord of the manor, to enclose two hundred acres. Similar ruthless action was repeated at Brascote and Naneby in the north-west of the same county.[11]

Dorset was not short of residences as he moved round his widespread estates. In Devon there was "the excellent manor house on the hillside at Shute with a fine park beside it"[12], and other manor houses at Wiscombe (also Devon) and Trelawn (Cornwall) and Gleaston (Lancashire).[13] It was at his manor of Groby in Leicestershire which was the subject of his greatest efforts of modernisation and improvement. Here, the old house of his Ferrers ancestors which had been acceptable to his father and grandfather was now dilapidated and hopelessly old-fashioned. Dorset began work on a large red-brick gatehouse, but after much effort abandoned it in favour of an altogether more ambitious scheme. This involved the construction of a completely new mansion, a home truly fit for a man of his station. It would stand in a much-enlarged version of his ancestors' deer park at Bradgate, and would be surrounded by the rocky outcrops and bracken covered wastes of Charnwood Forest. Here the inhabitants of the tiny settlement of Bradgate were eventually moved to accommodate the Marquess' plans and left their homes "in grief".[14]

Dorset had barely time to lay out and prepare the site for the house and perhaps lay the foundations before his death in September 1501. A month previously he had "banketted prively" with Edmund de la Pole, younger brother of the leading rebel at the Battle of Stoke and a fellow sufferer of the King's punitive policies. At 51 Dorset had reached old age but there were whispers that he had been poisoned.[15]

In his will, which is undated, he bequeathed his body to be buried in the Collegiate Church at his Warwickshire manor of Astley. He left provision for his wife Cicely and £1,000 from the profits of his widely scattered manors for each of his unmarried daughters. These included Mary who was to marry Lord Ferrers, and Cecily who was to marry Lord Dudley, cousin of John Dudley, later Duke of Northumberland.[16]

There are virtually no comments on Dorset's character by his contemporaries. The actions of his life suggest a man who was much influenced by his ruthless mother and who was carried along in the flow of events hardly of his making, with little ability to make sound political judgements. His position at court was maintained by his rank, his family connections and his usefulness to the King as a source of entertainment. But he was not a dumb brute of the tournament field for, with view to the future, he had placed his three sons under the tutorage of Cardinal Wolsey at Oxford.

# Chapter 6

# *In Fear of the King*
## Thomas Grey, 2nd Marquess of Dorset (1477-1530)

Evidently the first Marquess' meeting with de la Pole had not been sufficiently discreet for the King learned of the contact and Pole soon fled to the continent. Royal suspicion now fell on Thomas his son and 2nd Marquess, with the result that the young man was imprisoned in the Tower. His stay there was short, as the see-saw of royal favour quickly tilted once again in favour of the Greys. After his father's death, the young Dorset was released and given appointments to several lucrative positions. These included that of steward of Chartley Park, the home of the senior branch of his Ferrers ancestors.

The following year, 1503, saw the death of Dorset's grandmother, Lady Katherine Hastings. She had not remarried after the murder of her husband, Lord William Hastings, twenty years earlier. All her lands had been restored to her by Henry VII and, in recognition of her husband's service and loyalty to Edward IV, she had been treated well. Earlier in her life and "at divers times" Lady Katherine had been borrowing sums of money from her daughter Cicely, the first Marquess's wife. In times of need it was usually better to go to the family and avoid the money lenders in London. When she died she left Cicely "the tablet of gold which she now has in her hands as a pledge" together with a variety of household goods and fittings, trusting these would clear her debts.[1] She was buried in the parish church at Ashby-de-la-Zouch, close by the family castle and "between the image of Our Lady and the place assigned for the vicar's grave".[2]

Unwilling to follow her mother into extended widowhood, Cicely announced her intention of marrying Henry Stafford, later created Earl of Wiltshire. He was brother of the third Duke of Buckingham, the country's largest private landowner, many of whose estates, like those of Cicely, lay in the West Country. As a widow, Cicely was exercising her freedom to marry whom she pleased, although she knew that most of the other areas of choice available to her as a single woman would vanish once she had a new husband. She was aged 44 and had already borne 14 children. Now she was marrying a man who was 19 years younger than herself and even younger than her son, Dorset. In her own right Cicely was one of the wealthiest of peeresses, with estates giving rise to an annual rent roll in 1530 of £924.[3] Since she could see that her husband was likely to prove a financial liability she was clearly not marrying simply for material gain. Stafford had paid the King £2,000 for permission to marry her, half in cash and half as a bond for his good behaviour. Cicely granted to her new husband a life interest in her lands worth £1,000 a year, drawn from the properties she had inherited. This did not prevent him from running up debts which at the time of his

*The Tournament – the pageantry, ritual and spectacle which accompanied
the jousting were complex and formed a major part of all important state occasions*

*The Siege – the development of artillery using gunpowder brought a new dimension to siege warfare*

death in 1523 amounted to over £4,000. People remembered that Lord Dorset, her first husband, had been older than her. Was she now merely indulging a penchant for a younger man?

Whatever her motive, the announcement drove a deep wedge between mother and son. Dorset would now face the same problem his father had encountered when his paternal grandmother, Lady Ferrers, had taken her second husband. If Thomas was not to see his mother's West Country estates, always understood to be his inheritance, disappear into the clutches of the Buckinghams, he would have to take action. In 1504, before King and council, a solution was finally arrived at. Thomas was to enjoy the income of his father's estates in Leicestershire and elsewhere. Cicely, in turn, granted her new husband a lifetime interest in her other estates with a promise he would receive the remainder of her inheritance if Dorset should die. Otherwise, after her death, Thomas would inherit all her lands and titles.[4]

During his early years, Dorset had ample opportunity to follow his father as a champion jouster at court. Energetic displays of personal prowess continued to be an important element of life at a court full of aggressive males with super-charged egos. The pageantry, ritual and spectacle which accompanied the jousting were becoming increasingly complex and formed a major part of all important state occasions. In November 1501, shortly after his father's death, Dorset was called on to demonstrate his skills at the wedding of Prince Arthur and Catherine of Aragon. In front of Westminster Hall the lists were set up in a pavilion with turrets and pinnacles and other such wonders. In the procession of knights were three characters: William Courtenay in a dragon led by a giant; the Earl of Essex in a green mountain "with ... marvellous beasts upon the sides" and the Marquess of Dorset, who was preceded by a black-garbed hermit. In 1505 Dorset and other nobles were ordered to Windsor to greet King Philipe of Castille on his visit to England. This occasion, too, was one of great spectacle. "My lord marquess (of Dorset) rode a horse with a deep trapper (covering) full of long tassels of gold of Venus and upon the cropped ear of his horse a white feather, with a coat upon his back, the body goldsmiths work, the sleeves of crimson velvet with letters of gold". Other parading nobles were dressed in similar if perhaps not quite such extravagant finery.

When Henry VII married Elizabeth, daughter of Edward IV, there was good reason to hope that peace would come to a land weary of the conflict between the Houses of York and Lancaster. Throughout his reign Henry believed, with good reason, there were still those who were plotting unrest, insurrection and rebellion. One of the prime suspects was William Courtenay, heir to the Earldom of Devon and Dorset's uncle. Courtenay's father had been one of the nobles who, like Dorset, had been forced to sign bonds for his good behaviour. Later, in 1503, Devon saw his title would be extinguished when, for no obvious reason, Henry attainted his son and put him in prison. Later Dorset also fell under suspicion of treason yet again. This time there was no prospect of a quick return to favour; the King's worsening paranoia meant Dorset was facing his gravest crisis. In October of the following year the Marquess was exiled to Calais and the grim fortress of Hammes. Here, according to the *Chronicle of Calais*, "he was detained as long as King Henry VII lives and should have been put to death if he had lived longer."[5]

Fortunately for Dorset, the King died in April 1509. After eighteen months in captivity the Marquess now looked with renewed hope to an early release. But the new monarch, Henry VIII, took his time in reviewing the fates of the inmates, noble and otherwise, of his father's gaols. It was not until he was crowned and married that he finally sent orders for Dorset's return to England. A second snub was that the Marquess was exempted from the general pardon the King extended to so many of those his father had believed were his

*Left: Margaret Wotton, second wife of Thomas Grey, 2nd Marquess of Dorset*

*Right: Shute Barton, Devon, one of the properties of the Marquess of Dorset in the first half of the 16th century*

enemies. The final insult came with his summons to Parliament in the following October, in which he was addressed simply as "Lord Grey of Groby". His title of marquess was apparently in limbo and in danger of extinction. The King was letting Dorset know in no uncertain terms that he had a long journey ahead of him if he was to throw off his family's doubtful record of loyalty to the crown.

At some time before 1509 Dorset married Eleanor, daughter of Oliver St John of Lydiard Tregoze in Wiltshire, "a stout black man" as Leland noted. *Burke's Peerage* notes the union although there appear to have been no children.[6] Eleanor's sister, Elizabeth St John, had married Gerald Fitzgerald, the Irish 8th Earl of Kildare, in 1496 and Dorset's daughter Katherine, by his second wife, married the same Earl's son (later the 9th Earl) by his second wife.[7] It was these two marriages which established the Greys' Irish connection.

The date of Eleanor's death is unknown but in 1509 Dorset married Margaret Wotton, the widow of William Medley and daughter of Sir Robert Wotton of Boughton Malherb in Kent. Sir Robert was the Lieutenant of Guisne and Comptroller of Calais which meant he played an important role in the security of that strategic English outpost on the Continent. Dorset's link with a family which was held in high favour by the Crown was a helpful move towards re-establishing the Greys' fortunes. By Margaret, Dorset had four sons and three daughters, and probably some unrecorded offspring since he was widely regarded as a lecher.

At court Cicely Bonville, Dorset's mother, the dowager Marchioness and now Countess of Wiltshire, could only watch what must have seemed to her a re-run of the events which she had witnessed with her late husband. Like his father, the young Dorset had not been slow to take mistresses and enjoy the other pleasures that were in ready supply at court. For the next three years or so he was admitted to the monarch's intimate social circle and shared the many pastimes, principally drinking, wenching and jousting. Among the company were George Neville, Lord Abergavenny, Walter Devereux, Lord Ferrers and, to Dorset's annoyance, George Lord Hastings. Most of these companions were older than the King, who was barely twenty, and it was to them that he looked for instruction in the finer points of the pleasures such as jousting, wrestling, tennis and other sports which they shared. On one occasion, the Marquess in his cups told the King that "there never was a man merrier that had more than one woman in his bed, more than one friend in his bosom, more than one faith in his heart".[8] Drunk or otherwise, to play one's cards so ineptly in a game with an opponent who was invariably able to produce a Royal Flush was certainly the mark of a careless politician.

Fortunately for Dorset these were the days before matrimonial and religious problems dominated the King's life. The young monarch was a huge, strong and athletic man for whom suitable jousting partners were difficult to find. At the celebrations following the birth of the longed for royal son, Henry had led the tilt and Dorset and Wiltshire, his new father-in-law, answered the challenges.[9] As time went by these ageing courtiers were replaced by younger men who were contemporaries of the King and whose contributions at all levels of service reflected Henry's changing perception of himself both as a man and as a King.

The year 1512 saw England at war with France yet again. This time Henry had agreed to help his father-in-law, Ferdinand of Spain, and the Emperor Maximillian, in their dispute with the French King. Dorset was appointed commander-in-chief of the English army with the rank of Lieutenant-General. On 14th May and at the head of 10,000 men, he set sail from Portsmouth in 60 great ships and landed at Biarritz on the French coast on 17th June. What had begun on a high note of royal optimism was to turn into a debacle. Completely in character, Ferdinand put his own interests first and directed his army to attack Navarre. Further, he had sent a message to Dorset to advise him to advance via Pamplona. Dorset replied that his orders were that he should march against Bayonne. In the stalemate that followed disease struck the already demoralised English troops. Eventually mutiny broke out and Dorset was obliged to return home.

When he reached England it was to a withering blast from his monarch: the expedition had been a costly fiasco, England had been humiliated and the King had been made to appear a fool. When Henry demanded to know who was at fault, all present pointed in Dorset's direction. "Your Commander-in-Chief is doubtless a very distinguished nobleman," Ferdinand told Henry, "but he was entirely to blame." While a gallant knight in the lists and a brave soldier, Dorset had shown little ability to organise men and command them in battle. In his defence he pointed out that he himself had been very sick and, with all the diplomacy this blunt man could muster, told the King that his father-in-law was a scoundrel. Eventually the affair was hushed up by the royal council, but Dorset remained under a cloud.

Culpable or otherwise, Dorset found himself en route for France yet again the following year, along with his brothers and other leading noblemen including Charles Brandon, Duke of Suffolk. This time the King was in personal command of the army. Henry had persuaded the Holy Roman Emperor to join what was projected as a four-pronged attack against their common enemy, France. In May the King had beheaded Edmund de la Pole, Earl of Suffolk. The wretched man had been imprisoned in the Tower for his foolish political intriguing on the continent and the fact that his brother, Richard, had joined the service of France. The execution was a warning to anyone who might see the royal absence as an opportunity to commit disloyal acts. On 30th June 1513 the English fleet reached Calais and after three weeks of pageantry and posturing the army marched close to the town of Therouanne, 40 miles away. At the Battle of the Spurs, which in reality was a skirmish, the town fell and Henry's trumpeters proclaimed a great victory. Virtually every building was razed to the ground by the Emperor and King Henry returned home in good spirits. Dorset, now in favour, was left behind for a spell as English ambassador at Lille.

The machinations over France, which had not been defeated, continued to rumble on below the surface. Ferdinand secretly made peace with the French whom he no longer saw as a threat. Henry learning of this, and smarting under the eventual realisation that his expedition had been a very costly waste of time, also decided to make an ally of France. This was done by the time-honoured means of a marriage, on this occasion between his own younger sister, Mary, and the King of France. So it was that less than a year after his return from his earlier trip to France, Dorset now found himself commanded to accompany the Princess to her new home.

The tragedy of what might otherwise have been a happy occasion was painfully obvious to all. The bride was a bright and intelligent seventeen year-old girl whose fate it was to be saddled with a sick 53 year-old man. Mary had tearfully protested to her brother and at length an agreement was reached: she would do her duty on this occasion but on the understanding that she alone would choose her next husband. Few doubted who that would be: Charles Brandon, the Duke of Suffolk, with whom she was in love. In the splendid tournament which followed the royal marriage ceremony in France the action was less than sporting. According to the chronicler Hall, both Dorset and Suffolk almost killed opponents. Later, Suffolk "overthrew a man of arms, horse and man ... and yet the Frenchmen would no wise praise them'. More violence followed.

"It happened that the Lord Marquis one time, put for his aide his youngest brother called Lord Edward Grey of the age of nineteen years and to him was put a gentleman of France of great stature and strength, to the intent to pluck him over the bars but yet the young lord was of such strength and power and policy, that he so stroke his adversary that he disarmed him".[10] Dorset and the family returned home in triumph, the French King died soon afterwards and Princess Mary married her Duke.

For the next five years or so there is little news of Dorset. In May 1516 he was invested with the Order of the Garter and spent time jousting, playing tennis with the King's foreign guests and losing no opportunity to maintain his presence and position at court. On one occasion a mistake by Dorset in mishandling a lance resulted in Suffolk almost killing the unprepared King. It was a difficult situation but there is no record that Henry saw it as anything but a genuine accident. In the same year there were rumours that the Marquess, too, had met an early death as the sweating sickness swept through London; but he had left the capital in good time and had swapped the stinking streets of London in summer for the fresh air and safety of his Leicestershire estates.

One certain death the year following was that of Jane Shore who, after a long succession of lovers, had eventually married a Thomas Lynon. Thomas More, writing not earlier than 1518, described the woman Jane had become: "... lean, withered and dried up, nothing left but ravel skin and hard bone". Well into her seventies, "unfriended and worn out of aquainten and lacking a protector" the woman who had been the mistress of the highest in the land was reduced to begging in the streets of London. All the good deeds she had performed for the King's grandfather and his court had been, it seems, forgotten.[11]

*Henry VIII and The Field of the Cloth of Gold. From the painting at Hampton Court.*
*The 2nd Marquess of Dorset rides before the King and carries the Sword of State.*

During the five years following Jane's death events in Europe had been moving slowly towards war once more. Involved were France, Spain and the Holy Roman Empire, but armed conflict had been skilfully avoided by Cardinal Wolsey acting in the role of conciliator. Henry VIII and the French King, the leaders of two of Europe's oldest enemies, agreed to meet personally and sink their differences in a grand public show of goodwill. Negotiations completed, the King of England, accompanied by his entire court and most of the nobility, crossed the Channel to Calais in May 1520. Dorset, along with 112 men and four chaplains was accompanied by his three brothers John, Richard and Leonard and his infant son Henry. Also present were many others of his extensive and well-placed family: the Duke of Buckingham (a 'cousin'), the Earl of Wiltshire (his step father), Richard Grey (Earl of Kent), and the Earl of Kildare with his wife Lady Elizabeth (Dorset's daughter) and Dorset's sister Dorothy, Lady de Broke. On board too were his Leicestershire neighbours: Thomas Manners (Lord Ros) together with Sir William Skeffington, the executor of the 1st Marquess' will. In the melee which accompanied the embarkation, Dorset noticed George Lord Hastings and his servant the Nottinghamshire knight, Sir Richard Sacheverel, as travelling companions to the Marquess both were as welcome as the rodents that scuttled between the timbers of his ship.[12]

In support of this massive tour-de-force an enormous, elaborate and hugely expensive town of tents was erected with pavilions and squares where the fountains flowed with wine. Here at a point between Andes

39

and Guines in Picardy ("the Field of the Cloth of Gold"), the two monarchs met, with Dorset mounted on a white horse with black trappings and bearing the Sword of State before his King. In the festivities which extended over seventeen days, Dorset and Kildare put on impressive performances in the lists, much to their monarch's delight.

In spite of this extravagant show of international bonhomie, the political gains from the exercise were short-lived. On a personal level Dorset soon found the icy wind of the King's suspicion once more blowing down his family's corridors. His new Irish brother-in-law, Gerald Kildare, was the problem. The man's father was known to have a very doubtful record of loyalty to the crown. When Lord Deputy in Ireland he had advanced the cause of the pretender Lambert Simnel and was attainted for treason, only to be restored. The son, the 9th Earl, now seemed to be a man from the same mould. He was removed from the office of Lord Deputy by Cardinal Wolsey for what was termed maladministration, and left under a cloud. Kildare's reward for his performance in France was a spell in prison. Before his return to Ireland sureties of 10,000 marks were demanded by the King. To Kildare's relief, Dorset not only managed to somehow engineer the man's release but, with help from the family, had also come up with the money.[13]

After Kildare's death in 1534 his orphaned daughter Elizabeth, the "Fair Geraldine" of the poems of the Earl of Surrey, came to court to serve Queen Katherine Howard. At age fifteen Elizabeth married her first husband, the wealthy widower Sir Anthony Browne, who was aged 60 and Master of the Queen's horse. After his death she entered the service of the Princess Elizabeth at Hunsden and must have met Lady Jane Grey and her mother. The problem of the Kildares and the politics of Ireland were to return to the Greys long after Dorset's lifetime.

In spite of his Irish involvement, Dorset seems to have very slowly gained some of the King's confidence and favour. He realised that Henry no longer regarded him as a danger to his throne and, like many others, came to understand that loyalty, service and obedience were the ways to royal favour and patronage. The King, still without a male heir, saw any threats as more likely to come from other quarters. In 1520 he had Buckingham executed as a warning to would be challengers. The lack of armed response which such an act might otherwise have provoked was recognition of the strength of the monarch's control over his nobles.

Dorset was off to Calais again in 1522, this time to welcome the Emperor Charles V to England. The euphoria of the Field of the Cloth of Gold had melted into the Channel mist and the King of England and the Holy Roman Emperor were plotting together against France. "Plus ça change", Dorset thought, but his unavoidable duty was to carry out his sovereign's commands.

The following year he was given the important and sensitive position of warden of the marches of Scotland. Here, under his commander and great uncle, the Duke of Norfolk, he saw violent action in keeping down the troublesome Scots, who for centuries had been given to raiding across the border into England. For these and other services Dorset was well rewarded. Membership of the Privy Council was at last extended to him and he became a gentleman of the Privy Chamber.

At this time the royal court, though still much of a family affair, was dominated by the Privy Council which was no different in size and composition from the modern cabinet. Membership was restricted to those of proven loyalty to the monarch, who personally formulated and controlled all policy. An additional welcome bonus for Dorset was some manors in Warwickshire which had belonged to the late Duke of Buckingham. There were, too, the fruits of stewardships in various parts of the country together with a pension of 1,000 crowns from the French King. Not so welcome was the demand from Henry that Dorset exchange his manors in Essex and Northamptonshire for royal properties of the Duchy of Lancaster in Leicestershire.[14] Dorset was not the only victim of the King's territorial designs. Even Charles Brandon, the Duke of Suffolk and the King's own brother-in-law, had been persuaded to exchange lands with his dread liege lord. Parting with his properties near London was no small matter for Dorset; but then neither was any sign of reluctance to do so.

With the King's demands on his property seemingly now settled, Dorset felt sufficiently confident to return to the task of completing the mansion at Bradgate in Leicestershire which his father had begun. The second Marquess had added to it over the previous twenty years as finances, opportunity and his relationship with the King had permitted. An unforeseen problem had appeared in the person of Cardinal Thomas Wolsey, the Marquess' former tutor at Oxford. Wolsey had received his first benefice, Ilminster in Somerset, from Dorset's father, the first Marquess. For the first two decades of Henry VIII's reign the Cardinal had exercised his many skills in running the country for the young monarch. In the process, this prince of the church had grown very rich and had already rebuilt the Archbishop of York's palace in Whitehall and the stately house known as The More in Hertfordshire. His ambition was to complete his huge palace that was already under construction at Hampton Court on the bank of the Thames and upstream of the capital.

Such was the scale of the building at Hampton that the effect of the demand for skilled craftsmen was felt for many miles around and from as far away as Leicestershire. Dorset had written a letter to the Cardinal "from my poor house at Bradgate".[15] This was less a description of the state of the building but more an indication of the deferential style of address of the kind which most nobles, including the Earl of Surrey and Lord Hastings, used when writing to Wolsey or the King – if they knew what was good for them. Wolsey was to enjoy his creation at Hampton Court for only ten years. In the summer of 1525 Henry persuaded him to transfer the property to the royal collection. The relationship between monarch and cardinal had begun to sour and after Wolsey's eventual fall in 1530, the King continued the tradition of lavish royal building, thus perpetuating the problem of the supply of skilled labour.

The Tudor scholar and traveller John Leland, who visited Leicestershire in about 1539, observed of Bradgate that it had "a fine park with a lodge recently built ... by the (second) Marquess of Dorset".[16] Writing to his nephew in about 1528 Dorset had upgraded his opinion of his house to "my lodge" at Bradgate. But this "lodge" was no ordinary house. It was built of brick, a fashionable and very expensive material, and it extended around three, rather than four sides of a square. Its construction was a break with tradition in other ways: there was no moat, no great gatehouse and indeed no other sign of defence. The construction of this true country house, described by Dr Hoskins as "built for the pleasure of living and no thought of lawless attack", signalled that the times had indeed changed. A nobleman no longer felt the threat of violence and ruin from malcontented neighbours.[17] Bradgate House was a sign that the King had been successful in following up the policy his father had begun, that of reducing the feudal magnates to wealthy landlords, reliant on the crown for their continued prosperity.

Dorset's grand house at Bradgate placed him at the very forefront of a revolution in building. In many parts of England men of position and substance moved earth, stone, timber and bricks with a passion, building grand new houses or re-styling ancient ancestral piles. Edward Stafford, Duke of Buckingham and the King's cousin, built Thornbury in Gloucestershire where he entertained the King in 1519. Here, Dorset concluded, the grandness of the building may well have been seen by the King as a challenge to his own royal efforts and may have been a factor contributing to the loss of his lordship's head the following year. At Kimbolton, Sir Richard Wingfield, husband of Dorset's late aunt Catherine, the Duchess of Buckingham, was building what Leland described as "new fair lodgings and galleries".[18] Dorset's brother-in-law, William Lord Mountjoy, was at work at Apethorpe in Northamptonshire, Thomas Manners (Lord Ros) at Belvoir in Leicestershire and Charles Brandon (Duke of Suffolk) at Westhorpe in Lincolnshire. For the ambitious, wealthy and well placed nobleman these were interesting and challenging times.

Bradgate House stood in a prominent position in the deer park of 1,000 acres. The expansion of the ancient park of his Ferrers ancestors had caused Dorset's father trouble when he came to removing the village of Bradgate. For this act he was summoned in Chancery where he pleaded that he had rehoused the villagers elsewhere. Later his widow had been called to answer the same charge of depopulation; but nothing had come of it and the matter seems to have been dropped. The mansion at Bradgate stood on an elevated platform by the small river Lyn. It was supplied with water by means of a skilfully engineered channel which wound its way across the Park. It gave Dorset great satisfaction to know that the tops of the rugged hills in his new Park could be seen by the inhabitants of Leicester five miles away.[19]

The pleasures of living at Bradgate were soured by another conflict with the Hastings family. Edward, the son of William Lord Hastings, had died in 1506, a very wealthy man and had been succeeded by his son George. As a boy George had been a playmate to the young Prince Henry. At about the time Dorset arrived back from exile in Calais in 1509, Hastings was summoned to a seat in the Upper House of Parliament as a precocious sixteen year-old. Thereafter, George had trimmed his sails to the changing winds at court, especially when the storms over the King's matrimonial problems were gathering. He had become a royal favourite and had been created Earl of Huntingdon in 1529. Moreover, he had been appointed a Privy Councillor and had married a daughter of the Duke of Buckingham and Catherine Woodville. Not least, he had followed in his father's footsteps as Captain of the Yeomen of the Guard. This was a prestigious position since the corps had been formed by Henry VII for the express purpose of protecting the sovereign's person. Dorset must have reflected that Huntingdon had skilfully given loyal service, had carefully provided the advice and opinions expected of him and was now enjoying the rewards for so doing.

Another unwelcome development for Dorset was the fact that the dowager Lady Hastings had remarried. Her new husband was her receiver general (her most senior financial officer) Richard Sacheverell, who had been knighted after Tournai in 1513. At various times the couple lived with a large retinue of servants in The Newarke district of the town of Leicester. Sir Richard, in his new capacity as joint steward and with his stepson Francis Hastings, (later the 2nd Earl of Huntingdon) had, it was said, "used himself in a manner of comparison with the lord Marquess of Dorset".[20] From the start feelings ran high between servants of the respective camps and there were frequent noisy and violent clashes in the streets. There was a particularly unpleasant affray in the centre of Leicester between the men of Sir Richard and those of the Dean of the Chapter House of The Newarke, who was Lord Leonard Grey, Dorset's brother. Other disputes over respective rights, real and imaginary, in the nearby Royal Forest of Leicester are found in the records of the Court of the Star Chamber. A poisonous atmosphere hung over the town for more than a decade before Sir Richard died in 1534 and the matter was overtaken by more important events on the national scene.

Shortly before Dorset's own death his mother, Cicely, died. Her second husband, Lord Wiltshire, had been

*Alabasters in the church at Astley, Warwickshire. Left to right are Cicely Bonville, wife of the 1st Marquess of Dorset, Elizabeth Talbot, wife of Sir Edward Grey, later Viscount Lisle and Sir Edward Grey, Viscount Lisle.*

buried in 1522. She had not remarried and was left to clear up his substantial debts. Nevertheless she died a rich woman and with an income of £924 per annum.[21] In her will she ignored her late husband preferring to style herself "Marchioness of Dorset". Her titles of Bonville and Harrington now passed to her son together with her estates. Her life of 70 years had shown among other things, how a long-lived widow with a generous jointure and proper provision for dower could delay an heir's inheritance. Dorset was not to enjoy the benefit of her estates for very long for he died later the same year, aged 53. His wife and children were well provided for and he also left generous bequests to loyal servants, including £20 to the schoolmaster of his son and heir Henry. Last, and not least, he left his King one of his best geldings and £100 "to buy his Grace a saddle".[22] Did this record Dorset's recognition of merciful treatment from the tyrannical monarch or was the Marquess simply attempting to gain the most favourable provision for the wardship of his under age heir?

Dorset was buried near his mother and father in the church of his manor at Astley in Warwickshire. Almost 80 years later his vault was opened. Evidently the embalmers had done their work well for the body was found well preserved: "six foot wanting four inches, his hair yellow his face broad".[23] The only surviving portrait of him shows him on horseback at the "Field of the Cloth of Gold". He was obviously a stocky man, built like an ox and very strong, as all champion jousters were.

Like that of his father, Dorset's character has left few records by contemporaries and little can be gleaned from official records. His speech was said to be "soldier like plain, short, smart and material", hardly the mark of a successful politician. His inherited position and rank placed him close to the centre of life at the royal court but his spirited manner alone would probably have debarred him from high office.

# Chapter 7

# *A Matter of High Politics*

**Henry Grey, 3rd Marquess of Dorset and Duke of Suffolk (1514-54)**

Dorset's heir was Henry, his third son, who was aged thirteen-and-a-half at the time of his father's death. Shortly before his succession to the marquessate, and as Lord Grey, Henry had married Katharine Fitz-Alan, daughter of the Earl of Arundel. In turn, Arundel's heir was contracted to (and two years later married) Katherine Grey, Henry's sister. The Earldom of Arundel was an ancient and senior one whose creation preceded even that of the barony of Groby, one of the titles which Henry also inherited. The two Houses of Grey and Fitz-Alan now appeared destined to union with a bright future. Henry was certainly not marrying into a pauper family; Arundel's lands in 1524 were worth £2,200 per annum.[1]

However, Katherine Grey's marriage to Fitz-Alan was short-lived for in May 1532 she died. Unforeseen as it was, the death played into the hands of the Dowager Marchioness of Dorset, who saw an even greater prize on the marriage market for her son. This was the young Frances Brandon, daughter of the Duke of Suffolk, who had been a friend of the late Marquess of Dorset and who had been given the wardship of the young Henry. In London, the King had a new wife in all but name and was in the mood for a divorce. For Lady Dorset, the Brandon girl would make a fine addition to her family. Apart from a rich dowry she would bring, the Greys would certainly find themselves closer to the throne since Frances was a niece of the King.

In many ways the Brandons were a remarkable family. From solid East Anglian farming stock they had risen slowly, acquired a knighthood, and at the accession of Richard III, had been politically prominent enough to need to seek refuge with the Earl of Richmond in Brittany. William Brandon had died at Bosworth holding Richmond's standard. Later, Charles Brandon, William's younger son, had shared the playroom with Prince Arthur, the victorious Richmond's heir and grew up to be a close companion of the future Henry VIII. Richmond, as Henry VII, had been generous to Charles Brandon who had risen from knight to duke in five years. Brandon was tall, handsome and athletic and where the ladies were concerned he was no shrinking violet. A younger son, he had various liaisons and by the time he met Princess Mary Tudor it seems he had already been married twice. Gambling on his credit with the King, he had married, without the royal approval, the young widowed Mary whose marriage to the French King has already been noted. Far from giving his sister a fine dowry, Henry admonished her and imposed a huge fine on his new brother-in-law. The couple's first child, Frances, was born in 1516 and sixteen years later she was still unmarried. Princess Mary asked the King for his approval for the Greys' union with the Arundels to be annulled and this was duly given.

The breaking of the marriage contract turned out to be a bitter and expensive business for both families. It created a fund of resentment and antagonism on the part of the Arundels that was to return to haunt the Greys. Nevertheless, Henry under his title of Marquess of Dorset, married Frances in early 1533. Very shortly afterwards the Duchess of Suffolk died, aged 38. It was not long before her husband was married again, this time to Katherine Willoughby, daughter of Lord Willoughby de Eresby. The bridegroom was aged 44 and his bride, who was technically his ward, was 14, younger even than her husband's daughter Frances.

In 1523 the problems of the Greys' connection with Ireland surfaced once more. Thomas Fitzgerald, the 10th Earl of Kildare, had been made the King's Vice Deputy in Ireland after his father, the Lord Deputy, had been recalled to England on suspicion of treason. Thomas, hearing a false report that his father was to be beheaded, renounced his allegiance to the English crown and mounted a desperate insurrection, only to surrender a year later. He went to the Tower shortly after his father's death and, along with five of his uncles, was executed as a traitor.[2] He is remembered as "Silken Thomas" on account of the silk rope with which, legend has it, he was hanged. The King looked around in an effort to find another Lord Deputy who would remain loyal to him. Eventually Lord Leonard Grey, Dorset's uncle, was dispatched to Ireland with the title of Viscount Graney. The move was a failure. Graney was accused of treating the Kildares with undue favour and was brought home to London and found guilty of treason. His appointment with the axeman in July 1530 brought Ireland's relationship with England to a new low point.

As if the problems in Ireland were not trouble enough, Dorset was called to the colours in England when discontent with royal policy flared into rebellion. During the 1530s the King's matrimonial problems had been behind the break with Rome and the replacement of the Pope with the King as head of the Church in England. With the power which his new position gave him, Henry attacked the doctrine of the Catholic Church, introducing the ideas of the reformers on the continent and creating the Anglican Church which was subsequently "by law established". Banished, too, were many of the practices of Popery together with the signs and symbols which for centuries had played an integral part of church and parish life. Change had followed quickly upon change with the result that the adoption of the new theology was mostly confined to the literate, wealthy and well-placed. For the great mass of the King's subjects: the farmers, labourers, artisans and traders, acceptance of the new ways was to come much later and even not at all. People in the north of England, "very ignorant and rude"[3], were led in a widespread rebellion by leaders who had different reasons for their discontent with royal policy. The several uprisings were collectively known as the Pilgrimage of Grace. It was against such men that Dorset, under the command and supervision of the Duke of Norfolk, rode north in 1536 and successfully put down the rebels in their heartlands of the counties of Lincoln and York.

The theology and practices which formed the basis of the King's new religion gave Dorset no problems; neither did the rich pickings which accompanied another of His Majesty's moves: the dissolution of the country's monasteries and other religious houses. In April 1536 there were over 800 such establishments up and down the country; six years later there were none. Smaller houses had been ordered to surrender first and the Pilgrimage of Grace gave the King the excuse to follow up with the larger ones. With monks and nuns gone, the silent and deserted buildings and their contents were up for sale. Huge areas of land, from the rolling acres of Sussex to the windswept upland sheep pastures of Yorkshire, which had been held by the Church in mortmain (dead hand) for centuries, now came on to the market. For the wealthy and well-placed

*London 1543*

at the English court the opportunities for further self-enrichment had never been better.

The Greys' extensive estates lay in the South-West, East Anglia and the Midlands and they had properties in London; but their capital manor remained Groby in Leicestershire. Along with the Hastings family, they dominated this rich and fertile county but only with constant effort and vigilance. Their problem was that they needed the cooperation of the local gentry. These were the men of middling means who were riding on a wave of rural prosperity and were always set on advancing their own best interests against the designs and wishes of noblemen. When the time came for choosing the knights of the town and shire who would serve in the lower House of Parliament, arranging for the election of men sympathetic to the wishes of the noble lords was a matter which could not be neglected. Some men, like Sir William Skeffington and Sir Robert Burdett, were reliable clients of the Greys. Others, like John Beaumont and Sir Richard Sacheverel, were firmly in the Hastings' camp. For many years in Leicestershire an uneasy peace at noble level prevailed, that was until the monasteries were dissolved and a third force in the person of Sir Thomas Manners arrived on the landscape of local politics.

It is not difficult to appreciate how cheated by his royal step-uncle Dorset must have felt and how angry he was. Thomas Manners had served his King fully and faithfully, unlike the Kildares in Ireland, and had been created Earl of Rutland by a monarch who, like his father, put loyalty and service to the crown first. Manners's grandmother was Anne Holland, Duchess of Exeter, sister of Edward IV. Manners's mother was the half-sister of the Anne who married Dorset's grandfather, Thomas, the first Marquess. Further,

Manners's mother was due to marry Dorset's father, the second Marquess, but the arrangement had been called off and it proved to be a very expensive failure. Instead, the lady had married George Manners. Thomas Manners, now Earl of Rutland, was their son. Prominent at court and seated at Belvoir Castle in North-East Leicestershire, Thomas Rutland was to receive rich rewards at Dorset's expense.

When the monasteries in the county of Leicester were dissolved, Lord Rutland was given the four choicest properties. Even worse, the lands of Ulverscroft, one of the smaller houses, whose acres had been mostly donated by Dorset's Ferrers ancestors and which lay adjacent to his estates at Groby, were also given to Rutland. He had immediately sold them to Sir Andrew Judd, a skinner by trade, who had risen to become Lord Mayor of London and who was seen as an unwelcome upstart by noblemen of the likes of Henry Grey. Judd had no previous connection with Leicestershire but was one of the many merchants and traders who were prospering in the capital and who wished to invest their profits in land. It took eight years of persuasion and threats before Dorset could get his hands on Ulverscroft. One crumb of comfort for the peer was a grant of the site of the former Blackfriars monastery in the town of Leicester. This grant was made in 1547, almost a decade after the Dissolution had been set in motion. By the time the dust had settled on the whole affair in Leicestershire, the Manners's counted thirty-nine manors, the Greys sixteen and the Hastings eleven.

The Marquess must have been left wondering why he was so out of favour with his monarch. He was, after all, the King's nephew by marriage and both he and his wife were making sure they were seen to toe the royal line in all matters of state and church. One indication of the position and esteem a courtier held with his monarch was the scale of the traditional giving and receiving of New Year gifts. On New Year's Day 1540 Henry had presented the King with a brace of greyhounds; his mother gave "a garter, the buckle and pendant of gold". Other members of the family made other similar presentations.[4] The King smiled inwardly and was graciously pleased to accept them all, but there is no record of what he gave in return. Later that same year the King, on his tour of the northern shires, may also have visited Dorset at Bradgate where, as we have already seen, his father had built, in the words of Leland, "a fair lodge".[5] The King also planned to call at nearby Beaumanor where the widow of the newly executed Earl of Kildare lived, safe from the horrors of Ireland. Royal nephew or not Dorset, like his father and grandfather before him, appeared to carry little weight in court circles where the governance of the nation was decided.

There was much rejoicing in the royal household in October 1537. On 12th Jane Seymour, the King's third wife, had given birth to the long-wanted male heir, who was christened Edward. Some days later and over-shadowed by the music and fireworks at Hampton Court, Dorset announced the birth of a daughter who was named Jane. She was a cousin once removed of the new heir to the kingdom, and with all the advantages and dangers that such a close relationship entailed. Dorset's standing at court quickly recovered and thereafter he was to appear as a conspicuous figure at pageants and musical entertainments. Jane's birth propelled Dorset on a political career which quickly and inexorably gathered momentum, until it reached a certain point beyond which he had little or no control. A second daughter, Catherine, was born four years after Jane and at Dorset House, one of the Greys' London residences on the Thames near Westminster Hall. A third girl, Mary, completed the family whose links to the crown had once again become a matter of high politics.

Henry VIII died on 25th January 1547 having produced three children by his six wives. These were Mary, the eldest and daughter of Catherine of Aragon; Elizabeth, the daughter of Anne Boleyn and Edward, the son of Jane Seymour. The girls' claims to the throne were complicated by their father's matrimonial arrangements, political and religious considerations and the decisions of parliament. Well before the King's death, court and country – including Catholic Dissidents – were generally agreed that Henry's true heir was Edward, who at his father's death was aged nine; but the expectations of his two half sisters were soon raised by the fact that Edward began to develop signs of consumption (tuberculosis) which, in the mid 16th century, was usually seen as a death sentence.

At the centre of the problem was, of course, the matter of legitimacy. Ordinarily Mary, a Catholic, would be seen as second in line to her father's throne with Elizabeth, a Protestant, in third place. Mary had been bastardised in 1533 after the King's marriage to her mother had ended in divorce. The following year Elizabeth had been declared Henry's heir. After Anne Boleyn's execution in 1536 both daughters had been declared illegitimate so that the succession would be vested in the offspring of the new queen, Jane Seymour. In the event of Jane failing to provide a male heir, the succession would revert to the two princesses in order of age. In his will, drawn up a few weeks before his death, Henry repeated these terms but added that if this arrangement failed the succession should run through the offspring of his younger sister Mary – i.e. through the House of Suffolk to which the Greys, of course, had become firmly bound.

Once the King was dead the struggle for the wardship of the boy began and for the Greys the pace of political life began to quicken and develop momentum. The coronation took place on 20th February and Dorset was created, for three days only, High Constable of England and bore the Sceptre and the Dove at the glittering ceremony. It must have occurred to more than Dorset that here was a young heir safely crowned, unlike his earlier namesake who disappeared into the Tower and was not seen again. The present young King's Protector was his uncle, the Duke of Somerset, a man apart it seemed from the infamous uncle Richard of Gloucester, later Richard III.

It was during the early years of Edward's reign that Lady Jane Grey entered the marriage market. It was her parents' hope, of course, that she would marry the King, thus enhancing enormously their own wealth and position. Admiral Lord Thomas Seymour, the Protector's brother, stepped in with a promise that, if the Dorsets handed over a large sum of money, he could and would engineer the desired marriage. Primarily for that purpose, Jane moved into the household of Catherine Parr, the late King's widow, who had married the Admiral. Here she shared the house with the young Princess Elizabeth. It is difficult to understand how the Dorsets could have been so naive as to believe such an ill-founded plan could succeed. As a result of the power struggle of the young King's short reign, the Seymour brothers fell, were tried and executed. This left John Dudley, Earl of Warwick, as the new Protector and the real power behind the throne. It was to him that the Dorsets now turned and it was with his fortunes that their own became inextricably bound.

At the end of 1548 Jane returned to Bradgate to be with her sisters, Catherine and Mary. Her previous visit had been in the August of 1547 when the three girls were bridesmaids at the wedding in the chapel at Bradgate of Elizabeth Barlow. The bride, better known to history as Bess of Hardwick, was marrying as her second husband Sir William Cavendish.

Although surrounded by the grandeur of the house and its beautiful park, Jane was seldom happy. She shared none of her parents' interests such as hunting, hawking and gambling. In return, she came in for constant criticism for not meeting their expectations. Like many noble parents of the times, both mother and father insisted on strict discipline and obedience. Jane's education was in the hands of a tutor, John Aylmer, who taught her French and the classical languages of Latin and Greek. In 1550 she was visited by Roger Ascham, tutor to the Princess Elizabeth, who found her reading *Phaedon Platonis* in Greek while her parents hunted in the park. To the classics was added a firm foundation in the Protestant faith which, during her short life, Jane was to embrace with fervour. By thirteen she had developed into what Alison Plowden has described as "a stubborn, unusually bright, articulate and opinionated adolescent who did not neglect to inform sympathetic visitors that she regarded her parents' company as hellish."[6] It was the classic case of a wilful adolescent rebelling against narrow-minded and determined parents. Seen against the political background of the times, it was a prime ingredient in the disaster which followed.

Meanwhile in London, the young King was firmly under the control of the Earl of Warwick. In 1549 rebellion broke out in parts of south and eastern England against what were believed by ordinary people to be proposals by the government for land reforms and enclosures. The disturbances in East Anglia, led by Robert Kett, were suppressed by soldiers under Warwick who left Dorset in charge in London.

In February Dorset was appointed a warden of the Scottish Marches and was sent to quell trouble with the Scots. This meant a ride along the muddy and indifferent roads of the midlands and north, a journey which could take a week in bad weather. Writing from Berwick he complained to the Council in London that he was frequently raided by the enemy and that he was sent no money to pay his soldiers. Under the wretched conditions in the town he fell ill and became homesick. He was no soldier and did not function well under the pressures of military life. In October he was released from his post and returned home. During his absence, the men of Devon and Cornwall rose in arms against the laws which the young King, guided by Warwick, was proposing. These were set to change the face and fabric of the Old Religion. The new Prayer Book and the simplified liturgy it contained were particularly disliked. Although the rebellion was quelled and peace restored, the discontent continued to simmer below the surface.

When it became clear the King had consumption and would not make old bones, men of substance and position prepared to meet the inevitable crisis. It was with profoundly mixed feelings that Dorset found himself cast up by the tide of events on the same shore as Lord Huntingdon. George Hastings, the first Earl, had died in 1544 and Francis his successor had also firmly hitched his family's carriage to Warwick's team of horses. Huntingdon had conducted Somerset to the Tower on the occasion of that Duke's first internment and had shared with Dorset the judges' bench which eventually found him guilty of treason and had sent him to the scaffold. Huntingdon had also been prominent in putting down disturbances in Leicestershire and Rutland caused by rising prices and popular discontent with the speed of Warwick's religious reforms. Dorset had been called upon to try some of Huntingdon's prisoners. Henry Manners, second Earl of Rutland, also joined Warwick with strong support for his religious policy. With so many disparate supporters in the Warwick camp, the royal court was indeed a stage set for a drama of high politics and low cunning.

The rewards for supporting Warwick and the penalties for failing to do so were now appearing. In November 1551 Lord Arundel, the son of Henry's first father-in-law, was sent to the Tower for supporting Somerset. In contrast, and for his continued support of Warwick, Dorset was made Duke of Suffolk. This, of course, was the title his Brandon father-in-law had carried and which he had passed in turn to Henry, the elder of his two sons by his fourth wife, Katherine Willoughby d'Eresby. In 1551 the sweating sickness had spread through Cambridge where Henry and his younger brother were studying. The young second Duke had died on 14th July and Charles, the third Duke, followed him to the grave only half an hour later. The Brandon estates passed to Frances Grey and in October 1551 the Suffolk title was recreated as a reward from Warwick for her husband. The same week Warwick in effect granted himself the Dukedom of Northumberland.

Offices of profit under the crown now came to Suffolk thick and fast. In order to maintain a constant presence at court, essential if a nobleman simply wished to retain his position never mind advance it, the Grey family moved from Bradgate to a new home at Sheen on the banks of the river Thames. The move may also have eased the financial problem which Suffolk was experiencing with maintaining his houses at Astley in Warwickshire and Bradgate to a standard expected of such a bright and still rising star.[7]

Before the Dissolution Sheen had been a Carmelite monastery and the buildings, which had been converted into a comfortable dwelling, stood next to the royal palace of Richmond, a most sought-after location. The late Duke of Somerset had rebuilt it as a house and Warwick, who now lived across the Thames, was married there. Sheen House was also convenient for the Greys to visit Suffolk's widowed sister, Elizabeth, who lived at the Mansion of Audley End in Essex which her husband had created from the former Benedictine priory of Walden. Sheen was the most prestigious of Suffolk's London homes, although the others: Suffolk Place (exchanged with Henry VII for Cannon Row), Dorset House and the Minories all stood in the most fashionable parts of the capital. The Minories was once the Convent of the Little Sisters of St Francis and was the place where Henry's brothers, Lord John and Lord Thomas lived along with George Medley, their mother's relative.

In March 1553 the King, now approaching his end, made final plans for the succession to his throne. Under the terms of his father's will, it was not to pass to the descendants of Henry's elder sister Margaret, who had married King James IV of Scotland. Instead it was, as he had stated, to descend to "the heirs of the body of the Lady Frances our niece'. Failing that, it was to pass to the descendants of Frances' younger sister Eleanor.[8]

In the splendour of the ancient building of Sheen, Suffolk spent sleepless nights, pacing the dim, candle-lit corridors, where generations of more godly men had also contemplated a life built on riches and the future of a man's soul. There were the endless arguments with his wife who heard the court gossip which did not reach her husband. Words men spoke in public were not necessarily the same as those they whispered in private. Frances Grey was no fool; if her husband could not see where Northumberland's scheme was now leading, she could and she no longer wanted any part of it.

In April, with the King clearly beyond medical help, Sir Edward Hastings, Catholic brother of the Earl of Huntingdon, was ordered to raise 4,000 men from his Buckinghamshire estates to secure the throne for Jane. Also, and to bolster his own position and to draw Suffolk more surely into the web of intrigue, Northumberland arranged a series of marriages between the families of the principal parties. Jane married Northumberland's youngest son Guildford Dudley; Jane's sister Catherine married Henry Herbert, son of the Earl of Pembroke; and Northumberland's daughter married Lord Henry Hastings, Huntingdon's heir. On 6th July 1553 the King died and three days later at Sion House Jane was hailed as Queen by the lords assembled, including Arundel and Huntingdon. The deed was done and there was no turning back.

# Chapter 8

# *The Fall of the House of Grey*

**Henry Grey and Lady Jane (1553-54)**

The Princess Mary received the news of her brother's death and at once wrote to the council from Hoddesdon in Hertfordshire. Her letter was received on 10th July and her claim to the throne was rejected outright. The following day Jane Grey was brought by barge from Sion House down river to Westminster and thence to the Tower. One man present was the Genoese merchant Baptista Spinola who left this description of the girl. She was, he observed: "very short and thin, but prettily shaped and graceful. She has small features and a well made nose, the mouth flexible and the lips red. Her eyebrows are arched and darker than her hair, which is nearly red. Her eyes are sparkling and reddish brown in colour.'[1] He also noted that her complexion was good and that she had freckles. The shoes she wore had specially raised heels to make her appear taller. Perhaps not surprisingly the reception she received from the crowd was indifferent. "She is now called Queen," wrote Spinola, "but is not popular for the hearts of the people are with Mary."

Two days later, on the twelfth, Jane received the crown jewels from the Marquess of Winchester. At the same time Mary, forewarned by the Earl of Arundel of the danger that plans were being made to arrest her, moved promptly to Norfolk. Here she was proclaimed Queen by local gentlemen who gathered before her to pledge men and supplies in her cause.

The Council at Westminster met to decide their response. It was agreed that Northumberland should lead a force into East Anglia to arrest Mary. After his departure Suffolk made the mistake of allowing the Council members to leave the Tower, whereupon the majority re-assembled at Baynard Castle, Lord Pembroke's house, and the next morning declared for Mary at the Cross at Cheapside. A day later, Arundel brought the news to the feet of the Princess. Sir Edward Hastings, Huntingdon's third son, was also there with his men of Buckinghamshire drawn up in the Princess's support.

At Westminster on 19th July the final scene was enacted when Suffolk himself tore down the trappings of state which surrounded Jane and proclaimed Mary at the gates of the Tower. Northumberland saw his army melt away and found himself powerless. Seeing all was lost, he declared at the market cross at Cambridge that Mary was the rightful Queen. It was here, too, that he was apprehended by Arundel's men. Suffolk and Jane meanwhile had retreated to Sheen where they, too, were arrested. Five days later on Tuesday 25th July, Northumberland entered London a prisoner. The entire Dudley family was in custody when Mary entered her capital in triumph and on a horse led by Sir Edward Hastings.

*Baynard Castle, where a re-assembled Council declared for Princess Mary*

It was at this point that the influence of the Duchess of Suffolk with the new Queen came to the fore. Theirs was a relationship which had developed when the little Grey sisters had played with both young Princesses and had spent the Christmas of 1547 together at Hansden. Whatever the Duchess said in private had the desired effect and Suffolk was released. He had recanted his faith, had been fined £20,000 and had agreed to sit in judgement on Northumberland. The four-day trial opened on 18th August at the end of which John Dudley was duly found guilty of high treason and condemned to death. At the age of about 51 he went to the block protesting to his final breath his Catholicism and allegiance to his rightful Queen.

Recent research has suggested that the young Edward VI had not simply been the dupe of his overbearing uncle, Northumberland, and that he had played an eager role in the moves to establish Jane as his successor. But those persons living throughout the events of July and August 1553 believed Jane's claim to the throne, however presented, to be illegal. The foolish and naive Henry Grey had been deceived and brow-beaten by a ruthless, greedy and ambitious Northumberland who was almost twenty years his senior.

If the immediate crisis had passed, the processes of law still had to be followed. On 14th November 1553 Jane was arraigned for high treason and found guilty. The penalty was death and the date for her execution was set for 9th of the following February, although few believed the sentence would be carried out. Her father had his attainder reversed and Huntingdon, who had been languishing under suspicion in the Fleet prison like a common criminal, was also pardoned and given his liberty.

Towards the end of November 1553 news that the Queen intended to marry King Philip of Spain swept the capital. The prospect of having a Spaniard sharing the English throne sent shock waves through the

country. Voices were raised in protest and rumours circulated that men were gathering arms across the shires. Spies and informers added to growing confusion. One such was Edward Courtenay, a young man who had lost his way in the rapidly changing politics of the capital. On his word, the government came to learn of the involvement of Suffolk, who was Courtenay's uncle, in a planned rising under the Kentish gentleman Thomas Wyatt, son of the eminent poet.

This time the result of Suffolk's intrigues was an even greater disaster. At Sheen he received a summons from the Council on 25th January which he may have believed was an order to lead a force against Wyatt's men gathered at Rochester. The next day Suffolk fled with his brothers Thomas and John to their estates in the Midlands. By 29th January they had reached Bradgate where they made a short stay to feed and rest the horses and before riding to Leicester. Here they read a proclamation against the proposed Spanish marriage to an indifferent crowd of townspeople. The following morning they reached Coventry only to find the town gates closed and the inhabitants shouting against them. Realising the vital support from his own tenants would not be forthcoming, Suffolk paid off his men and instructed them to disperse. In desperation he and John made for their manor at Astley and hid, only to be betrayed by a servant. Suffolk, tired and ill, was taken in a hollow tree, Thomas under a pile of hay. Their captor was Huntingdon who, it was said, had requested the task from the Queen.

The five day rebellion had been no more than a gallop across the open fields of the Midlands; but this time there was to be no mercy for the leaders. On 17th February, before a bench presided over by the Earl of Arundel, Suffolk was convicted of high treason and on 23rd was executed. He was aged 36. Two days later it was the turn of Jane and her husband. Wyatt, whose efforts at rebellion had also failed, and Suffolk's brother Lord Thomas paid the same price.

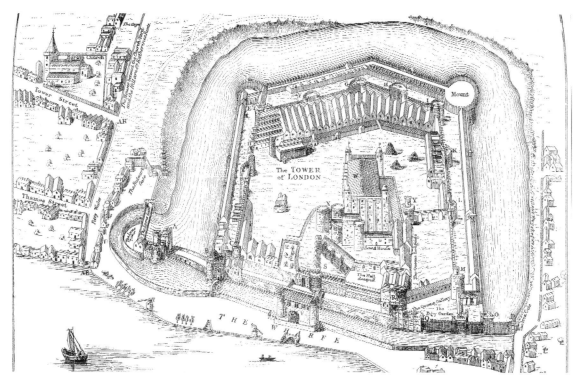

*The Tower of London about the time of Lady Jane Grey*

Writers who have commented on the character of Suffolk are agreed that he was an educated man, a thinker on matters of religion and one who firmly espoused the tenets of the reformed church. The anonymous writer of a contemporary document known as the *Chronicle of Queen Jane*, who describes himself as a "resident of the Tower", said of Suffolk that "to his friends he was gentle and courteous" and "was easy in deed than was thought expedient, of stomach stout and hardy, hasty and soon kindled, but pacified straight again", regretting if he had made a hasty wrong judgement. The same writer describes him as "upright and plain in his private dealings".[2] So he may well have been, but he was easily led by an overbearing Northumberland and his lack of a grasp of the politics of the snakepit of the royal court meant that inevitably events slipped further and further beyond his control.

During the time her husband, daughter and son-in-law were held in the Tower under sentence of death, Frances Dorset was received by the Queen at court. Three weeks after her husband's execution the Marchioness created a sensation by marrying her groom, one Adrian Stokes. She was now 37 and he was a ginger-haired lad of 19 years. He came from a fairly good yeoman family and two years earlier had joined the Grey household where, it would appear, he had done more than simply groom and exercise the horses. Whatever else her reasons for the match, Lady Suffolk was making it clear that she was bowing out of politics. Any offspring she may have with Stokes would have no more than a very distant claim to the throne. After Jane's reign she had effectively saved the Duke; thereafter he was on his own with his ill conceived plots. His removal from the scene after the fiasco with Wyatt had been inevitable but perhaps not entirely unwelcome to her.

*Astley Castle, Warwickshire, granted to the widow of the Duke of Suffolk*

The Duchess had been able to intercede on behalf of Lord John Grey, her brother-in-law and the youngest of the Grey brothers. She told the Queen that the foolish young man had been dominated by Henry and Thomas who had persuaded him that the only way out of the crisis was to stick together. In June John was lodged in the Tower; but he had some other influential friends at court. The first was his wife Mary who was a Catholic and the daughter of Sir Anthony Browne, the Queen's Master of Horse. Browne's wife, we have seen, was John's Irish relative, the Fair Geraldine. Lady Mary Grey went through "painful travail and diligent suit" on her husband's behalf.[3] John's brother-in-law, Anthony Browne, newly created Viscount Montague, was also very much in favour with the Queen. Montague's other sister, Mabel, had recently married Gerald Fitzgerald, 11th Earl of Kildare. In addition, there was Lady Catherine Grey who was a close friend of Montague and who was reputed to have Catholic sympathies. Finally, there was little Lady Mary Grey, aged eight and youngest sister of the unfortunate Jane, to shed tears in the cause of her errant uncle John. The Catholic presence probably managed to persuade the Queen that the main danger from the Greys was over and that she could afford to be seen to be merciful. Not only was Lord John released from the Tower but was also allowed to live in the Minories where he could be watched, and he was granted manors to support himself.

The pardon rolls bearing the names involved in the movements against Queen Mary reveal how little support for Suffolk and the other leaders there had been from men of position and substance.[4] The Earls of Rutland and Huntingdon, both as scheming and unscrupulous as Henry Grey, made their peace with the new regime. In their own interests they now moved for control, on behalf of Her Majesty of course, of those parts of the realm where they held lands, particularly Leicestershire. Even the impetuous William, Lord Grey of Wilton, was pardoned and acquired the post of Master of the Queen's Hawks.[5] It was fortunate for the mischievous Edward Courtenay that he had spent the months of crisis in the Tower. On his release he went into exile and died in Padua in 1556.

Hardly had the Queen finished arranging the cushions on her throne than her supporters crowded round to collect their rewards. There were many estates and offices of profit available for disposal and few more valuable than those of the late Duke of Suffolk. With his attainder went his titles and his entire possessions, although the remaining members of the family had at least escaped the stigma of "corruption of the blood".

The first measure was to provide for Suffolk's widow who, we have seen, married beneath her former station. Some of her husband's Leicestershire lands, notably Groby (but not Bradgate), Beaumanor, Bardon and the great park of Loughborough were granted to her for life. So too was the manor of Astley and other properties in Warwickshire, some manors in Hertfordshire and a few manors in Devon and Somerset which formed part of the Bonville inheritance of Cicely, wife of the first Marquess. Lady Suffolk was also allowed to live at Sheen where her young husband made the most of his nearness to the court. Stokes the groom had done well for himself; his new wife was a rich woman.

The Queen treated Huntingdon, too, with much kindness since he was related, through his wife, to the Countess of Salisbury, the Queen's former governess. To him went Suffolk's Leicestershire manors of Loughborough and Burley together with the valuable site of the former abbey of Leicester on the northern edge of that town. Lord Rutland was not so fortunate and does not appear to have benefited from this hand-out of Grey lands. He already held many thousands of acres in north-east Leicestershire, Derbyshire and Lincolnshire and may have been seen by the Queen to be already powerful enough in the Midlands.

Far from being kept alive but out of sight and effectively imprisoned by poverty, Lord John Grey and his wife were granted extensive lands from his late brother's estates. Manors in Leicestershire, Derbyshire, Warwickshire, Essex and Suffolk came their way. The grants were more modest than those given to the Duchess Frances who also held lands in Lincolnshire in her own right, but they certainly helped to maintain a lord in lordly circumstances. At the court of Queen Mary, one did not look a gift horse in the mouth too readily.

Also at the Queen's disposal were the enormous estates forfeited by the former Dukes of Somerset and Northumberland. It was fortunate that the crown had such resources available with which to reward loyal servants and favourites. Career administrators in the machinery of royal government were also not overlooked. One such was Edmund Peckham who received Grey estates in the south-west, especially in Somerset and Devon. Even Robert Cole "principal cook of the household" received lands in Leicestershire.[6]

During Mary's short reign, Lady Catherine and Lady Mary Grey lived with their mother at Sheen. They maintained themselves with income from lands passed to them from their Brandon grandfather. Catherine had been repudiated by the Herberts; no son of theirs would remain married to the daughter of a traitor. The Greys of Wilton had made the same decision about Lord Arthur who was betrothed to the eight-year-old Mary Grey. Both girls were to marry eventually but under conditions which were to lead to only more strife for members of this most unhappy family .

# Chapter 9

# *The Greys at Pirgo*

**Lord John Grey (?-1564)**
**Sir Henry Grey, 1st Baron Grey of Groby (?-1614)**
**Sir John Grey (?-1611)**
**Henry Grey, 1st Earl of Stamford (c1600-1673)**

Queen Mary died on 17th November 1558 and following Elizabeth's peaceful succession to the throne the Greys' fortunes took a turn for the better. Lord John was included in the new Queen's entourage as she made her first progress through London, hailed by the same cheering crowds who had acclaimed her sister five years earlier. He was also present at court as head of the family. This was rehabilitation indeed. To obtain a place at court a nobleman had to be invited or he waited patiently for what he judged to be a suitable opportunity to apply. No matter what his rank, he did not simply turn up and join in.

On the first New Year's Day of the reign, Lord John gave his monarch a costly cup "of mother-of-pearl garnished with silver and gilt", a suitable token of gratitude which in any case the Queen expected. His wife, the Lady Anne, gave "a purse of red silk and gold knit in gold and silver' at a cost of £56. Elizabeth's gifts of cups and bowls, also in gilt, to the pair were equally generous.[1] The Queen was signalling her satisfaction with Sir John's position. Also at court with the Greys was Katherine, the young Willoughby heiress who had married Charles Brandon, Duke of Suffolk when she was fourteen, although she had been intended for William Clinton, Earl of Lincoln. This second Duchess of Suffolk had spurned William too, and had then gone beneath her station by marrying Richard Bertie, her gentleman usher. Lincoln had eventually married a daughter of Francis Hastings, the second Earl of Huntingdon. It was all most confusing, not to say embarrassing at times, determining and following the correct order of precedence and trying to remember who was speaking to whom, especially on royal occasions.

Even from his earliest days at court Lord John found keeping up the position expected of him became more and more beyond his means. A lord was expected to have a fine house, servants, fine clothes and a carriage. He wrote to William Cecil, the Queen's principal Secretary of State, asking for help. His letters were not left to gather dust. Shortly afterwards he was granted manors in Somerset, part of the Bonville inheritance of his late grandmother Cicely. These, together with a large number of his family's former estates in Leicestershire, including Bradgate, went some way to alleviating his financial problems, at least for a while.[2]

Lord John was also granted the royal manor and park of Pirgo, part of the royal liberty of Havering-atte-

*Lady Catherine Grey, Countess of Hertford and her son Edward Seymour, Lord Beauchamp (artist unknown)*

Bower north of the town of Romford. The mansion, which was set in pleasant and rolling countryside, was a large and ancient structure and contained a small chapel. In 1594 it was described by the surveyor John Norden as "a fair house" and was depicted on a map of c.1618 as a large gabled building.[3] It had been bought by Henry VIII and repaired in 1543. Before his downfall along with Suffolk and the other Protestant reformers, Sir John Gates, Master of the Guard to Edward VI, lived at Pirgo as a retreat from his residence near the court in London. At various times the Princesses Mary and Elizabeth had stayed at Pirgo which now became Lord John's chief residence.

Along with the grant of Pirgo, Lord John's attainder was reversed and his family was restored "in the blood". This measure was extended to his nieces Catherine and Mary who had been living with their mother and Adrian Stokes. Since her husband's execution, Duchess Frances had divided her time between her several properties including those of Astley in Warwickshire and Beaumanor in Leicestershire. She died in November 1559, received a state funeral by the Queen's command and was buried in Westminster Abbey.

The new monarch, Elizabeth, was under no illusions about the threat to her throne posed by her cousins, the Grey sisters. Even within her Council opinion was divided as to the legitimacy of her own succession and as to who might follow her as long as she remained without a legitimate male heir. While the Grey girls were at court they could be kept under surveillance and suitable measures could be taken at the first signs of trouble from them. Catherine was now eighteen, a slender and good looking girl who had her Tudor grandmother's auburn hair. Unlike Duchess Frances she had an air of reticence which men found appealing. There was no shortage of suitors at home or from abroad, but the Queen had warned her not to even think of becoming betrothed. The potential problems to the monarch of marriage to Catherine Grey by any man of rank and substance were many and complex.

Catherine, however, was in love with Edward Seymour, first son of the second wife of the late Duke of Somerset, and now restored to the title of Earl of Hertford. He was known by some as "Little Hertford" on account of his small size and vacillating character. Whatever his physical assets and disposition, he did ask Catherine to marry him and opened negotiations with her mother to formalise the affair. Unfortunately Duchess Frances was sick and unable to seek an audience with the Queen, or even to pen an appropriate letter. Meanwhile Elizabeth had learned of the affair and had extracted from Catherine a promise that she would not marry without express royal approval. If, and it was a very big "if", the Grey sisters were allowed to marry, suitable partners would of course be chosen for them. The Queen had seen what an ambitious race the Seymours were and how they could not be trusted.

At court every eye was focussed on the Queen's own dalliance with her favourite Robert Dudley, her Master of Horse and son of the late Duke of Northumberland. Dudley's wife, Amy Robsart, had died under mysterious circumstances and rumour was that he had got rid of her so that he could marry the Queen. Making the most of the opportunity of being out of the royal spotlight, Catherine married Seymour secretly in October 1560.

At the time of her marriage Catherine was already pregnant and soon after was unable to conceal her condition. She and her husband were sent to the Tower but were kept in separate apartments. Her child, Edward, was a healthy male who was baptised in the church of St Peter ad Vincula in the Tower. Richard Davey has pointed out the grim irony attached to the ceremony: the witnesses must have stood on the flagstones covering no fewer than six of the infant's immediate forebears, including his two grandfathers and his aunt (Lady Jane Grey), all of whom had lately perished by the axe.[4] For the Queen the birth of every new descendant of the House of Suffolk only added to the web of intrigue surrounding her position and the succession to her throne.

The following year, 1562, the Queen caught smallpox and became dangerously ill. The corridors and back rooms of the palace buzzed with whispers and intrigue. Since she was unmarried there was no direct heir, let alone a male one. There was not even an appointed successor. First in strict order was Mary, the Queen of the Scots, who was descended from Henry VIII's eldest sister, Margaret Stewart. Second in line was Margaret Douglas, daughter of the same Mary by her second marriage. Then came Frances Grey, Duchess of Suffolk, followed by her two daughters, Lady Catherine and Lady Mary. To add to the already fraught situation was Henry Hastings, the third Earl of Huntingdon, whose great grandfather was the Plantagenet George, Duke of Clarence and brother of Edward IV. Huntingdon's mother had often reminded those who would listen of her son's claim. Now the Queen appeared to be at death's door there was renewed discussion of the prospects of this apparent outsider from the House of Hastings. Elizabeth, however, made a complete recovery and ordered a review of the conditions of her prisoners in the Tower. Catherine was living in reasonable comfort. She had her parrots, which ruined the furniture, her monkeys and her lapdogs.[5] She and her husband were supposed to be kept apart but clandestine meetings took place with the result that in February 1563 a second son, Thomas, was born. The Queen's response was like a broadside from a roaring cannon. Hertford was fined £5,000 for supposedly deflowering a virgin of the royal blood, £5,000 for breaking his prison and a further £5,000 "for repeating his vicious act". The enormous total was later reduced to £3,000 with a warning, if one was needed, that the royal patience was exhausted. Under normal circumstances he and Catherine could expect to be kept in the Tower indefinitely, but in the same summer a serious outbreak of plague in the capital caused Elizabeth to move them elsewhere, out of reach of infection.

Hertford was sent to his mother's home under house arrest. The unfortunate custodian of Catherine and her younger son Thomas was her uncle, Lord John Grey, who received his unhappy and almost penniless niece, her servants and her menagerie at Pirgo in August 1563. He was not pleased to see them since, the nuisance of her parrots apart, he was expected to act as gaoler and ensure there were no unauthorised contacts with the outside world. Furthermore he could not expect an adequate allowance for her keep. Lord John, a melancholy man by nature, took no pleasure from the company of a young woman who seldom smiled and was often in tears in her "miserable and comfortless estate".[6]

His concerns about the payment for his niece's residence were well founded. He was still suffering from the financial effects of a visit by the Queen two years earlier, and was hard pressed to find the £6-16s-8d a week which Catherine and her servants were costing him. He wrote again to Secretary Cecil pleading for help. Catherine was, Lord John insisted, "a penitent and sorrowful woman in the Queen's displeasure". The response was an instruction to Hertford to shoulder the responsibility for his wife and son himself. Added to Lord John's worries was the problem of Catherine's poor health. The long corridors of Pirgo Palace in winter were cold, damp and draughty; Lord John could hardly keep up the place let alone heat it properly.

Cecil's lack of action, caused by his inability or unwillingness to move the Queen to relax the terms of Catherine's house arrest, began to tell on both uncle and niece. In yet another plea to Cecil in September 1563, Lord John described the desperation both were experiencing:

*"I assure you cousin Cecil ... the thought and care she taketh for want of her Highness's favour, pines her away: before God I speak it, if it comes not the sooner, she will not long live thus, she eateth not above six morsels in the meal. If I say unto her, "Good madam, eat something to comfort yourself", she falls aweeping and goeth up to her chamber; if I ask her what the cause is ... she answers me "alas uncle, what a life is this to me, thus to live in the Queen's displeasure; but for my lord, and my children, I would to God I were buried."*[7]

The following year Lord John's situation worsened with the publication of a book by John Hales, an extreme Protestant, which set out the case for Catherine Grey's claim to the throne. Hales was sent to the Fleet prison in April and Lord John fell under a cloud as it was believed he and Hales had discussed the contents of the book before its publication. For a time he was detained at court under close royal supervision but was eventually released.

As a precaution against any unrest Hales' book might provoke, the Queen moved Catherine to the care of Sir William Petre, who had served on the commission set up to investigate the circumstances surrounding Catherine's marriage to Hertford. His home in Essex was the prestigious Ingersgate Hall, which was not unlike Bradgate and which had been built partly from the profits from lands confiscated from Catherine's late father. There she remained in captivity for two years before being passed on to Sir John Wentworth at nearby Gosfield Hall. Wentworth protested in vain that he and his wife were too old for such an onerous task. He died in 1567 and Catherine was moved yet again, this time to Cockfield Hall in the remote Suffolk village of Yoxford. Here she died in the following January of tuberculosis or a similar chronic infection, quite possibly caught from her monkeys or parrots.

Lord Hertford was in the custody of John Spencer at Althorp when he learnt of the death of his wife, but he was not given his freedom for another two years. In 1591 he entertained the Queen at the Seymours' house at Wulfhall in Wiltshire. Four years later he married his second wife, Frances, sister of the Earl of Nottingham, who died in 1598. His third wife was the widow of a wealthy wine merchant who brought a welcome injection of cash to the family.[8] Hertford died in 1621 at the remarkable age of 83. His son, Edward, obtained letters patent from the crown which ensured that the first Duke's son by his second wife could make claim to the dukedom and other honours.

Mary, the third and youngest of the Grey sisters, was unlike either Jane or Catherine. The few sources available describe her as very small and at best as very plain looking. In August 1565, when Mary was 19, the Spanish ambassador wrote to his master that "she is little, crooked-backed and very ugly".[9] Little is known about her early life before she married Thomas Keyes. He was a widower aged 40, a mere sergeant-at-arms and the father of several small children. Perhaps most bizarre of all, he was a giant of a man at six feet eight inches. The wedding took place on either 10th or 12th of August after an evening party in his rooms at Westminster and was witnessed by at least three people.[10] When word reached the Queen the two were separated; Keyes was sent to the Fleet prison and Mary to the close custody of the Queen's servant William Hawtrey at Chequers. The following year she was transferred to the care of her aunt Eleanor in the Minories in London. At neither place was she happy, but her entreaties to the Queen went unanswered. In 1571 her husband died and the following year she was released from her prison-like custody and sent to Adrian Stokes at Sheen. Towards the end of her life she recovered some favour at Court and when she died in 1578, aged 33, she was buried in Westminster Abbey.

Lord John Grey's final years were not happy ones. In addition to his involvement with John Hales he spent time in the Tower for meddling in the Mary Queen of Scots affair. On his release he retired to Pirgo where he died in 1569, supposedly of melancholy but more likely of his family's problem – gout.

Royal interest in the Greys now rested with Lord John's son Henry, born in 1547 and the oldest of four brothers. He had been often at court in the company of his father and seems to have gained the Queen's trust. In 1573 he was elected MP for Essex and three years later he was appointed a Justice of the Peace for Haveringham in the same county, a post he held without a break for the following 27 years. Evidently he prospered to the point where he was able to buy the estate of his distant cousin John at Enville in Staffordshire. Thereafter he set about recovering the lands the family had so recently lost.

The death of Lady Mary Grey in 1578 removed what the Queen regarded as an important threat to her throne and thereafter Sir Henry's favour with his monarch blossomed. Between 1583 and 1594 hardly a year went by without his receiving the reversion of parcels of former Grey lands in Leicestershire which had earlier been granted to others. In the 1580s he regularly entered the lists before the Queen at the Ascension Day joustings at Whitehall. As part of the defensive measures taken to meet the threat from the Spanish Armada, Henry, as deputy Lord Lieutenant of the county, was ordered by the Privy Council to prepare for the defences of the Essex coastline. He was knighted the following year and held various royal appointments such as Master of the Queen's Buckhounds. His Court connections alone made him head of the most important family on the Haveringham social scene.

The return to influence of the Greys, especially in Leicestershire, greatly concerned the Hastings. After the executions of 1554 they had seized the opportunity to become the dominant family in the county; but this was not without problems which centred on the family's financial affairs. Francis Hastings, the 2nd Earl of Huntingdon, had forfeited the trust of the monarch when he married Katherine Pole, whose family was still considered a political risk. In order to meet the debts of his father and grandfather and to provide for his four brothers and five sisters, Henry the 3rd Earl, known as the "Puritan Earl" on account of his strongly held religious beliefs, found it necessary to sell land worth £16,000 from his Botreaux inheritance in Devon and Cornwall. At Leicester he had served the town and county well as their local lord, but following the scare of Elizabeth's illness in 1562 he had found himself in the political wilderness for more than a decade. Such were his financial problems that the family were unable to make the desired move to their manor of Stoke Poges which gave them ready access to London. Instead, they were obliged to remain in their Leicestershire manor of Ashby, and to continue as close neighbours with Greys. By 1580 the Hastings had accumulated debt to the point where further sales of land, to a total of £36,000, were made. With a large family, keeping up a lordly appearance and dominant social presence was an expensive business.

Of the Earl's brothers, Sir George bought the manor of Loughborough and the hall and park of Castle Donington in Leicestershire. Edward the second brother, lived at Leicester Abbey, the site of the former great monastic house on the edge of the town where Cardinal Wolsey had been buried. Francis, the third brother, was MP for Leicester before moving to Somerset to oversee the administration of the remaining properties in the west country. Walter, the youngest brother, was a Catholic and ruled over the family's interests in Leicester Forest, close by the town. In spite of their debts the Hastings, almost by their very numbers, had no competitors for the political and social leadership of Elizabethan Leicestershire.

The rise of the Greys and the problems of the Hastings were signs of changing fortunes in Elizabeth's reign. The Queen was set on clipping the wings of families whose power was not of her own making or whose position was not to her advantage. Against the jostling of other would-be players in the dramas of the Court, she alone demanded centre stage in the role of Gloriana. There were rewards enough for favoured subjects who regularly, diligently and faithfully served her; but there was no place in matters of state for those who were content to act merely as the big fish in a shire pond. A presence at court was in every respect as important as it was expensive.

In 1601 Henry Grey's son, Sir John, felt confident enough to challenge the Hastings on their own ground, standing for knight of the shire for one of the two seats for Leicestershire. Sir Henry had spent his youth soldiering in the Netherlands, under the Earl of Leicester, in a bid by England to curb the growing power of Spain. As part of his election strategy, Sir Henry called in a favour owed him by the Earl of Rutland. This required the votes of his lordship's tenants against the Hastings candidates. In the event the expected support was not forthcoming. Sir John was defeated by the last minute intervention of Huntingdon's nephew and was obliged to contest a seat in far away Cornwall. This he saw as a serious snub which only served to revive old animosities and give rise to a fresh and lengthy episode of antagonism between the two families.

Queen Elizabeth died early on the morning of 24th March 1603. Within hours of the announcement Henry Grey and a group of others were riding hard through the rain to Edinburgh to inform King James VI of Scotland that he was now also King James I of England. Four months later Henry Grey was created Baron Grey of Groby. That same year he also left the house at Pirgo and moved the family back to Leicestershire. After an absence of fifty years the Greys were home once again at Bradgate.

*Henry Grey, 1st Earl of Stamford, as a young man (C. Jonson)*

# Chapter 10

# *Earl versus Monarch*

## Henry Grey, 1st Earl of Stamford (c1600-73)

King James found all was not well in Leicestershire where the resurgence of rivalry between Greys and Hastings was affecting the efficient administration of local justice. The conflict had intensified after the death in 1595 of Henry Hastings, the "Puritan Earl" of Huntingdon who, as we have seen, led his family to dominate the County's affairs during Elizabeth's reign. His successor as fourth Earl was his brother George, a less Godly man and a much less skilful politician. At the turn of the century, when the Greys were making moves for a seat in the House of Commons, Huntingdon managed to antagonise those members of the gentry who would normally have considered themselves his family's supporters. It was a turn of events which was to cost the Hastings dearly.

At the heart of the problem of local government was the administration of "purveyance", which was the claim by the crown to goods at less than market prices. Much resentment was felt by those of the middling sort (the gentry, squirearchy, merchants and the like) who were called upon not only to meet the totals demanded but also also to supervise and administer their collection. When problems arose there was little scope for manoeuvre about meeting deadlines and making deliveries. Consequently, the local justices, who were responsible for the administration of purveyance, tended to treat the levy as a local rate. The fourth Earl of Huntingdon died in 1604 leaving his grandson, a minor, to succeed him. This provided the opportunity the Greys had been waiting for since it gave them the opportunity of once again seizing the political initiative at county level. Lord Grey boldly asked the King's chief minister Cecil to award the Hastings' offices to him. This request was granted, but following vigorous protests from the Hastings camp the decision was reversed. After much acrimony a compromise of sorts was reached. Although this did not solve the underlying problem of purveyance or settle the matter of the post of Lord Lieutenant, which was left vacant until a compromise which might be acceptable to both sides could be negotiated, it did at least keep the two families more or less on speaking terms[1].

Eventually, however, the Lord Lieutenancy was given to the young Earl of Huntingdon. The Greys were outraged and the political temperature rose abruptly. Matters were made worse by the very partisan way in which Huntingdon, an arrogant young man, now made appointments to county positions and conducted affairs. Even his ancient uncle Walter, who it was whispered had been questioned over his possible involvement in the Gunpowder Plot, was found a lucrative post. The general discontent with purveyance in general, the way it was being collected together with series of additional minor incidents came to a head in

1610. The result was that Sir John Grey, an irascible and short-tempered man, challenged Sir Henry Hastings to a duel. Bloodshed appears to have been avoided only at the last minute and on the field chosen for combat. As far as the two families were concerned the battle lines for future conflict had been redrawn.

By 1610 purveyance was becoming even harder to collect. Questions were being raised in Parliament by Sir Thomas Beaumont of Stoughton, a Leicestershire gentleman, who sought to challenge the very legality of the demands. In response to this show of impertinence, King James replied that he regarded purveyance as legal and, his secretary stated, that if it was not delivered "his majesty knew what he had to do". By sniping and manoeuvring the Greys managed to force the Hastings family into a position where their integrity for administering all royal affairs was cast in doubt. But in 1611, with Sir Henry Hastings floundering with the millstone of purveyance round his neck, Sir John Grey caught smallpox and died. The tide of politics turned once again. Unable to press home their advantage, the Greys were powerless to prevent the Hastings recovering their position in Leicestershire and from preventing them establishing a dominance of the electoral process. This local command of power was to remain theirs for a further three decades to the Civil War.

Purveyance was only one aspect of the monarch's policy and style of government which was troubling the Greys. Although by upbringing a Protestant, the King soon managed to antagonise many of his puritan subjects by his disdain for the Presbyterian system of his native Scotland and the intolerance he displayed toward its followers. In contrast, his Catholic subjects were not treated with the severity expected of him, although after the Gunpowder Plot of 1605 his attitude changed abruptly. The authorised version of the Bible of 1611, also caused dissent and provoked much protest. This was a serious setback since it was hoped the book would bring together those Protestant sects who could barely tolerate one another, never mind Catholics.

A further problem for the Greys, and a good many other loyal Englishmen, was the King's view of government, known as the "Divine Right of Kings". This was a doctrine that held that the monarch derived his authority to rule directly from the Almighty, with optional reference to the views of his subjects. This, James maintained, enabled him to govern very much as his conscience dictated since he and he alone was answerable to God. A struggle with Parliament was the inevitable outcome since most of its members did not share the King's views and were becoming ever more bold in saying so. A rising tide of dissent was heard not only in the taverns, from around the yeoman's table and in the dining rooms of the rich and influential; the representatives of borough and shire were raising their voices in open protest in the capital.

In the course of time James dismissed Elizabeth's advisors whom he had inherited with the crown. Instead he relied on his own appointed favourites such as George Villiers, a very handsome Leicestershire yeoman's son, who rose from obscurity to become the Duke of Buckingham in only eight years. The King bought judges, which corrupted the justice they administered; he imposed taxes which were not sanctioned by Parliament; he declared the right to put aside the results of elections which did not please him and he contested the right of members to speak their minds in Parliament. The collection of delicate religious and political compromises with which the late Queen had managed to hold her nation together was beginning to fall apart.

Lord Grey of Groby died in 1614 and was buried in the vaults of Bradgate House where a monument in the chapel records his life. He was succeeded in the title by his grandson, also Henry, then aged about 14

*Combe Abbey, Coventry, in 1810. It was formerly one of the properties of Thomas, Lord Grey of Groby.*

and the eldest son of the late Sir John Grey. The following year the young Henry matriculated at Trinity College Cambridge which awarded him an MA degree. Little is known of his early life other than that he lived at Bradgate. As a minor, he was unable to mount any opposition to the Hastings. But with his marriage in 1620 – the year *The Mayflower* left the shores of England for the New World – the tide of events once again began to move in favour of the Greys.

Henry's marriage to Anne Cecil must be seen as something of a perhaps not unexpected triumph for the Greys. She was the youngest daughter of William Cecil, later the second Earl of Exeter and grandson of William Cecil who had guided the ship of state through the stormy seas of Elizabeth's reign. William Cecil the Elder had privately believed that the true heir to Elizabeth's throne was the elder of the surviving Grey sisters. The exact nature of his efforts behind the scenes which resulted in the slow but certain restoration of the Greys to prominence can only be imagined.

The wealth as well as the goodwill of the Cecils now flowed in the direction of the Greys. Exeter's three daughters, who were his co-heiresses, brought huge dowries to their husbands. With Diana,who became the wife of Henry de Vere, Earl of Oxford, it was worth £30,000.[2] For Henry Grey it was the immensely wealthy estate of the castle and manor of the ancient borough of Stamford in Lincolnshire, part of the great fortune her great-grandfather had built up during his years as Secretary of State to Elizabeth.

Five years after Henry Grey's marriage to the Lady Anne, King James died and was succeeded by his son

Charles. In the first Parliament of his reign the House of Commons lost no time in presenting a list of its grievances. In particular, the House insisted on the right to be consulted on the appointment of the King's ministers. Charles rejected this and their other demands and it soon became clear that the "Divine Right" was to guide this King in matters both spiritual and political as much as it did his father.

In 1628 Charles I summoned the Lords of the Upper House and the gentlemen of the Commons to his presence. This time he found them in an even more truculent mood and with a longer list of grievances, which they presented to him under the banner of the "Petition of Rights". A trial of strength was averted, at least temporarily, by the King agreeing to their demands but with no intention of keeping his word. At least he might be spared being harassed by the likes of Henry Grey who would now be free to channel his considerable energies in other directions. The King's confidence that he had the upper hand was such that in the same year he created his influential, if troublesome, subject as the Earl of Stamford. Six years later, on his journey from Leicester to Nottingham, the monarch visited his lordship for a day at Bradgate. Charles may have been more interested to see for the first time the home of the late Lady Jane rather than to honour Stamford. Whatever the King's motive, the visit could not have been an enjoyable occasion for either man. Beneath the formality of monarch with subject, guest with host, the atmosphere was decidedly frosty.

It is not difficult to understand why Stamford and his monarch were at loggerheads. The Earl had been raised as a presbyterian. He did not accept Charles, or any king for that matter, as head of a church whose leader drew authority from such a preposterous view of his relationship with God as "Divine Right". He also did not approve of the ways in which the Church of England was being shaped. It was supposed to be a Protestant church, the result of a glorious Reformation, but as each week passed Archbishop Laud – as a critic wrote, "that red faced little butcher's son from Reading" – pressed forward with his high church ways. Arminism it was called, full of the language, signs and rituals which differed little from those of the Church of Rome. Wherever men like Stamford looked, there were Popish lords and commoners like Laud who were gathered round the throne at the feet of Charles' French Catholic Queen. Stamford could see no escape from this King and his "Divine Right", which gave rise to so much division among men and which threatened a terrible fate for the country.

The King dissolved his fractious Parliament in 1628 and attempted to rule for ten more years without further reference to the electors. While his policies looked backwards and inwards, trade and commerce was looking forwards and outwards. Merchants and sailors were setting out to the wider world beyond the continent of Europe and, in so doing, were challenging the maritime and commercial power of the old enemy, Spain.

At home Stamford and other prominent and like-minded puritans, such as the Lords Manchester, Brooke and Saye & Sele, were employing their presbyterian zeal to improving their estates. If this involved a harder attitude towards tenants, that was part and parcel of their puritan belief of developing among all men the virtues of hard work and self reliance. In Somerset, Stamford was prosecuted for enclosing open land and there was a similar problem on his Leicestershire manors of Broughton Astley and Breedon-on-the-Hill[3]. He was granted permission to improve the 4,000 acres of windswept bog known as Wildmore Fen near Boston in Lincolnshire for development with a view to eventual sale. About this time he set about acquiring a patent for a new way of dressing flax from which he hoped to make a profit of £4,000 to £5,000 a year. In Leicester a brewhouse was planned in order to provide, as Stamford put it, "good and wholesome drink at reasonable prices" all, of course, to his lordship's considerable and certain profit.

By the beginning of the 1640s Stamford was benefiting from rising land revenues which added to his already considerable income. His estates produced a gross rental of approximately £4,000 per year. This brought him alongside twenty or so other peers, many newly created, of similar means. These included the families of Brudenell, Digby, Feilding and his distant northern kinsman Lord Grey of Warke. Yet flourishing as these new-style entrepreneurs were, the richest families in the kingdom such as the Howards, the Percys, the Seymours and the Manners still towered over them in terms of wealth. Many of Stamford's equals were the very men called upon to collect and pay towards the King's demands such as "Ship Money", "Forest Dues" and the like. At the same time they believed the King was effectively inhibiting the success of their commercial ventures and shamelessly giving favours to Catholics. There was almost no important matter of policy on which Lord Stamford and his monarch could agree.

In his turn Stamford must have been a difficult man to deal with in many ways. Although William Mercer, author of *Angliae Speculum*, refers to him as "most courteous and right stately Stamford", the Earl's portrait together with the comments made of him by others suggest a different character[4]. He had a haughty disposition, was easily irritated and had difficulty getting on with his neighbours. These qualities coupled with an avaricious nature, a callous disregard for the poor, his hostility to the church and the fact that he was not above physically laying into anyone who annoyed him, made him anything but popular among those with whom he sought to deal.

By the Lady Anne, Stamford had five daughters and four sons. The oldest of these, Thomas Lord Grey of Groby, was to play a prominent part in the approaching Civil War. The second son was Anchitel, who was named after the supposed distant ancestor and who married Anne Aston, the daughter of Sir Henry Willoughby of Risely, Derbyshire. Members of the Willoughby family also showed an entrepreneurial streak and were active in coal mining. It was by way of Anne Aston's dowry that the mines in Derbyshire and Leicestershire came to the Greys. The revenues from the Nottinghamshire pits were to form a valuable source of income for later Earls of Stamford. Of Stamford's other children the oldest daughter, Elizabeth, married Sir George Booth, later Baron Delamere of Dunham Massey in Cheshire. This was the first of two links between the Booths and the Greys, the second of which in the following century, would see the mansion and grand estates at Dunham and Ashton-under-Lyne pass by marriage to the Greys.

In 1639 King Charles was forced to give up managing his kingdom without Parliament. Among other ill-advised schemes, he had foolishly attempted to force the English Prayer Book on the people of Scotland. Protests had turned to riots which had turned to war. The resulting peace was an uneasy and unsatisfactory compromise and the King looked to Parliament for money. The assembled Commons told the King in no uncertain terms that they would not grant him money until he had settled their religious and political grievances. Charles, greatly offended, sent the members back to their homes and turned once again to face the Scots. When diplomacy failed they marched south into England and a desperate monarch called on Parliament for money sufficient to at least halt their advance. The newly assembled Lower House, the benches packed with gentry, merchants and lawyers, was destined to be remembered as the Long Parliament since it sat continuously, in various forms, throughout the troubles of the following two decades.

Apart from its longevity, the Long Parliament was notable and important in other ways. In a remarkable about turn in their fortunes, many candidates with powerful traditional backers had found themselves defeated at the polls. The upset was nowhere more marked than in Leicestershire where three of the four seats for the town and county were won by the Greys. For the shire the electors returned Sir Arthur Haselrige, a covert republican, and Lord Grey of Ruthin, a sound Parliament man. The townsfolk of Leicester produced a similar surprise by electing Lord Grey, Stamford's son, who was only seventeen years of age. Beyond any doubt the Hastings clan had taken a beating and had lost local control of the polls. The time when Lord Huntingdon could write to the mayor of Leicester at election time to inform him who should represent the town was now at an end. Although Huntingdon was no Catholic and did not support the Catholic clique around the throne, he lacked the sort of puritan zeal his predecessor, the third Earl, had shown and which the electors now demanded. Across the kingdom there were clear signs that men now cared less for a candidate's family background and more for his attitudes towards the important issues of the day. It was in the composition of this new Parliament that the first signs of the emergence of political parties in England appeared.

As a leading peer of the realm Stamford was closely involved with developments of the Scottish invasion. In 1639 he was with the King's Army to treat with the Scots at Berwick. On one occasion he had dined with their leader General Leslie, a fellow presbyterian, an act which had caused the King to rebuke Stamford with the words, "you have done them too much honour".[5] In spite of this, and as late as 1641, Stamford had been recommended to the King for the post of governor of the strategically important island of Jersey which guarded the Channel approaches. Charles thought otherwise; Stamford could not be trusted.

The early months of the Long Parliament witnessed rowdy scenes as members packed the benches to argue across the floor for and against the stream of demands: no more bishops and church courts which meant, in effect, no more church dependence on the crown; no more Star Chamber, and therefore no more prosecution of royal enemies; no more Ship Money and other illegal dues and, finally, ministers must be made answerable to Parliament and not to the King. These demands were collected together and debated under the title of the "Grand Remonstrance", which was passed in November 1641. This challenged head-on the monarch's most deeply held and often restated belief that he alone, under God, was ordained to govern the nation. It was during the debate on whether or not printing of the Grand Remonstrance should go ahead that swords were drawn for the first time in the Commons. Armed conflict across the nation now seemed inevitable.

# Chapter 11

# *Civil War*

## Henry Grey, 1st Earl of Stamford (c1600-73)

In common with many other English counties, Leicestershire found itself divided in its support for King or Parliament. Of the great noble houses of the county, the Stamfords and the Rutlands were for Parliament as were the majority of the wealthier gentry such as the Babingtons of Rothley, the Hartopps of Buckminster, the Pochins of Barkby and the Herricks of Beaumanor. As a family, the Greys were not altogether united in one cause. Stamford's uncle Ambrose Grey, resident at Enville in Staffordshire, had always been a King's man and so too was his son, Henry, Stamford's cousin. Also for the King was Henry Hastings, 5th Earl of Huntingdon, then a very sick man. His oldest son, Ferdinando acted as head of the family and offered what was to be only luke warm support for Parliament. His younger brother Henry, however, was a zealous royalist and carried with him such Leicestershire families as the Faunts of Foston, the Halfords of Wistow, the Farnhams of Quorndon and many of the lesser gentlemen of the county. It was during the closing days of 1641 that men of substance and honour took to wearing swords on public occasions and demanded to know a stranger's politics before giving him more than the time of day.

In the November of that year (1641) the King received news from Ireland that his Catholic subjects had risen in rebellion against the Protestant settlers. An army and a nobleman to lead it was needed to crush this resistance to English rule. The royal appointment to the post was dismissed by Parliament as untrustworthy. It was not a post to be considered by the King alone; the liberties of all Englishmen were at stake.

It was the passing of the Grand Remonstrance in the same month which finally provoked the King to direct action. On 4th January following, Charles entered the chamber of the Commons with a troop of soldiers and attempted to arrest five of the leading puritan members, including Sir Arthur Haselrige; but the birds had flown. Thereafter, both sides now moved swiftly to prepare for the impending conflict. In February the King sent the Queen to the Netherlands with the crown jewels and instructions to raise money to buy arms. On the 12th of that month Stamford rode into Leicester with a troop of horse. Parliament had appointed him Lord Lieutenant of the county and he now took it upon himself to remove the magazine of weaponry – muskets, pikes, halberds, armour, powder and shot – to Bradgate, out of reach of the enemy. On 19th March the King reached his northern capital of York as the Commons passed the Militia Bill which gave them control of all military and naval appointments.

York welcomed the King and there he set up his court. Meanwhile, Stamford and Lord Parham had been

Within the image: Henry E^l of Stamford
ob: 1673

*Henry Grey, 1st Earl of Stamford, as a general in the army of Parliament (attributed to J B Gaspars)*

chosen by Parliament to carry to the King a petition from both Houses. This recorded the members' objections to Charles' declared intention of going to Ireland on the pretext of putting down the insurgents. It was a timely move by Parliament; the fear was that he intended to lead the wild Irish against his own Protestant subjects.

Charles' loyal reception at York was not repeated at Hull, the principal seaport of the north. Days earlier Stamford had been sent by Parliament to confer with the governor, John Hotham, who had agreed to hold the town against possible royalist seizure. When Charles arrived outside the walls, Hotham closed the gates and refused him entry. At about the same time Stamford at Bradgate wrote to the Mayor of Leicester informing him that Parliament had given him (Stamford) powers of raising militia and ordering the assembling of the town's trained bands for inspection. Thus far the initiative in the county had been with Parliament, but elsewhere the enemy was organising too.

Within the sombre towering walls of his castle at Ashby-de-la-Zouch, the infirm Earl of Huntingdon had retired from active politics and had allowed his two sons to follow their own consciences. Ferdinando, the elder, opted for Parliament but his brother Henry, aged 31, set about a vigorous campaign for the Royalist cause, rallying men and gathering supplies. For these actions he was branded a most desperate malignant by Parliament. Henry Hastings and the young Lord Grey, Stamford's son, now marked the other as his own personal target. The wretched war which followed was to raise to new heights the enmity between the two families which had begun two centuries earlier.

The first clash came in June 1642. On the 4th Stamford was in Leicester to arrange musters for the trained bands in different parts of the county. At the same time a royal messenger arrived and demanded an explanation from the Earl for his actions. Stamford and his men drew their swords and to cries from the excited market day crowds of "Popish Lord!" and "a Stamford!" drove the royal messenger from the town.[1] In spite of this show of popular support for the Earl's actions, the Mayor and Aldermen, meeting in emergency session in the gloomy Guildhall, now hedged their bets. If, they eventually decided, instructions to the contrary from his majesty did not arrive before seven in the morning of the day designated for the musters, Stamford would be given control.

On 12th June 1642 Hastings received his Commission of Array, the first of a long series issued country wide by the King. This document bestowed on him powers similar to those which Stamford had received from Parliament. After eleven days of hectic preparation Hastings left Ashby at the head of a band of about 300 men, mostly rough, untrained and coal-blackened miners from his pits in Derbyshire. With colours flying and drums beating they marched via Loughborough to the Horsefair Leys in Leicester, to make known the King's commands to the people of the county. The worst fears of the mayor and aldermen were realised; they were now faced with demands from both sides for control of the local militia. Leicestershire's high sheriff then moved to read out Parliament's Commission which declared the royal document invalid and named Hastings a "delinquent". In the shouting and confusion which ensued, jostling turned to fighting and only a downpour of rain, which dampened the powder in the muskets and put out the smouldering match, saved certain bloodshed.[2]

The following days were busy ones for Stamford who had missed the action at Leicester. There were orders to be dispatched, tenants to be rallied, musters to arrange, recruiting to organise and daily contact by mounted messengers to be maintained with Parliament in London. For these actions he was formally declared "traitor" by the King. In turn, Parliament formally impeached Henry Hastings. The struggle for the control of a county divided in its loyalties had begun.

The Greys were particularly mindful of what they stood to lose. First and foremost was their mansion at Bradgate, so splendidly open and undefended when it was first built but now so vulnerable to Royalist attack. Stamford's fears were quickly realised. Within four days of the King raising the royal standard at Nottingham on 22nd August, a party of Royalist horse, lead by Prince Rupert and Henry Hastings, appeared before Bradgate. They plundered the house, took away all the arms and spoilt those goods they could not carry. Cattle and horses were driven off and Stamford's tenants were robbed and terrified. A Parliamentary chronicler records the degree of bitterness existing between Hastings and Grey. "Where are the brats, the young children?" the Royalists had demanded. "God damn them! They would kill them that there might be no more of the breed of them".[3]

With a decision they were later to regret, Parliament decided Stamford must have command of their forces in the west of England. In truth they had little choice in the matter; to have overlooked this leading and influential peer would have been to invite trouble. Thus it was that in August 1642 Stamford began the campaign with a brief rendezvous with his commander-in-chief, the veteran soldier the Earl of Essex, on Dunmore Heath in Warwickshire. Thereafter, Stamford parted company with his son and Sir Arthur Haselrige and led his blue-coated regiment, raised at his own expense, on the march to Hereford. With drums beating and his colours – golden lions on a sea of blue with his motto "by my power" – fluttering in the breeze, he entered the town on 30th September to a less than rapturous welcome by the townsfolk. At about the same time the King left Shrewsbury for London and found his way barred by Essex and the main Parliamentary army. On the open grassy slopes of Edgehill the two armies came face to face. For Parliament, Lord Grey commanded the 3rd troop of Sir William Balfour's Regiment of Horse. Present too was Ferdinando Hastings, commanding Balfour's 7th. Facing them, among the Royalist Horse under Prince Rupert, was Henry Hastings. To the booming of cannon, the crackle of musket fire and a struggling mass of men and horses the two noble houses of Grey and Hastings faced each other, this time as leaders in a most bitter conflict.

In Hereford, Stamford set up his headquarters in the bishop's palace and prepared the defences of the town which were said to be " useless ... for any purpose of immediate protection".[4] As governor, the Earl declared that honest men need fear no harm provided, he should have added, they were in tune with his lordship's religious and political views. To the largely Royalist and neutral townsfolk such a blunt warning was bad news. Over the following weeks refugees from the depredations of the King's forces elsewhere in the west of England were billeted free of charge on Hereford's catholic residents. Houses of those suspected of helping the King were searched for arms and plundered. Even the clergy were not safe. As a result of a tip off by a neighbour, Thomas Swift of Goodrich, a retired vicar, came under suspicion as a Royalist sympathiser. According to the Royalist newssheet *Mercurius Rusticus*, soldiers showed no mercy. They ransacked the vicarage and cleared it, "even of the lumber", leaving the wife and ten children to face the winter alone as best they could.[5] To counter the high church practices of Hereford's clergy, Stamford brought in his own preacher, one John Sedgewick, to share with the town the true word of Presbyterianism.[6]

Stamford's orders at Hereford were to engage and destroy the remnants of a force of the Royalist Marquess of Hertford which was thought to be marching to the King's permanent headquarters at Oxford. Near

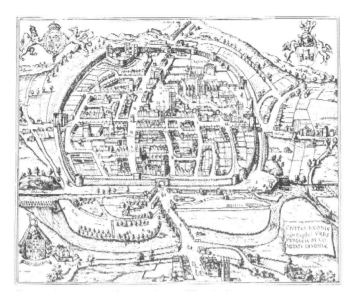

*Plan of Exeter, 1583*

Tewkesbury and again near Hereford, Stamford's men inflicted crushing blows on the enemy, killing many and taking large numbers of prisoners. Eventually Stamford was ordered to proceed to Plymouth via Gloucester and Bristol. Plymouth, with access to the Channel, was an important Parliamentary outpost, but the garrison was now under threat from the forces of Sir Ralph Hopton and, more distantly, Prince Maurice. Stamford was also appointed commander-in-chief and on 21st February he had considerable success in driving Hopton from his quarters near the town. In April Stamford was with his troops at Exeter. He was suffering from gout and dispatched his deputy, James Chudleigh, to lead the men into Cornwall, where they defeated the Cavaliers at Sowton Down. On 15th May Stamford, now rested, led his regiment in person westwards; but at Stratton Down his forces were soundly repulsed and he withdrew to Exeter. The defeat had been nothing short of a disaster for Stamford, but there was news of worse to come. Prince Maurice was advancing with orders to take Exeter.

The siege of Exeter occupied the summer of 1643. After three and a half months Stamford surrendered the town on 5th September. As one of the articles of capitulation the Earl had managed to negotiate his own personal safety together with a free pardon. In his defence he said later that he had been assigned incompetent officers, but the fact that his rank and file failed to enlist in the Royalist forces and were taken prisoner to London suggests otherwise. On his return to London Stamford found himself in disgrace. To some in government it had been only too obvious that he had been holding Exeter until his pardon arrived.

On his return to Bradgate the Earl had time to take stock of his situation. One way or another the war so far had cost him dearly and he had received little recompense for his efforts. In October he petitioned Parliament for money and that "some malignants house that was ready furnished might be allotted to him as a residence for his family."[7]

While his father laboured on behalf of Parliament in the west, Lord Grey of Groby served energetically in the same cause nearer home. In January 1643 while the Earl was in Bristol, Grey at age twenty had been appointed commander-in-chief of the Parliamentary forces in the Midlands. That month he had failed to take the castle at Ashby-de-la-Zouch but had succeeded against the enemy at Luffenham in Rutland and at Rockingham in Northamptonshire. On account of his family's property at Stamford, he was appointed governor there. Also vulnerable to surprise attack was the town of Leicester. His reluctance to move his men too far from the town brought criticism from a certain Colonel Cromwell who complained to Parliament that his lordship had failed to keep an agreed rendezvous. Grey's individual and hot-headed approach to military affairs eventually resulted in his replacement as commander-in-chief. Instead he was appointed along with Lords Rutland and Ruthin as one of the commissioners to go north in order to help seek the aid of the Scots. At about the time of the fall of Exeter, Lord Grey saw action with the force which relieved Gloucester and he was in the victorious Parliamentary army at the first battle of Newbury in the September of 1643.

Following Lord Grey's appointment as commander-in-chief for Parliament in the Midlands, Henry Hastings was given the equivalent command of the opposing Royalist forces. He had served actively and with considerable success in the west Midlands. In early June of 1643 he entertained the Queen at Ashby Castle on her return from the Netherlands. Four months later the King created him Baron Loughborough. He and Lord Grey had not clashed directly since Edgehill, and the war had yet to produce a decisive outcome.

In Cheshire "young" Sir George Booth of Dunham Massey had attempted to negotiate a truce with the local Royalists but it was declared null and void by Parliament. Nantwich was held by Booth for Parliament, whereupon the Royalist commander Byron laid siege. Booth refused an offer of surrender in January 1644 and, partly due to the rising of the river Weaver, the siege fell away.

After almost two years of warfare Stamford retired from active service. Although he received the formal thanks of both Houses of Parliament for his efforts, his ability as a general came in for criticism and his command was given to others. He had suffered much financial loss and found Parliament slow to reimburse him. His gout grew worse and long hours in the saddle were becoming unbearable. In May 1644 he petitioned Parliament for permission to visit the hot baths in France. He was given leave and voted £1,000 towards his costs from the property of Lord Stanhope.

The same year saw a Scots army under General Leslie crossing the Tweed into England. An agreement called the "Solemn League and Covenant" had been signed four months previously. Under the terms of this the Scots agreed to assist Parliament against the King. The main condition was that the Church in England must be reformed "according to the word of God", by which they meant along Presbyterian lines. Now the Royalists were fighting two enemies and this intervention was to prove decisive in their eventual defeat.

With the benefit of hindsight it is possible to detect at this stage of the war the signs of the turning of the tide in favour of Parliament, but at Westminster Stamford's discontent with the war and its effect on his economic and political affairs grew. In May 1645 he was impeached by both Houses, a matter later dropped, for assaulting Sir Arthur Haselrige during the course of the latter's Parliamentary duties. A week later he asked for Parliament's protection for his wife at Bradgate and that she should be spared the billeting of Parliamentary soldiers in the house or park. The Countess also informed Parliament that, since her husband's estates in four counties had been "plundered and spoiled by the enemy" and that "she was in great want", she demanded maintenance for herself and her children.[8] As a result £500 a year was voted to her from the estate of Sir Henry Bedingfield of Oxburgh Hall in Norfolk.

Lady Stamford's problems were made worse by the battle for Leicester in the same month. The formation of the New Model Army by Oliver Cromwell in April 1645 gave Parliament the military advantage that was to win the war. The King and the Royalist forces under the command of Prince Rupert arrived at Ashby Castle. On its way to Leicester the main body passed close enough to Bradgate to cause panic among members of Stamford's family, his household and tenants. In no less fear were the mayor and council of

*King Charles I leads the Royalist attack on Leicester, May 1645*

Leicester. Supposedly protected by Lord Grey, who at this time was occupied elsewhere, the townsfolk now faced the prospect of ruin if they did not surrender to the King. The corporation closed the town gates and asked for more time to consider the matter. Quickly tiring of their prevarication, Prince Rupert ordered the army to open an artillery bombardment of the southern district known as The Newarke which broke down the walls. Women and children put up a spirited defence by plugging the gaps with bales of wool; but the struggle was one sided. "The town (was) miserably sacked without regard to church or hospital" reported Sir Edward Walker, the King's Secretary for War, and the King and his army moved southwards towards London.[9]

Near the village of Naseby in Northamptonshire the Royalists came across the main Roundhead army under Sir Thomas Fairfax. On 14th June the last great battle of the Civil War was won by the disciplined troops of General Cromwell's New Model Army. The defeated King now fled north, pausing briefly at Leicester before making for the safety of Ashby Castle where he spent one night.

Four days after his decisive victory, General Fairfax moved north with his army against Leicester. Henry Hastings was offered generous terms to surrender but refused. The following day the Parliamentary gunners set about a massive assault on the town. Hastings now realised his decision had been an error; the defences were weak and the townspeople refused to fight. Stripped of his bravado, he capitulated and, minus their arms and colours, he and his men marched out to the jeers of the Roundheads.

By the end of 1645 it was clear that the King was beaten. In the following March the last Royalist army surrendered at Stow-on-the-Wold in Gloucestershire and one by one the remaining Royalist garrisons capitulated. At Ashby, Henry Hastings refused to surrender the castle and made plans to withstand a siege. Elsewhere the war was over and in June 1646 the King gave up Oxford to Parliament although he surrendered himself to the Scots.

*Thomas Grey, Lord Grey of Groby, regicide son of the 1st Earl of Stamford (M Wright)*

# Chapter 12

# *The Death of a King*

### Thomas Grey, Lord Grey of Groby, Regicide (1623-57)

Early in 1646 Parliament ordered Lord Grey to Ashby Castle where the grim granite walls sheltered a royalist garrison under a defiant Henry Hastings. In January the defenders had made several successful sallies into the surrounding countryside for food and provisions; but as the days passed their situation began to grow desperate. On 7th February a troop of Parliamentary cavalry from Leicester encountered little opposition when they broke the town's defences and pillaged the homes and shops of the inhabitants. Without any real prospect of relief Hastings' control of the fortress inevitably slipped away. There was overcrowding, a shortage of food and, even worse but hardly surprising, an outbreak of disease.

By the end of February the situation had become critical and Hastings began negotiations for a surrender. The terms of this were agreed by both Houses of Parliament and signed on the last day of the month. Considering the trouble the castle under Royalist control had been to the Roundhead forces, Parliament was not ungenerous. On 2nd March the commander and the surviving men of the garrison marched out, "with their horses, arms, ammunition, bags and baggage" and "with trumpets sounding, drums beating, colours flying, match lighted … and muskets loaded". Hastings and other gentlemen were escorted to either Hull or Bristol where transport was provided to take them to either France or Holland.[1]

With the King's forces defeated and the war seemingly won, Lord Grey, now 23, found time to attend to family matters. Two of his sisters were already married. Elizabeth was the wife of Sir George Booth, "young Sir George", of Dunham Massey in Cheshire. The previous year Booth had warned Lord Grey of royalist designs on Leicester and had pointed out the inadequate state of the town's defences. Diana Grey, the younger sister, was the wife of Robert Bruce, later Earl of Ailesbury. Lord Grey married in June 1646 Dorothy Bourchier, the nineteen year-old second daughter and co-heiress of Edward, 4th Earl of Bath. Dorothy's mother was the former Dorothy St John, daughter of the 3rd Baron St John of Bletsoe in Bedfordshire. This was a strongly Parliamentary and later republican family and the bride's cousin had died fighting against the King at Edgehill. A further link with the Parliamentary cause was that Lord Grey now found his brother-in-law was Basil Feilding, who had married Elizabeth, the sister of his new wife. Feilding was the Earl of Denbigh and had been colonel of horse at Edgehill under the Parliamentary commander-in-chief, the Earl of Essex.

The death of Essex in September 1646 was a particular blow to Lord Grey. The old veteran was a distant

Ferrers kinsman but, more important, he had acted as young Lord Grey's patron in his early and inexperienced days in both Houses of Parliament. Essex's family life had been unhappy and the young Lord Grey seems to have filled the role of the son the Earl never had. Now it was left for Grey to find his own way through the jungle of Parliamentary plotting and intrigues in revolutionary times, a task he was to manage with great skill. The death of his former mentor also saw the young lord move away from the Presbyterian beliefs of his family and towards more independent and eventual republican views.

At the opening of 1647 the King was a prisoner of the Scots in the north of England. He hoped to divide Parliament from their northern allies by agreeing a separate peace which was to be followed by a Scottish invasion of England. However, negotiations had broken down when Charles failed to agree to the terms of the Solemn League and Covenant. In the same month the exasperated Scots handed back their prisoner for the £400,000 they claimed the war had cost them. This move the defeated Royalists eagerly trumpeted as the "selling of their King as Judas sold his master". Parliament appointed Stamford as a supervisor for the implementation of the terms of the treaty with the Scots. Riding northwards along the route he had travelled only eighteen months previously, he cursed the muddy roads, the driving rain and his gout. He could hardly refuse this assignment, not least because Parliament still owed him money to compensate for his losses in the recent conflict. On 12th February 1647 he was at Berwick to negotiate and in Edinburgh the following month to conclude the formalities. Thereafter all his thoughts were on returning home.

At Westminster, Stamford found that events had moved quickly during the weeks he had been away. With no King, administrative procedures which had required the royal signature had broken down. Censorship had been abandoned and there now poured forth from a thousand presses the views, considerations, exhortations and rantings of a factious multitude. Fired by religion and now free to speak their minds, narrow-minded sects of every description competed to expound their own views of the truth and to demand a particular form of religious and social justice.

Indeed the nation was in turmoil. Sober men might well observe in horror when the squire felt obliged to leave his house in fear for the safety of his family, when the parson was ejected from his living and when plain men's goods and livestock were stolen. In their work and in their attitudes, the majority of Members of Parliament were becoming ominously at odds with the army. The former, mostly Presbyterians like Stamford, had fought to tame the powers of the monarchy but had no thought to abolish it. They were also now in favour of reducing the size of the army and sending it to put down the rebellion in Ireland. The military, on the contrary, were mostly Independents, not willing to be disbanded until they had received their back pay and until they had seen what they regarded as an acceptable and radical conclusion of their quarrel with the King. The more zealous army commanders branded Charles as the anti-Christ and claimed that they, "the Saints" or "the Elect", were there to rule until the Saviour's Second Coming. To his father's great dismay it was to this group that Lord Grey now firmly attached himself.

The King, a prisoner on the Isle of Wight, continued his efforts to re-establish himself as the person who alone could prevent the collapse of the social order. In secret negotiations with the Scots he agreed – with no intention of keeping his word – to establish the Presbyterian religion in England in return for a military solution to his restoration. When the Scots subsequently invaded England they were soundly defeated in battle at Preston, a victory seen by the Parliamentary commander Cromwell as yet another sign from the Almighty of the righteousness of the cause his men had fought for all along. The members of Parliament, in

*Ashby-de-la-Zouch Castle, Leicestershire, was slighted by Parliament at the end of the Civil War*

turn, saw their power and authority slipping away from them to the army.

Stamford and Lord Grey were now going their own ways. After Preston, Grey was appointed governor of Ashby Castle and it was to this stronghold that he brought the captured Scottish commander, the Duke of Hamilton. During the unrest preceding the Scots' invasion, Henry Hastings had returned to England and had been present at the conflict at Colchester, one of the failed local risings timed to aid the Scots. The town capitulated only after a lengthy siege, but by this time the walls of Ashby Castle had been blown apart by the Parliamentary engineers, making it an indefensible and uninhabitable ruin. After a spell in the Tower of London for his defiance at Colchester, Hastings was released and fled to Holland where he was received by the exiled future Charles II.

As the weeks of 1648 slipped by, Lord Grey's sympathies fell ever more in step with those of the Independents in the army and their radical and republican politics. In November 1648 the army laid before Parliament a demand that the King – "Charles Stuart, this man of blood" – should stand trial. In order to produce a verdict which would command common agreement among those hostile to the King, only members of the House of Commons who were in sympathy with a radical outcome would be allowed to vote on the matter. Accordingly, on 29th December, one Colonel Pride stood on the steps of the chamber of the Lower House checking a handwritten sheet and, amid shouting and jostling, turned away or arrested those whose names were not listed. At his elbow, to help identify the lesser known faces, stood Thomas, Lord Grey of Groby. The resulting much-depleted chamber, the Rump Parliament, elected Lord Grey to carry to the Upper

House the ordinance that the King should face trial. This was rejected by the Lords and it was said that Lord Grey was heard to remark that "he would himself perform the executioner's office rather than let the King escape from justice".[2]

To the sound of church bells north of the border the people of Scotland proclaimed Charles Stuart, the King's son, as King of Scotland and the Scottish ministers and their generals made plans for another invasion of England. In the Great Hall at Westminster the trial of the King opened on 20th January, with Charles refusing to recognise the authority of the court to try him. The right to govern according to his conscience, the King told the court, was the gift of the Almighty to whom alone kings and princes must answer. The court was unimpressed. Such a defence was not admissible, John Bradshaw, the president of the court, ruled. Since the King had made war on his own subjects he had broken that trust and, for the elect, there was no room for such an earthly king. Lord Grey on the judges' benches put in a particularly good attendance at the proceedings which lasted three weeks. Eventually the verdict was announced. The King, in Bradshaw's words, "The tyrant traitor and murderer and public enemy of the good people of this nation ...", was found guilty and sentenced to death.[3] When signatories for the death certificate were sought only 59 of the 135 commissioners who had been nominated to act as judges could be persuaded to append their names. Second only to that of Bradshaw and before that of Oliver Cromwell was the bold, enthusiastic hand of "Thos. Grey".

John Throsby, the 18th century Leicestershire historian, recalls how his great-grandfather was in conversation with Lord Stamford at Bradgate when an elated Lord Grey arrived from London with news that the King had been sentenced to death. "Well, Thomas, King or no King?" Stamford asked his son. "No King, my lord," replied the son. "Then no Lord Grey," rejoined the father and left in disgust.[4] Stamford was not alone in appreciating that no king meant no lords and the inevitable downfall of the whole social hierarchy.

The execution of the King took place on 30th January 1649. Early in the following month the monarchy, "Unnecessary, burdensome and dangerous to the liberty, safety and public interest of the people of this nation" was abolished, along later with the House of Lords and the Church of England and its bishops.[5] On 13th February a Council of State elected by the Rump, was established to govern the country. In May England was declared to be a "Commonwealth and Free State" under God. Prominent among its members were Lord Grey and Lord Denbigh. Grey's religious approach to constitutional meddling was now given new rein. The following year the Parliament set about passing acts to create a society of saints, where the death penalty was laid down for such crimes as swearing, blasphemy and adultery. These and other bold moves antagonised many otherwise passive sections of the population and served only to create a deep pool of national resentment.

This discontent encouraged royalists to make further efforts to topple the government. Having wreaked havoc in Ireland among the Catholic rebels, the Parliamentary army under Cromwell returned home to defeat the Scots in battle at Dunbar in September 1650. This was followed in 1651 by a further victory over the Royalists at Worcester. General Cromwell now took a personal role in the government of the country which, in spite of high taxation, was already short of money. Most of the state valuables had been sold off: the royal palaces, the King's art collection and what was left of the crown lands.

Such sales, of course, were once-only sources of revenue; so too were the fines from delinquents. These were imposed on defeated Royalists who were then invited to re-purchase confiscated lands on terms which the Parliamentary Commissioners calculated they could afford. Such persons were seen as either "delinquents", relatively minor offenders, or "malignants", the hardliners. Lord Grey was on the committee which was appointed to look at affairs in Staffordshire and was able to ensure that investigations against his cousin Henry of Enville were never proceeded with. The allegations that the man had maintained a garrison against Parliament at the hall and that he had been in arms for the King early in the war were quietly passed over. At the same time there was little mercy shown for the Hastings family. With Henry Hastings exiled abroad, his brother Ferdinando, the 6th Earl of Huntingdon, was left to face the demands of the sequestrators. At various times lands were sold to pay the fines and to enable the Earl to pay his own and his father's debts. One way or another the recent conflict had cost his family dearly.

The years immediately following the King's death saw Lord Grey seize every opportunity to enrich himself from the spoils of war. He was a member of the Council of State which had wide executive powers. In March 1650 he was granted the custody of a London royal park known to later generations as Hyde Park. In the same year he received an income of £5,120 out of the estates of Philip Stanhope, the Earl of Chesterfield. Poor Chesterfield was particularly unfortunate: two sons were killed in battle and his own house pillaged by roundhead forces. With his losses totalling £50,000 he was now the victim of the jackals of Parliament. For Lord Grey the fact that Chesterfield was the uncle of both Ferdinando and Henry Hastings made his receipt of these estates an act of sweet revenge. The following December a further £1,000 per year was voted to Lord Grey as "a mark of favour and respect" and for services to the Commonwealth. He was also given the house, park and lands at Holdenby in Northamptonshire and went on to purchase, on easy terms, the largest portion of the estate of Lord Craven worth £3,000 per year. This included the property of Combe Abbey near Coventry with its park and deer where his son Thomas, the future 2nd Earl of Stamford was born.[6]

The Rump Parliament was short not only of money but also of a sense of direction. Well into the routine of framing and passing bills it began to resist the pressure from the army to draw up legislation specifically designed to prepare for the rule of the saints and Christ's Second Coming. To Cromwell and his officers the chamber was becoming ever more conservative; it seemed most concerned with looking after the interests of its members and lacked the will to do what was expected of it. The Rump, in turn, feared the wilder elements in the army who, given the opportunity, might unleash and impose by force their outlandish ideas on the disillusioned, unhappy and confused populace. When eventually the Rump made moves to perpetuate its power, the army under Cromwell intervened and drove it out. The experiment in Commonwealth government had come to an end.

The Rump's replacement was an assembly composed of 144 men nominated by the army. This collection of place men became known in later years as the "Barebones" Parliament after its fanatical leader "Praise God" Barbon. The Assembly made a start with a number of sweeping reforms but proved to be fatally faction ridden, with the result that after only five months a large group of members asked Cromwell to intervene. In response, the military under Cromwell drew up another constitution which made provision for a Protector (Cromwell) and a Council of State. This was a written constitution and known as the "Instrument of Government". It was designed to prevent the Protector or Parliament achieving the absolute control which King Charles had claimed. Thus was born what was later to be known as the First Protectorate and which, steered by the hand of Cromwell, lasted until 1656.

The existence of this new form of government saw the mutual distrust between Lord Grey and Cromwell intensify. At heart Cromwell was a man of deep inner convictions who believed he had been raised from obscurity by the Almighty to guide the English to become a just and godly nation. At the same time, and by the standards of his times, he was a tolerant man who wished to allow limited dissent by those of tender consciences, even to Catholics and Jews. He was, too, a man of great common sense, a skilful politician who unlike his more impatient colleagues, realised that his vision for the future would not be built in a day.

Conflict with Lord Grey thus became inevitable since Grey was everything Cromwell wasn't. To all but himself perhaps, his Lordship's position constituted a great paradox. The heir to a rich and important Earldom, he vigorously espoused what he saw as the desires of much humbler men. At the same time he enriched himself shamelessly under a system which he despised and under which he had maintained a position of great influence by skilful manoeuvring. He was very intolerant of those who did not share his views and who stood in his way.

It was Lord Grey's unpredictability which made him dangerous and Cromwell took great care to keep him out of London and busy on military duties in the Midlands, searching out royalist attempts at regrouping. Grey went on to express sympathy with the Levellers, an extremist group in the Parliamentary army who, through their leading propagandist John Lilburne, advocated fundamental reform of government, of the Parliament and of society itself. Eventually Lilburne was banished to Jersey. While the Levellers as a political force faded away, Lord Grey espoused the views of yet another fringe group of radical republicanism in the army. These were the self-styled "Fifth Monarchy Men". They were individuals who were inspired by the execution of Charles, the great "Anti-Christ", and who expected the rule on earth of King Jesus in their own lifetimes. In this expectation they, the heralds of the Second Coming, would seize power. On 12th February 1654 Lord Grey was detained at Bradgate on the orders of Cromwell. In the words of Colonel Hacker who arrested him, his lordship was "much distempered with the gout" but nevertheless he was moved to Windsor as a precaution against any attempt by his fanatical supporters to seize him.[7]

On his release from Windsor six months later he became the sect's figurehead leader. In a series of meetings in Shoreditch, he and the other chief conspirators plotted to overthrow the Protector. What separated this plot from a hundred other similar wild schemes was the interest shown by the Spanish in advancing finances to the plotters rather than supporting exiled royalists as a means of toppling Cromwell. On the eve of the planned uprising Lord Grey, together with the other leaders, was arrested. Later he was released, but this time only on payment of a large sum of money against his good behaviour. In 1656 he stood for Parliament but to his surprise was rejected by the same electors of Leicester who had supported him in the past. This time he had gone too far; not only the freemen of Leicester but the mass of ordinary Englishmen were showing that they were tired of the army, the fanatics, the competing factions, the failed experiments and the rantings of the minorities, all of whom claimed the ultimate source of political power and authority.

Fortunately perhaps, Lord Grey fell victim to his gout which was brought to a vast height by the violence of his passions and he died in the spring of 1657 aged 34.[8] Thereafter, a series of crises exposed the fundamentally unstable structure of power and authority in the nation which had marked the years since the King's death. Tired of their unwillingness to tackle what he saw as the nation's ills, Cromwell dissolved the Protectorate Parliament. For a time he tried a new form of local government whereby England was divided into eleven districts each administered by a major-general. This military option was seen by the populace as plain despotism – slavery of government by the sword – and proved enormously unpopular.

After the elections which followed for a second Protectorate Parliament, Cromwell was obliged to exclude 100 members who were hostile to his plans. A new Upper House of nominated members was established to replace the old House of Lords; but antagonism between it and the Lower Chamber caused the Protector to dissolve both in February 1658. Seven months later Cromwell died of the kidney failure known as pylonephritis resulting in uraemia complicated by a vesicle stone and of the tertiary malaria he had contracted in Ireland.[9] The Second Protectorate came to an end with a solution to the problem of how to square the wishes of the populace with dictatorial rule as far away as ever.

Cromwell had nominated his son Richard as his successor but Richard was not even half the man his father had been and the inadequacies of his short term as Protector were reflected in the contemporary epithet "Tumbled Down Dick". From Bradgate the Earl of Stamford watched what he saw as the further break up of the nation into anarchy. In London the army once again seized power in yet another bid to bring peace and stability to violence and chaos. Stamford had been one of many Presbyterians who had taken up arms against the King to prevent just the sort of injustice he was now witnessing. He had, he decided, been right all along; a monarch with suitable restraints to his power was an indispensable part of English government.

When a series of Royalist risings was planned Stamford declared for the King at Bradgate. Aged 59 and suffering from gout he was in arms in the saddle once more, this time in support of a cause he had fought against so bitterly fifteen years earlier and which had cost him dearly. For this latest action he was arrested for high treason and committed to the Tower. When General Monck marched south from Scotland with a section of the Army, the monarchy was restored and Stamford gained his freedom.

*Thomas Grey, 2nd Earl of Stamford (JB van Loo)*

# Chapter 13

# *Restoration and Disillusionment*

## Thomas Grey, 2nd Earl of Stamford (1653-1720)

King Charles II entered London in May 1660 in a colourful and noisy procession of clattering regiments of cavalry, column after column of marching infantry and with wealthy citizens in carriages. It was a multitude, the diarist John Evelyn said, which took seven hours to pass through the Capital's streets. Away from the cheering crowds was the welcome from the fawning lords in Whitehall, including the Earls of Stamford, Rutland and Huntingdon. At such a reception the King was moved to remark that since all around him appeared never to have wished him absent in the first place, it must have been his own fault that he had been away for so long. From the lord in his mansion to the humblest ploughman in his cottage, the restoration of the monarchy promised a return to a kind of stable government which twenty years of division and bitterness had failed so miserably to deliver. Even the most cynical observers, and there were plenty of them, could see that a legitimate sovereign on the English throne was giving rise to a spirit of optimism throughout the land.

The package of policies and reforms outlined by King Charles II in his Declaration of Breda did promise well for the future. With the restoration of the monarchy came the return of the House of Lords with its ancient rights, privileges and procedures. Less welcome to Stamford was the reappearance of the Church of England and its bishops. Yet he could take satisfaction in the fact that at last a monarch was to rule with a Parliament which was to control taxation. This would surely limit the power of the King. Also it would ensure that hated monster, a standing army, would never again allow the monarch to intimidate his subjects or even attempt another coup d'etat. It appeared that the second Charles would also extend the hand of religious toleration to as many of his subjects as obediently asked for it. On an entirely different matter, and much to the relief of Stamford and Rutland, but the dismay of Huntingdon, all lands bought by individuals during the Commonwealth were to be retained by their purchasers; only estates acquired by grants from the Protectorate Government were restored to their former Royalist owners.

The new King's general amnesty did not exempt everyone from royal justice. Persons singled out for retribution were the regicides and others who had been active in promoting the execution of his father. Some were already dead of course. One such was Thomas Horton of Noseley in Leicestershire who had risen to the rank of colonel of horse in Cromwell's army. He had signed the death warrant in 1649, and had lost his life in Ireland before a year was out. Others who had died in the later months of the Commonwealth were not necessarily safe in their graves. The body of the late Protector himself was disinterred and his remains exhibited to public gaze at Tyburn.

Many who had been involved in the King's trial were very much alive. Of those men from Leicestershire who were known to Stamford, Colonel Francis Hacker of Stathern, who arrested Stamford's regicide son at Bradgate, and John Cook of Husbands Bosworth, who had conducted the prosecution case against the King, were tried, found guilty and joined the queue for the gallows. Peter Temple of Sibson, Henry Smith of Walcote and Thomas Waite of Wymondham, all Leicestershire men and signatories of the death warrant, were more fortunate. Their sentences were commuted to lengthy periods of captivity. Some regicides had fled the country and, with a few exceptions, were allowed to live out their lives in obscurity, safe from the hired assassin.

When he saw the manner of the men who were elected to the second Parliament of the reign, which opened at Westminster in the spring of 1661, the guarded optimism which Stamford held for his declining years faded. Packing the benches of the Lower House were the country gentlemen, former royalists and others whose speeches, values and attitudes harked back to the bad old days of the 1630s. Stamford and those who had risked their lives in arms in the cause of the King's restoration supposed these men had been elected to draw a line under the actions and memories of the earlier years. In particular, they were expected to sweep away as much as possible of the remains of republicanism. Yet here they were again, petty minded little busy-bodies, seeking to further their own best interests and make their fortunes, determined at all costs to regain the influence their kind had enjoyed a generation earlier.

Although Stamford held lands and tenements in Lincolnshire, Derbyshire and Northamptonshire, his main interests still lay in the town and county of Leicester. Even here the electors had caught the national mood. The five thousand or so franchise holders of the county had elected John Manners, the 23 year-old son of the politically indecisive Earl of Rutland – a soft harmless man[1] – together with George Faunt of Foston, a covert Royalist, who was actually returned unopposed.[2] The news from the borough where Stamford liked to think his will held sway, was even more gloomy. His third son John Grey, had secured a majority for the seat from his fellow corporation members but he had been rejected by the burgesses: butchers, bakers, tailors, worsted-stocking makers and others of a lowly sort, in favour of an upstart called Sir John Prettyman. The second elected member for the borough was Sir William Hartopp who Stamford guessed, correctly, would be no more use to him than either Prettyman or Faunt.[3]

This second Parliament of Charles II's reign lost no time in endorsing the monarch's wishes with a programme of legislation which bore an unpleasant likeness to that which his father had promoted. The royal prerogative was restored and with it the monarch's control over the army and navy. In religion, the ties between church and state were strengthened. This meant the resurgence of the Anglican Church, which lost no time in meting out the same lack of tolerance in matters of public life that it had received from the Dissenters during the Republic. For Stamford and his fellow Presbyterians, the religious boot was now firmly on the other foot. There was more than a whiff of incense and a jingle of bells in the kind of changes which were about to be set in train.

Stamford's fears that the new monarch had what might be described in present day terms as a "hidden agenda" were to prove well founded. Behind the swarthy good looks of the King – the Black Boy of the inn signs – and the courteous manner and apparent desire to please all about him, lay a clever, cynical and unprincipled leader. A commanding presence which drew deference, clever words which engaged attention and a flurry of worthless promises were the weapons of a man whose political morality was one of survival.

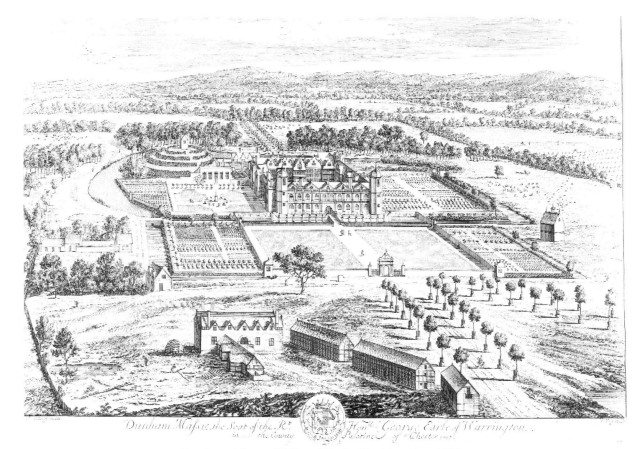

*Dunham Massey Hall and Park, Cheshire, circa 1700*

Taking care to dissociate himself entirely from the calumnies of his late brother Thomas the Regicide, Stamford's second son Anchitel Grey entered Parliament as the member for the borough of Derby, which he went on to represent for many years. His connection with the town was, as we have seen, through his marriage to Anne, daughter and coheir of Sir Henry Willoughby Bt., a man whose wealth was drawn from his coalmines. With Anchitel in the Lower House and Stamford in the Lords, the Grey family was able to maintain a close contact with current events. From his seat on the backbenches the young MP made copious notes in shorthand, principally for his own convenience, on the business of the House. Since at that time no proper official documentation was kept of what members said, the notes turned out to be the only surviving records of the progress of many of the debates between the years 1667 and 1694. Such was their value that they were later published in ten bound volumes. Anchitel died in 1702 of cancer aggravated by the family affliction, gout.

This Anchitel was the same man who had taken part in the Cheshire rising of 1659 (which had been led by his brother-in-law, "young" Sir George Booth) in support of the new King. Unlike the Greys who had been catapulted to national prominence by marriage in the late 15th century, the Booths exemplified those many worthy English families who, over the generations, rose from relative obscurity to attain moderately high office in their country's service. At about the same time that Sir Edward Grey acquired Groby manor by

*"Old" Sir George Booth of Dunham Massey (English School 17th Century)*

marriage to the Ferrers heiress in the late 15th century, Sir Robert Booth, second son of John Booth of Barton-on-Irwell in Lancashire, came into possession of the barony of Dunham. During the late 15th and 16th centuries the Booths married predominantly into the gentry families of Cheshire and Lancashire whose lands between them included much of the north and south of those counties respectively. By a series of judicious marriages with local heiresses, the Booths acquired several distinct estates. At the time the Greys were regaining their ancestral lands at Bradgate in the later years of Elizabeth's reign, the name Booth was gaining in prestige in the area of Dunham Massey in Cheshire.

Seven generations after his ancestor Robert, George Booth was made Sheriff of Chester in 1597 and a baronet by James I. In the 1620s the Booths were influential members of Cheshire society. When the Civil War broke out the family sided with Parliament. At age 77 George Booth, a patriot in the Elizabethan mould, played a leading role in the attempt of 1643 to reconcile the King with his Parliament. Along with Stamford and other peers, he did not support the trial and execution of the King or the abolition of the monarchy. "Free, grave, godly, brave Booth, the flower of Cheshire," as a puritan pamphleteer described him, died in 1652 at the amazing age of 86.

"Old" Sir George was succeeded by his grandson "young" Sir George who was a man who followed his grandfather in both politics and religion. He had represented Cheshire in the Long Parliament of 1645 but was excluded from taking his seat in the Rump by his own brother-in-law, Thomas Grey, the regicide. Disillusioned with the ramshackle political state of the nation, "young" Sir George Booth along with Anchitel (the first Earl of Stamford's second son) led an uprising, "Booth's Rising", against the government in 1659. At first he was successful in raising his tenants and the gentry of Cheshire to arms, but both men were no match for the veteran General Lambert who was sent against them. George and Anchitel made their escape but the former, disguised as a woman, was arrested at Newport Pagnell when an innkeeper became suspicious of his guest's need for a shave. The following year George was rewarded by the King at his coronation with the Barony of Delamer.

After 1661 Stamford became too infirm to be a regular attender at the House of Lords and preferred the peace and quiet of Bradgate. Delamer too returned to his estate at Dunham and observed the wisdom of his cousin's misgivings about King Charles. By 1667 the monarch had dismissed his first minister, Lord Clarendon. Corruption in public life was rampant, morals at court were extremely lax and the country was unsuccessfully waging a naval war against the Dutch. The rumours that the King might declare himself a Roman Catholic put an end to any faith Stamford may have had for the restored monarchy. He had seen it all before.

It was in 1673 with the first strong signs that the policies of the King might once again lead to civil strife that Stamford died in his 74th year. The portrait of him in the military dress of the civil war reflects a man with a haughty and irritable disposition. This was not improved by the mediocre military performance he had shown as a leader of men in combat or by the problems stemming from the gout which accompanied him for more than 40 years. He was buried among his ancestors at Bradgate. His widow died three years later.

Stamford's first son, Thomas the Regicide, was already dead and the title passed to the Earl's grandson, also Thomas. The second Earl was now aged about twenty, a bright young man who found himself in an exciting world so very different from that in which his grandfather had been raised. Thomas had matriculated from Oxford University at the age of thirteen and in 1708 became a Fellow of the newly-formed

Royal Society. Even if the King's political and religious policies appeared set on taking the country back in time, the signs of change and progress in almost every other aspect of the nation's affairs were all around. A commercial revolution was bringing prosperity and a rising level of affluence to many sections of the community. England was becoming a trader to the world, the countryside was experiencing a revolution in agricultural production and there was a great increase in the production of coal. This allowed more and more people to become town dwellers and the cities also grew in size. Medicine, science, technology, the arts and the field of military affairs were all bursting out of their old constraints and establishing new frontiers, just as they had done during the years of Elizabeth's reign.

Only months after his grandfather's death Stamford married Elizabeth Harvey, a young society beauty and the daughter of Daniel Harvey of Combe in Surrey. Daniel Harvey's grandfather was a Kentish yeoman and Daniel had built a fortune by following his father into the family business of trade with Turkey. For his daughter's dowry he had reputedly advanced a sum of £10,000 which in due course was added to the Stamford estates. There were many noblemen who envied the second Earl his tall, slim and lovely wife and his secure financial position. In spite of his grandfather's losses during the Civil War, Stamford's estates were free from the sort of crippling loans, mortgages and annuities which a noble family could so easily accumulate over the generations. Stamford had no brothers and only two sisters for whom he would eventually have to find dowries. Provision for his grandmother, another potentially expensive affair, was to last only three more years and his own mother had long ago remarried.

The Earl's primary sources of income were the rents and dues from his farming tenants. Also there were the rising revenues from the developing coalmines at Amblecote in Staffordshire where his affairs were managed by his uncle Anchitel. Not least was his income from offices as high steward of the Honour of Leicester and as Lord of Trade and Foreign Plantations. Although his annual revenues could not rival those of his Leicestershire neighbour the Earl of Rutland, who was one of the richest of peers in England with an annual rent roll topping £14,000, an income of £6,000 a year made Stamford a good marriage prospect, even though he was the son of a regicide.

But, alas, the Earl's marriage to Elizabeth was not a happy one. Lady Stamford did not take to life at Bradgate. She was accustomed to the busy and eventful social round of the capital and to life on the fringe of court circles where, if the wagging tongues are to be believed, she did not want "just pretence to keep her bed".[4] Life at Bradgate was so boring, her husband was making no headway at court and his long term political career was likely to lead nowhere. Although Lady Stamford supported her husband during his spells in the Tower for opposing the King's policies, she fell more and more under the influence of her mother and sister, both of whom were active court gossips. In addition, Stamford's disposition was made no better by the constant interference with his domestic problems by his mother-in-law. People sympathised; the woman's own husband had accepted the appointment of Ambassador to Turkey for what were to be the remaining four years of his life in order to be away from her.

In a letter to her sister, Lady Stamford is said to have written of Bradgate that while the house was tolerable, the country was a forest and the inhabitants were all brutes. If she was to escape from Bradgate and her unexciting husband she would have to take drastic action. Her sister suggested she should set fire to the house and flee by the light of the flames. Tradition points to a fire in the north-west tower where the Earl slept and where, according to the Leicestershire historian John Nichols, the burnt ends of the beams

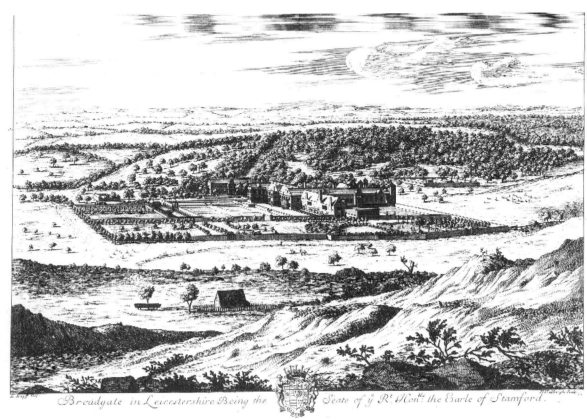

*Bradgate House and Park, Leicestershire, circa 1700*

could be still be seen in 1804. The Countess did narrowly escape with her infant daughter Diana, but the house was saved by the water in a large leaden reservoir in the roof which doused the flames.[5] It is not clear who left whom but after only eighteen months of marriage the couple separated and Lady Stamford died in 1687 aged 30.

Time spent at Bradgate enabled Stamford to attend to his varied and expanding financial affairs and, as a leader in county matters, to keep a finger on the pulse of local politics. In 1673 the county of Leicester was still represented in the Lower House by John Manners (Lord Roos), and George Faunt, both protagonists of the King's legislative programme. The borough was served by Sir William Hartopp and Sir John Prettyman, who were both similarly disposed. After a scandalous divorce from his first wife, Roos had married Stamford's aunt, the widowed Diana Bruce. The lady died after only eight months of marriage but the political embarrassment it caused lasted much longer.[6] Late in 1676 Sir John Prettyman died and Stamford's second brother John Grey, of Enville Hall, managed at a cost of £800 to secure the seat against a challenge from Hineage Finch, the Lord Chancellor's son.[7] The battle for the county seats now rested with the families of Grey and Manners, since the Hastings were still licking their wounds from their misfortunes in the Civil War. Henry Hastings, Lord Loughborough, died unmarried in 1666 and his relatives no longer posed a serious political threat to the Greys in Leicestershire.

Meanwhile at Westminster tension was building in a maze of intrigues as the King pushed forward with his programme of backward looking legislation against mounting opposition headed by the Earl of Shaftesbury. In the autumn of 1678 a crisis arose with a supposed Popish plot to murder the King, to bring a French army to England and to place the Duke of York on the throne. Violent mobs were on the streets breaking windows and shouting opposition to the monarch. They were stirred up and inflamed by the rantings of a wild-eyed renegade clergyman called Titus Oates and skilfully managed by Shaftesbury. An Exclusion Bill was proposed which was aimed specifically at preventing succession by the Duke. The following year James' Protestant daughter Mary, who had married William Prince of Orange, was proposed as Queen. The King dissolved Parliament to prevent further discussion and the opposition's attention turned to his illegitimate son James, Duke of Monmouth. This move was once again defeated by the King dissolving Parliament. Thereafter, and until his death in 1685, Charles ruled without any reference to either Lords or Commons and in so doing generated a head of opposition to the crown much the same as that which his father had created 40 years previously.

As a result of the Exclusion Bills, division across the nation for and against the King's policies hardened and deepened. Some men supported moves against toleration of Dissenters and Catholics and in favour of the Church of England and wanted no war with France. They also saw the monarch as the fount of power and authority, a view suspiciously reminiscent of the "Divine Right of Kings" and its demands for passive obedience. Such men became known as "Tories". Their opponents were for religious toleration, control of Parliament by its members, and a war with France and any other continental foe if this was in the national interest. Such men became known as "Whigs" and it was from these early beginnings that political parties in the modern sense of the term emerged.

Stamford's activities and speeches in the House of Lords and his overt alliance with Lord Shaftesbury's circle quickly marked him out as a Whig, a label the Greys were to carry with pride for another century and a half and more. In this he was supported wholeheartedly by his cousin Henry Booth, who had been elected to the Commons as knight of the shire for Cheshire and who was even more outspoken on the subject of Parliamentary reform. In 1682, two years before his frail and aged father the first Lord Delamer died, Henry had demonstrated his independent spirit by entertaining the Duke of Monmouth at Dunham. Here, as one onlooker observed, "as he (the Duke) sat at meat the doors were opened and the rabble suffered not only to gaze upon the room but to come in and view the Duke".[8]

In the following year, 1683, the situation for both Stamford and Henry Booth rapidly worsened after an unsuccessful attempt was made to assassinate King Charles and the Duke of York. This occurred at Rye House near Hoddesdon in Hertfordshire after the royal brothers had spent a day at Newmarket races. Bradgate House was searched and Stamford was sent to the Tower on suspicion of high treason. The searchers, Lords Beaumont and Sherard, missed the arms which were later said to be hidden between the mansion's two great ovens.[9] Henry Booth too was arrested in Cheshire and joined his cousin in the Tower where both men were lodged at the King's pleasure.

From the news and gossip reaching him in the Tower, Stamford was concerned to learn of the return to royal favour of the Hastings family in the person of Theophilus, the 7th Earl of Huntingdon. For many years the family had been missing from court circles and national politics. Emerging from the civil war on the losing side, they had suffered much for their loyalty to the King. The vigorous pursuit of the royal cause by Henry, Lord Loughborough, the 5th Earl's second son, had proved the family's ruin. Deep in debt from his losses in Ireland and needing to support a large family Ferdinando, the 6th Earl, had then failed to meet the demands of the sequestrators of Parliament and had landed up in the stinking Fleet prison in the company of common criminals. An Act of Parliament had allowed him to sell lands to clear his debts and he returned to Ashby to live quietly until his death in 1655. The efforts of his son and heir Theophilus, the 7th Earl, to regain the family fortunes were dashed when an Act confirmed the earlier sale of lands. Many other Royalists had compounded for their estates at twice their annual value or ten years rent, but the Hastings plight was such that their estates had to be sold. Thereafter Lord Huntingdon sought a wealthy wife and by early 1669 marriage with Mary Langham, sole heir of the wealthy Sir James Langham of Cottesbrooke, Northamptonshire, "was as good as concluded".[10]

However advantageous the match appeared to her father, the lady evidently had other ideas as to whom she wished to marry. At the last moment she was snatched from beneath his nose by no less than Henry Booth, Stamford's cousin, whom she married the following year. Huntingdon, a loser in love and poorer by £20,000, swore revenge.

At the height of the Exclusion Crisis of 1669, Huntingdon blundered. At a dinner with the mayor and council of Leicester, and in a borough where Royalist sympathies were strong, the Earl had shocked the company by insisting that a toast be made to the Duke of Monmouth. For this act the King banished Huntingdon from the court. Two years later the Earl was back in royal favour. The months of exile in the peace and quiet of his mansion at Donington had provided the opportunity for a period of reflection on his condition. The result was a fundamental shift in political outlook with the aim of placing the Hastings at the centre of national affairs where they surely belonged. At the time when both Booth and Stamford were deep in the suspicion of the Rye House Plot, Lord Huntingdon was admitted to the Privy Council. He had also been promoted to captain of the band of Gentlemen Pensioners, a group whose function it was to protect the King's royal person. Huntingdon had shed his Whiggish credentials and had become a Tory and King's man. At a time when another constitutional crisis was looming, the deep and ancient political animosity between Grey and Hastings was all set to break surface once again.

*Henry Booth, 2nd Baron Delamer and 1st Earl of Warrington (Sir Godfrey Kneller)*

# Chapter 14

# *Whigs and Tories*

## Thomas Grey, 2nd Earl of Stamford (1653-1720)

The sudden death of King Charles in February 1685 brought the nation to the brink of turmoil. For the Greys his departure also produced a family crisis much like the one they had experienced two centuries earlier when another King, Edward IV, had also died unexpectedly. Charles had left a string of healthy bastards but he and his queen had not managed to produce a legitimate male heir. His successor was his brother James, Duke of York, an aloof and arrogant man who was determined to restore the monarchy's absolute control and return the nation to Catholicism.

For both Stamford and Henry Booth the year 1685 was one of recurring problems. On the death of his father, "young" Sir George, the previous year, Booth had succeeded to the title of Baron Delamer. Less than six months into the new reign the Duke of Monmouth, the late King's illegitimate son, led a military rebellion which King James had put down on the marshy expanse of fields near Sedgemoor in Somerset. Delamer was deeply involved, since Monmouth's plan had been to march north and meet his lordship and other supporters in Cheshire. Delamer was therefore not surprised to find himself in the Tower on a charge of high treason. Stamford, at Bradgate, was also arrested on the same charge and once again joined his cousin in captivity behind the same walls. Dates were set for their trials and both men began preparing their respective defences. Later, Stamford was released on bail and, because of the prorogation of Parliament, nothing became of his prosecution and he eventually received a pardon.

The release of Delamer, considered the more dangerous of the two, followed a different course. In January 1686 he was arraigned in the same Westminster Hall where King Charles I had been tried almost fifty years earlier. His judges were a panel of 27 peers brought together specially to produce a favourable result for the King. Among these lords was Theophilus, Earl of Huntingdon, who saw an opportunity of dealing a blow to the man who fifteen years previously carried away his intended wife, Mary Langham. Even worse for Delamer, the Lord High Steward for the trial was the gout-ridden Chief Justice Jeffreys who had dealt so cruelly with the wretched survivors of Sedgemoor. But the prosecution's case had been badly prepared; and throughout the proceedings Delamer defended himself so successfully that the trial came to a premature end in his favour. Such was the popular support for him that his acquittal was greeted in London with "great joy of the whole town".[1] What had turned into a *cause célèbre* was to prove more than just a vindication of the good name of Booth; it was to mark a victory in the battle against James' authoritarian view of government which was later to cost him his throne.

During the years 1686-88 Stamford and Delamer retired to the peace and quiet of their respective country estates and watched as Huntingdon moved closer to the centre stage of national politics. Following Delamer's acquittal, Huntingdon had been prominent in signing the proclamation confirming James as the rightful heir to the throne. Thereafter, the King made him colonel of a regiment of foot. Now Huntingdon was committed to fight and, if needs be, die for his sovereign. Other lucrative royal favours followed including the office of Chief Justice of a large number of the royal forests.[2] In the eyes of his royal master it seemed his Lordship could do no wrong.

In Leicestershire, Huntingdon moved into conflict with not only Stamford but also with the Earl of Rutland. As part of his efforts to control local government, Charles II had begun a policy of replacing hostile and outspoken local worthies with those he felt would be more sympathetic towards the royal cause. In common with many other communities the town of Leicester, "this old and ragged city" as the diarist Evelyn found it, had seen its borough charter revoked and its Anglican and Presbyterian JPs replaced by gentlemen of Tory or Catholic sympathies.[3] Huntingdon had arranged with the King for the issue of a reformed charter and with him, Huntingdon, the safe pair of hands, in the post of Borough Recorder. Charles had told Rutland, his Lord Lieutenant, "to take care of the Leicestershire election ... (to ensure) ... that persons of approved loyalty and affection to the government be chosen'.[4] Rutland had recently succeeded his father as Earl and after representing the county in the Lower House knew only too well where all this was leading, and refused to obey. For his defiance he was dismissed, just one casualty in a countrywide purge along with other Lord Lieutenants from other overtly Whig families, such as Lord Scarsdale in Derbyshire, Lord Shrewsbury in Staffordshire and Lord Newport in Shropshire.

Shortly afterwards came the news that many citizens had been dreading; the Queen had produced a male heir and the royal succession was no longer in doubt. It was the last straw for many leading Whig families who now invited William of Orange to seize the throne. Even many Tory Anglican gentlemen, who had lost their places in county government, deserted James and throughout the nation the King's support collapsed. In the December of 1688 Delamer, together with Lords Halifax and Shrewsbury, were sent to persuade James to vacate his palace in favour of a place in the country. When William of Orange landed in November 1688, Delamer took the field with 50 armed and mounted men in Manchester, where crowds shouted for Prince William. At about the same time Stamford met the Earls of Devonshire and Manchester together with Rutland at Nottingham. A few days later Delamer and Stamford joined the Prince of Orange at Hungerford. Even men like the Earl of Chesterfield, whose father had lost so much in the service of Charles I, again risked all, this time against his legitimate sovereign. After James had fled to France on 23rd December, Parliament voted that the crown was vacant and with William's acceptance a bloodless revolution – the Glorious Revolution of 1688 – had come about.

The new King lost no time in distinguishing between winners and losers. For his services in the north and his proven opposition to all that the previous two monarchs had stood for, Delamer was admitted to the Privy Council and became Chancellor of the Exchequer, the second most senior post at the Board of the Treasury. This was followed by the Lord Lieutenancy of Cheshire and a number of stewardships, the whole culminating in April 1690 with the title Earl of Warrington. It was a triumph for Delamer who saw all his efforts rewarded. Yet at the same time he found himself unable to adapt to the highly charged atmosphere of Court and Parliament. His irritable manner, his inability to get along with his fellow members of the Treasury and his strongly held views on the need for ever more restrictions on the royal prerogative brought about his early retirement from official circles.[5] In 1690 he returned to Dunham where, at least in the county of Cheshire, the name Booth had never been held in higher esteem.

Stamford was pleased with his cousin's success but also envious; there was nothing for him in the lists of honours and rewards which poured from the royal palace, and it was to be six more years before he would be admitted to the Privy Council. Now that his cousin Warrington was out of Court circles he had no one with access to the King's ear who could speak for him. The ways to riches and advancement still mostly lay through the royal court unless, of course, a man was an eminent lawyer, an exceptionally distinguished soldier or a hugely successful merchant; and of course Stamford was none of these. King William's Dutch advisers, who spoke a strange tongue few outsiders could understand, had reminded the King that Stamford's other cousin John at Enville and his cousin, the Earl of Ailesbury, were unreformed Jacobites and that Stamford's father had been a leading regicide. Perhaps it would be no bad thing, they advised, if Stamford was given a few more years to demonstrate the depth of his family's commitment to the new government.

Early in March 1691, a few months before the new Lord Warrington was made mayor of Chester, Stamford at age 38 married for the second time. His bride was Mary Maynard, the 20 year-old daughter and co-heir of Joseph Maynard of Gunnersbury in Ealing. Mary's father had skilfully steered his family through the political turmoil of the Cromwell years and had risen to become Sergeant-at-Arms to Charles II. His success as a lawyer enabled him to purchase and rebuild Gunnersbury House. By 1689 he had become one of the Lords Commissioners of the Great Seal to King William and Queen Mary and now was a committed Whig.

In January 1694 news reached Bradgate that Warrington was dead. He had died more respected than loved as is the case with many men who live with a burning and unbending passion. In a contemporary pamphlet entitled "The King of Hearts" he is described as "a restless malcontent even when preferred (in favour)", a description which one may readily attach to not a few politicians of the early 21st century.[6] He was certainly a man who lived on a short fuse and his religious views were strongly tinged with a narrow-minded puritanism from which he found compromise with others difficult. Yet his heart was undoubtedly with his family and close friends, as shown by the collection of prayers he left behind for the use of his wife and children.

Unfortunately, Warrington bequeathed to his oldest son George, who was a minor, a huge legacy of debt. This had been accumulated both by himself and his father, the 1st Lord Delamer, who had "much beautified" the hall at Dunham "by building the north side thereof (in fact the south side) ... and hath encompassed a large outward court with a brick wall and a fair gate of stone."[7] The house, set in its large park, was said to be one of the finest in Cheshire, and here his Lordship entertained "a great store of gentlemen and gallants'.[8] Warrington's expenditure during his energetic and eventful life had gone unchecked. The style of living in the house, the servants, the clothes, the carriages and other costs of "living in the keeping of one's station", had much increased with the arrival of the Earldom. Frequent attendances at Parliament meant the need for an establishment in the capital. He had entertained Monmouth lavishly and the costs he had incurred in the support of William of Orange had been great. His four Parliamentary elections had cost by his own admission a total of £1,000 and his trial costs were in the region of £2,000. The first Lord Delamer had made no provision for annuities for his other sons and had set aside nothing for his daughters' portions, omissions which would account for a total of about £19,000. By 1661 the debts totalled £30,000 and

*Mary Booth (née Langham), the wife of the 1st Earl of Warrington (Sir Peter Lely and studio)*

about 25 years later had reached a figure of £50,000. Not surprisingly, perhaps, the young 2nd Earl recalled his father weeping over the family finances.[9]

King William had not entirely lost sight of Stamford. In 1694 he was at last admitted to the Privy Council and in November of the same year the King visited Bradgate as part of a tour of senior loyal citizens in the Midlands and North. This was the first time the Stamfords had had the King to themselves and they were determined to impress. For the one-day visit much alteration and addition was made to the house, which by then was hopelessly old-fashioned and had all too obviously been little adapted over the years to changing times. Temporary stabling for 100 horses was hurriedly thrown up and the bridge over the small river Lyn in front of the house was widened to accommodate the royal carriage. A large solar window was inserted into the great hall and here, overlooking the bracken-covered hills of the park, the Earl and the King discussed the outstanding matters of the day. A walk in the gardens, lately enlarged and newly adapted to the style current in the King's native land, would surely impress on the royal mind the worthiness of his majesty's loyal servant?[10]

If Stamford was expecting a great display of royal favour he was to be disappointed. He later became the Chancellor of the Duchy of Lancaster and was appointed colonel of the Devon Militia, but there was little else. He was never to receive a post in national government, the revenues from which might at least have gone some way to clearing the cost of the royal visit to Bradgate, never mind checking his growing financial problems.

Stamford's ambitions for control of the local scene in Leicestershire fared no better with the new era in politics which was dawning. With Parliament meeting every year, service to the House of Commons was becoming an important route to political success. The control of the membership of the Commons added to the prestige of noblemen who made management of elections an important priority of both time and resources. The county's squirearchy and lesser gentry, who were almost exclusively Tory, resented such interference, especially where the seat for the borough of Leicester was concerned. In the election of 1689 Rutland secured all four seats for the Whigs but in direct competition to Stamford's candidates and personal interests.[11] A further blow to Stamford's influence came three years later when he was once more in competition with Rutland. Although he spent freely with the electors, he was unsuccessful once again. A pattern of changing allegiances of the politics of the county and borough over the following two decades was to put a severe strain on his Lordship's finances. In spite of Stamford's efforts, the Rutlands emerged to dominate the local scene in Leicestershire for the remainder of the 18th century and in much the same way as the Hastings family had done two centuries earlier.[12]

For Stamford it was the tragedy of William's reign that the monarch died without children and that he was succeeded by his sister-in-law Anne, the second daughter of Charles II. Anne was a Stuart, a Tory at heart and a staunch Anglican. She was determined to rescue the established Church from the growing influence of the Dissenters and other such unsympathetic groups and to restore it to what she believed was its rightful place in the affairs of the nation. Since, as monarch, she controlled both foreign and domestic policy and appointed her own ministers, she was able to remove those servants whom she had inherited and disliked. For Stamford her succession was a disaster; he was dismissed from all his offices and replaced by other peers whom the Queen considered politically more reliable.

For much of the time when English armies under Marlborough were winning victories on the Continent,

Stamford was at Bradgate picking up the pieces of his political career and trying to sort out his finances. At least he could take some satisfaction in the knowledge that Lord Huntingdon had been eventually cashiered from the army on a charge of financial corruption and his regimental command given to another. In 1690 Huntingdon was one of the six lords still under suspicion of subversion who were excepted from the Act of Indemnity. When the threat of a Jacobite invasion was ended by an English naval victory at La Hogue, Huntingdon's house at Donington was searched. The ashes of burnt correspondence were in the hearth and the stables contained a large number of horses which his Lordship could not satisfactorily account for.[13] Even a spell in the Tower did not manage to refresh his memory of events. In 1701 the foolish Earl protested against the Act of Settlement which provided for a Protestant succession to the throne. He died shortly afterwards and his son George carried the title of 8th Earl for only four years during which he spent much of the time fighting for queen and country abroad.

At around the time of the death of Queen Anne in 1714 and the peaceful succession to the English throne by George of Hanover, Stamford and his second cousin, George, the 2nd Earl of Warrington, were in deep financial trouble. Whereas the latter's problems began to show some signs of recovery the former's were steadily growing worse. Indeed, so well known were Stamford's problems that during the late Queen's reign his Lordship was identified as a member of a seven strong group of peers known at large as the "Poor Lords". Admittedly Stamford was not in the same position as Lord Parham of Willoughby, who was granted a pension of £200 a year simply to enable him to maintain some pretence of noble status.[14] But Stamford's situation was such that he decided to accept a pension from abroad, in return for which he was expected to vote in the Lords in favour of the Hanoverian succession. After Stamford's death in January 1720 Lord Ailesbury, his cousin said of him, "That poor headed Earl ... had received a paternal estate but entailed so that he cut down all his vast fine woods, ruined the mansion house (Bradgate) and took money by advance on this estate and spent it ... his maternal estate, upwards of £3,000 per annum, he ate up absolutely, all sold."[15]

While Stamford was squandering his fortune, Warrington had decided to spend as long as it might take to reverse the financial mess his father had left him. Immediate payment of some outstanding debts was met by the sale of properties in Warrington. He was later to recall that for many of the early years, "I had not a shilling to live on ... I would not wish my worst enemy to go through the straits I have left, to be driven to the like melancholy dilemma." Of the hall (Dunham), he wrote that it was "..in such a rotten condition and barely furnished with worn out goods that it would have been better not to live in it than to attempt to keep it up", and he believed "it could not have lasted safe another generation".[16] The Earl decided to withdraw from life at Court and make all necessary economies. He also tackled the problems of the estate where so many of the rents had not been raised for a generation or even collected.

After several years of a very frugal existence his efforts at financial retrenchment still appeared hopeless. "My encumbrances being greater than I could struggle with" he told his younger brother in 1715, "to make money (is) the chief view of marriage".[17] The income required to support the basic aristocratic lifestyle in the last decade of the 17th century was between £5,000 and £6,000. Warrington's was barely that of a lesser gentleman. There was nothing for it; he would have to find a rich heiress.

When the efforts of his uncle George to find him a wife came to naught, two agents were engaged at the cost of £1,000 to trawl the market for a suitable candidate and to negotiate a match. In the City of London

*A panoramic view of Dunham circa 1750 by John Harris*

there were some daughters of very wealthy merchants who had an eye for a title. The 1st Duke of Chandos' third wife had brought him £40,000 and the 3rd Duke's third wife a staggering £150,000. Warrington's Cheshire neighbour, Thomas Grosvenor, had married Mary Davis whose dowry included all the land in London between Oxford Street and Chelsea. Clearly, there was now no shame to such a move. Thus it was that Lord Warrington married Mary Oldbury, the daughter of London merchant Sir John Oldbury. Although Mary's dowry could not match that of Mary Davis, her £40,000 was a very handsome figure. In the event only a little over half that sum was ever handed over, for her marriage to the Earl turned out to be a disaster.

Although she could claim descent from the Bohuns, the ancient Earls of Hereford, Mary was out of her depth in the aristocratic world and was never accepted by the likes of the Cholmondleys, the Cottons, the Warburtons and the Grosvenors and the rest of Cheshire society. "She is a limber (flabby) dirty fool" wrote one of her contemporaries and contrasted her with her husband who was "the stiffest of all stiff things".[18] Another observed that "some few years after my lady had consigned up her fortune to pay my lord's debts they quarrelled and lived in the same house as absolute strangers to each other at bed and board".[19]

The Countess, however, was not prepared to retire quietly and retreat into her husband's shadow. On the contrary, she went out of her way to humiliate him. She was fond of sports and would drive to the races at Knutsford on the same days as her husband. Her own coach was pulled by four powerful black horses and it was her delight to overtake Warrington's carriage on the rough roads of the times. Approaching home she would call to her coachman, "A sovereign for thee if thou can get in first" and she would fly past her husband's coach, gaily waving her handkerchief. On another occasion she visited Altrincham when the local Sanjam (i.e. St James') Fair was being held. Here she drove through the grounds upsetting stalls, frightening women and causing a huge sensation. She was also a great attender at athletic games, particularly those between the men of Lancashire and Cheshire held on Cinderland Moss. From the start she would "constitute herself the arbitress of the proceedings and crack crude jokes with the young men".[20]

The Earl's experience of matrimony caused him in later years to write a treatise on *Considerations on the Institution of Marriage*. In this he presented the case for the desirability of divorce, then a ruinously expensive business, on the grounds of the incompatibility of the partners. He was also only too well aware that he was responsible for any debts his wife ran up. There was no escape for him and he had to wait a total of 38 years until his Countess died, for release from what he and others saw as his wretched condition.

Mary's financial contribution to the marriage, however, did have the desired effect on Warrington's finances and in 1724 he also inherited the bulk of the estate of his younger brother Langham. By 1730 the Earl was in a position to renovate and improve Dunham Hall which the traveller Celia Fiennes noted was "an old fashioned building" but with "good walled gardens".[21] The Earl retained the Jacobean house set around a courtyard with the Great Hall set opposite the entrance. Of the rooms which he remodelled and which have remained little changed to the present day, it is his Library which reflects his interest in politics, genealogy and history. His taste of furnishing remains evident in the austere mahogany and walnut furniture. Outstanding of interest are his many pieces of silverware which are of heavy gauge and high quality and which were commissioned by the Earl from the Huguenot refugee craftsmen of the time. The collection, built up over many years, reflects the family's Protestant tradition and the Earl's good taste and, not least, his eye for a bargain.

Even before he began work on the house, Warrington was laying out anew the large acreage of surrounding park. There had been a park at Dunham since medieval times but the Earl was not happy to have his re-modelled house in old-fashioned surroundings. Trees were the one thing the Earl held particularly dear. Contemporaries remarked, somewhat unkindly, on his passion for planting which included 100,000 oaks, elms and beeches. Warrington replied that it gave "inward satisfaction in my own breast".[22] He also pointed out that his activities would benefit his descendants because, aesthetic considerations apart, his plantations were likely to prove to be particularly fine long-term financial investments and spare his descendants the financial misery he had suffered.

By the time Kip had made his engraving of Dunham in 1697 the avenues of trees planted to north and south of the house were well established. They showed the Earl's ownership of a large area of countryside, asserted dominance of the landscape and demonstrated his patriotism. An avenue to the south of the house followed and this completed the symmetry captured in John Harris' unique views of the park, which were painted before the Earl's death in 1758. They record a landscape typical of the style of twenty years earlier, a time when formality was first being challenged by Charles Bridgeman at Stowe and William Kent at Rousham and before the genius of Capability Brown and the reforms of the English landscape movement burst upon the scene. From a lifetime of toil and much personal sadness the Earl could at least leave to his much-loved and only child, Mary, an estate in good heart, a house worthy of his title and a delightful park full of valuable timber.

# Chapter 15

# *Return to the Shires*

**Harry Grey, 3rd Earl of Stamford (1685-1739)**
**Harry Grey, 4th Earl of Stamford (1715-68)**

Queen Anne's dismissal from office of Thomas, the 2nd Earl of Stamford, marked the departure of the Greys of Groby from the stage of national politics. Apart from the appointment of John Grey to a minor post, no member of the family would ever again occupy a high office of state, be given responsibility for administering the resources of the crown or even sent to fight for King and country in a distant land. The Glorious Revolution of 1688 had given rise to a situation where the government of the country was now firmly in the hands of the aristocracy; but the second Earl had clearly failed to get off to a good start. At a time when a quarter of the leading peers held office at either Westminster or at court, the second Earl's political career ended in a whimper. The commentator Macky said of him, "He doth not want sense, but by reason of a defect in his speech wants (needs) elocution." He was, he added, "a very honest man himself, but very suspicious of any man who is not of his party".[1] The writer Dean Swift remarked of the Earl that "he looked and talked like a weak man, but it was said he spoke very well in Council."[2]

Stamford died in 1720 and his widow two years later at her house in Bloomsbury. Both were buried at Bradgate. They left no children and the Stamford title passed to Thomas' cousin Harry Grey, son of John Grey of Enville who was the third son of the 1st Earl of Stamford. John had supported the Jacobite cause in 1715 and was an open supporter of the Prince in exile. So, too, were other members of the family, including the new Earl's nephew, John Ward, an MP. Although Harry Grey had sat for a short time in the Commons prior to his father's death, he had been overlooked for even minor office. There were many other men of equal or greater ability and of proven loyalty to his majesty than the Greys of either Enville or Groby.

The 3rd Earl married Dorothy Wright, daughter of Nathan Wright, in July 1704. Wright was a Leicestershire man of no particular ability but he had nevertheless risen to become keeper of the Great Seal, a post from which he was able to amass a large fortune. The 3rd Earl's marriage produced five sons and five daughters but it was not a happy one. Lord Stamford appears to have been subject to fits of rage which were accompanied by heavy drinking, hardly qualifications for a senior post in government. Later he began to beat his wife who eventually left him.

Stebbing Shaw in his *History of Staffordshire* describes one of the marked eccentricities of this strange man; "Once he fancied lime unwholesome; so built a small House of wood framed, and straw, which instead of a ceiling was covered with dimity [a stout cotton cloth woven with raised strips and fancy figures] sewed

*George Booth, 2nd Earl of Warrington with daughter Mary, later wife of*
*Harry Grey, 4th Earl of Stamford (Michael Dahl)*

together." This ramshackle structure in the grounds of Enville Hall was struck by lightning whereupon the Earl built "another odd piece of building upon a sandy bank upon the common, which till then was a rabbit burrough. This consisted of several rooms built about one, an octagon, as a centre, to which there was only a skylight. In the parlour floor there were two or three trapdoors into a cellar. One room was first hung with dimity ... Then wainscoted with deal, and at last with cedar". To finish he made "a square wall eight or nine feet high five hundred yards on each side in length and at great expense..."[3] Perhaps Lord Stamford should not have been too surprised that he continued to be overlooked for high office.

Lady Stamford died in 1738 and her husband a year later. They left two sons, Harry and John, and five daughters. Harry, the elder son, succeeded his father as 4th Earl of Stamford and in May 1736 married Mary Booth, Lord Warrington's daughter.

The wedding ceremony took place in the fashionable church of St James in Westminster and must have been seen as the society wedding of the year. In many respects it was an extraordinary event. Members of the congregation were witness to the cooperation, at least for one day, of a group of individuals whose antipathy to one another was well known. The two respective fathers-in-law, both eccentric individuals, were accompanied by wives whom they hated. It had been decided that the two women could not reasonably be excluded from the ceremony since their absence would only spark off yet another round of society tongue-wagging.

The same gossips were not slow to dissect the reasons why the union had come about. Lord Warrington, only the second holder of his title, was marrying off his daughter and sole heir, whose Booth ancestry was old and honourable, into a family whose noble lineage stretched back in almost unbroken male line to the late Middle Ages. Stamford for his part had found his son a rich heiress whose wealth in the long-term at least would pass to his grandchildren and their descendants. In the meantime, the bride's dowry would go some way to solving the financial problems which were the legacy of his own misdemeanours and those of his cousin, the improvident 2nd Earl. Those present in the church noticed too, the compromises that each of the parties had reached. Warrington, the archetypal unbending Presbyterian Whig gave away his daughter in an Anglican ceremony to a man whose family was firmly of the established Church, and some of whom were well known to be Tories of professed Jacobite sympathies.

Social and religious considerations apart, the marriage highlighted other important matters of the times. Both bride and groom were direct descendants of the first Earl of Stamford (c1600-1673) but, since Harry was his great-grandson and Mary was one more generation removed, the matter of consanguinity – interbreeding in farmyard terms – was not the problem it was in other noble families of the times. At least at first sight, the matter of fertility (or lack of it) was cause for concern since both Mary and her mother were sole heiresses. Over the centuries many noble lines had died out because of their inability to produce children, especially boys. Such deficiencies sometimes became a matter of high politics.

In the case of the Booths the previous five generations of the family had managed a disastrous record, not from infertility but rather the inability to raise offspring beyond childhood and then to marry them so they would launch the following generation. In this the Booths were not alone, for the same problem had dogged other noble families, friend and foe alike, including the Hastings. The Greys' record of procreation and survival over the same period was marginally better and to Lord Warrington the prospects of having grandchildren and great-grandchildren must have appeared as good as he was likely to get. Time was to show that the heart of the matter lay not with any Booth infertility. The simple fact was that Warrington and his wife so hated each other that the sort of contact which successfully begets children had simply not taken place.

The union of the Houses of Booth and Grey also highlights the wider political, social and economic forces at work during the early part of the 18th century. When George of Hanover came to the throne in 1720 he spoke no English and was unable to preside over his council of ministers. Walpole, his acting chairman, and eventual de facto first minister, could converse with his sovereign in private only in Latin. The Walpole years, spanning the two decades 1720-1740, saw the emergence of cabinet government and with it a gradual shift of power from the Lords to the Commons. The first two Georges were very sympathetic to those who had brought them to power and gave the aristocracy much of a free hand in running the country. There developed among the Whig majority a group of 150 or so rich, landowning aristocratic families who were united by ties of politics, economics, self interest and marriage. These families, which just about included the Greys, constituted an effective oligarchy which governed the country during the first half of the 18th

*Harry Grey, 4th Earl of Stamford (JB van Loo)*

century. They were, as Edmund Burke told the Duke of Richmond, "The great oaks that shade a country and perpetuate your benefit from generation to generation."(4)

The Grey-Booth marriage also played a part in cementing these ties further. At a stroke the Stamfords had more than doubled their acreage and, in the eyes of their tenants and others of the lower orders, had enhanced their lordly status enormously. At the same time they made no pretence of being in the same league as the Russells in Bedfordshire, the Cavendishes in Derbyshire and even the Manners, now Dukes of Rutland, in the Greys' own county of Leicestershire. Nevertheless, towards the end of his life the 4th Earl of Stamford, with estates large or small in eight counties, could be counted among England's top 400 wealthiest landowners.

Shortly after their marriage the newly-weds moved into the mansion at Bradgate where their first two children were born. Their stay was brief and after the 3rd Earl of Stamford's death in November 1739 they moved to Enville.

The decision to leave Bradgate was not a difficult one. Although it was the ancestral home of the Greys, the house, now two centuries old and built in the early Tudor style, was hopelessly old fashioned, in a poor state of repair and very unsuitable for a well-placed nobleman of polite society of the times. Dunham, with grumpy old Warrington still in residence and likely to live to an old age, was hardly the place for a young couple. Besides, Stamford had no connections with a Cheshire society which his mother-in-law had scandalised and his irascible father-in-law had managed to antagonise. Warrington had left the estate in trust to his daughter with remainder to her male heirs. He was well aware that a family's assets could quite easily disappear into the black hole of an in-law's financial affairs as the result of an unexpected death or some ingenious or unscrupulous legal move. After Lord Warrington's death in 1758, Mary managed her inheritance herself with skills learned at her father's knee. At Enville the 4th Earl had much more opportunity to indulge himself in gardening in the new fashion. By the 1740s there was already a long tradition of noble gardening. The move to Enville at this time allowed the Earl to be in at the beginning of what was to be known as the English landscape movement through the work of Brown, Repton and others. In 1739 the doors and windows of Bradgate were bricked up and the house abandoned. The ensuing years saw the building, which two centuries previously had been *the* house of its time, decay rapidly to the point where it became no more than a lonely romantic ruin, home to wailing peacocks and the wild park deer.

King George I gave his Whig ministers very much of a free hand in the running of his kingdom, but it did not follow that all his supporters benefited from the opportunities this presented. In this respect the Greys were once again noticeably unsuccessful. The 4th Earl of Stamford was a committed Whig but openly opposed Walpole, particularly regarding his policy governing England's naval conflict with Spain over trade with South America. As plain Lord Grey, the 4th Earl had been elected to the Commons as a member for Leicestershire in 1738, a few months before his father's death. Perhaps it was hardly surprising that the first minister did not look kindly on him. With no relative at court with access, however modest, to the King, any faint hopes of a career in government which Grey may have harboured stood no chance of success. In any case, His Majesty, so happy with the peace and prosperity which Walpole had brought to the nation, was not moved to upset his First Minister by pleas from a man who was the son of a drunkard, the grandson of a Jacobite and a member of a family with a none too reliable record over the centuries of loyalty to the crown. It was also likely that Stamford was simply not up to meeting the demands of a top job in government. By moving from Bradgate to Enville the Earl in effect turned his back on the political hot house of Parliament and, as one of the lesser "mighty oaks", embraced instead the lifestyle of a grandee landowner.

It was less than a day's ride by horseback or carriage from both Bradgate and Dunham to Enville in south Staffordshire. The village lies only a few miles to the west of Birmingham but still manages to retain a measure of the atmosphere of peace and calm which the 4th Earl and his Countess found. In much the same way that the manors of Groby and Bradgate had descended from the first son of Reginald Grey of Ruthin (died 1441), so Enville was the inheritance of the third son. As the fortunes of the senior line of the family in Leicestershire had risen and fallen and risen again during the 16th and 17th centuries, the Enville Greys had prospered modestly and quietly. In 1525 Edward Grey had served as sheriff for his county and had died the father of 17 children.[5] John, his grandson, had no heir and sold Enville to his distant cousin Henry Grey of Pirgo who, as we have seen, was grandfather of the 1st Earl of Stamford. Thereafter the house and estate descended from Stamford's second son Ambrose.

Surrounded by the rolling hills at Enville, the fourth Earl soon found himself a place among the county families of south Staffordshire. There, as elsewhere in 18th century England, one's position in the social order rested on the ownership of land, the display of arms and the bearing of titles. Lacking the first, one had little prospect of acquiring the other two and for much of the century the opportunities for an untitled man, however wealthy, to reach the peerage were very limited. Members of the aristocracy expected deference from, and control over, their social inferiors. In return they saw their duty as to govern, come what may. They believed themselves to be a balance between the autocratic tendencies of a monarch and the demands and clamourings of the ignorant multitude. In the changing climate of government, the role of Enville had also changed. Whereas once Stamford's grandfather, as lord of the manor, had held his manorial courts at the hall, now they were held in more public buildings. By the time of the 4th Earl, Enville had become an entirely private family residence with access restricted to those considered worthy of entrance. Above all it was a place to impress social equals, to overawe the lower orders and, in achieving both, maintain the status quo.

Although "this beautiful mansion" (as Plott, the Staffordshire historian, described Enville in 1686), was modernised only slowly, much time, effort and money were expended on the estate and especially the gardens. Since the time of the 1st Earl of Stamford, additions to what was then a fairly modest estate had been put in hand and further purchases made by the 4th Earl. On the rolling hills around the house, Stamford began laying out the gardens which were to make Enville famous for more than a century as a place of gardening excellence.

There had been a deer park to the west of the house in medieval times and it is possible there had been some small scale garden development at the end of the 17th century. This would have been according to the style favoured by William III and his Dutch followers: hedged or walled enclosures in which were set out square or rectangular flower beds, each separated by gravel paths and lined with trees and bushes trained and clipped to perfection. There may also have been a parterre, a bastion, a raised terrace and possibly a bowling green, all of which produced a landscape of formality and control. This directly reflected the belief of the time that God's command to Man to go forth and subdue nature could be answered in one's garden which was also a place where signs of one's intellect, learning and piety would become apparent to visitors.

At the time the 4th Earl set to work, such ideas were being challenged by the philosophy and changes in

*Enville Hall Staffordshire, circa 1686*

society now known as the "Age of Reason". It was held that an individual's relationship with God must be seen in a new way – that is if one believed there was a God and the Stamfords were devout believers. Miracles and divine revelation were less important than praising God in his manifest works, and it was held that one might come particularly close to the Almighty in the garden. Leading writers and thinkers such as Pope and Addison maintained that the landscape should reflect such changes. Parks and gardens should be laid out informally and should be two parts of the same structure, a line of thinking which culminated with the view that swept away walls and fences and which saw all nature as a garden.

While his father-in-law at Dunham continued to plant his trees in straight lines in the fashion of a fading age, the young 4th Earl of Stamford set about challenging such geometry by laying out a landscape with an approach which, in 1740, was really in its infancy. William Kent had introduced these new ideas at Chiswick when he had laid out the gardens for Lord Burlington. At Rousham in Oxfordshire a few years later, he transformed a modest riverside estate into a linked series of separate vistas which used such features as temples and cascades to evoke the features of the landscape of classical Greece and Rome. Elsewhere during these years, the young "Capability" Brown was learning the business of gardening before marking his genius on the landscape in the 1750s and beyond.

In what can be seen as a bold and pioneering spirit Lord Stamford set about the task of transforming Enville according to ideas he had developed from his books, his conversations with friends, his London connections and yet all without the benefit of a Grand Tour. He also had the assistance of a number of local people including the architects Sanderson Miller of Radway in Warwickshire and William Shenton of The Leasowes near Halesowen. The Earl adapted with great skill the rolling scenery around the house. He did

*Enville Hall Staffordshire, circa 2000*

this by planting trees and placing buildings which drew the admiring eye to a series of views within panoramas, or as Stebbing Shaw had it; "lay in setting the stronger features of nature to admiration". Between 1744 and 1760 Stamford brought in features which transformed an area of over 700 acres to one of contemporary sophistication. On the island of a specially constructed pool he built an octagonal Chinese temple which was reached by means of a painted bridge. To the west was a Gothic summerhouse which gave fine views over the estate. A rotunda with a domed lead roof and supported by six Corinthian columns had open walls and seats where the weary traveller could rest. This was, as Heely wrote, "a handsome building ... situated upon an eminence that gives the eye the most ravishing variety of landscape."[6]

On the brow of a hill against a wooded skyline was a large folly known as the Gothic gateway which still gives, as Dr Pococke so admired two and half centuries ago, commanding and particularly fine views to the north. From a spring on a neighbouring hillside a cold plunge bath was constructed. Here a single pool provided the opportunity for a cold dip in an age when such a thing, taken on a regular basis, was considered beneficial to the health. From a point lower down the same valley the water descended through a height of over four hundred yards to the Temple pool by two cascades, the upper one stepped and reminiscent, on a smaller scale, of that at Chatsworth. By the side of the pool was a boat house, a comfortably furnished square brick building built over arches, below which the boats were moored. Visitors were treated to a display of the cascades in full flow with the water "foaming and bellowing, as if the mountain were enraged, pouring down a river of water as white as snow." There were many other features and in 1759 Dr Wilkes was full of praise for the Earl's achievements: "He has done with so much art and so elegant a manner that few places in England can rival, and none of the same compass of ground can exceed it."[7]

With such idyllic surroundings it is perhaps not surprising that the 4th Earl and his Countess spent much of their time at Enville. When one considers that both partners were the products of what today might described as broken homes, the marriage they made can be seen as a happy and successful one.

By 1750 their family was complete with three sons and two daughters, one of whom, Anne, died as an infant. The eldest son was christened George Harry after both grandfathers and the second boy was called Booth, names which in the fashion of the times acknowledged the union of the two families. When grandfather Warrington died in his 84th year, George Harry was only a few weeks away from his majority, although he had to wait a further fourteen years before receiving the entire Warrington inheritance.

Although far from the political jungle of court and Parliament in London, a man of Lord Stamford's wealth and position was still required to perform important duties at a local level. By birth he was one of the privileged few who were there to govern those who were there to be governed. In 1744 he was appointed Deputy Lieutenant for the counties of Staffordshire and Lincolnshire. His brother, John, was appointed to the Board of the Green Cloth, the administration of which had given rise to the clash between his family and the Hastings a century and a half earlier.

Stamford could not have found his duties sufficiently onerous to upset his life as a country gentleman although there were times to the contrary. In 1745 the final military challenge by the Jacobites to the House of Hanover brought panic to the quiet corners of northern and midland England. The hordes of the rebel army swept southwards from Scotland into England and rampaged almost unchecked on through Kendal and Preston to Manchester. Fortunately for the Stamfords, their Warrington estates in Cheshire and Lancashire escaped the attention of the fast-moving invaders, although Stamford did take the precaution of moving the valuable silver collection to Enville. In December of that year the invaders reached Derby; Bradgate house and park, on the road to Leicester and London, lay completely unprotected. At Donington, only 12 miles from Derby, the 9th Earl of Huntingdon faced the same situation but where his sympathies lay only he knew. Fortunately for their lordships the Scots left Derby and turned for home. With the defeat of the Pretender at Culloden in 1746, the Jacobite challenge was extinguished and the nation breathed easily once more.

In October of the same year, 1746, Lord Huntingdon died. He had married Selina, the daughter of his neighbour Earl Ferrers. Shortly afterwards she had been converted to the teachings of John Wesley's Methodism. This was a protest against the established Church's feeble response to the challenge to religion fostered by the moral laxity which accompanied the Age of Reason. With tireless and fanatical fervour and using all the advantages of her privileged position, Selina led a personal crusade in an attempt to bring her sinful fellow citizens back into Grace with their Creator. The total disregard for the social and political implications of the theology she preached were not lost on her husband and friends. Donington Hall was turned into a centre for dispossessed Anglican clergy who became her ministers; the park was ploughed up to grow food to feed them and family jewels and treasures sold to support them. Even Lord Stamford could find it in his heart to pity her husband. A stranger in his own home, this quiet and courteous man stepped back and allowed his wife to have her way, if only because, the cynics said, "she was the better man". After Huntingdon's death Selina lived for 45 more years before succumbing to cancer at age 83.

With the passing of the 2nd Earl of Stamford in 1720, both Hastings and Grey had adopted a low key approach to politics since there no longer seemed any prospects of members of either family capturing glittering prizes at national level. The fact that the Greys were not resident on their Leicestershire properties after 1739 did not mean they had abandoned their social and political concerns in borough and shire. Their landed interests in the county had to be protected against the other large landowners, Whig and Tory, especially the Rutlands, the Huntingdons and the newly-ennobled Sherrards of Stapleford, who might seize or engineer opportunities to take advantage.

Another problem for the Greys in Leicestershire was a large group of politically active and vociferous Tory country gentlemen, such as the outspoken Sir George Beaumont of Coleorton and James Wigley Esq. of Scraptoft. Such men lost no opportunity to press their rights, real and imaginary, for an increased say in local government and banded together with the borough corporation which in 1749 this was said by Lord Egmont to be "totally in the Tories" and was of strong Jacobite sympathies. The Greys drew support not only from their own tenants but also from the emerging working class, such as the stocking frame knitters of borough and county. During the years of the 3rd Earl (1720-39) it had fallen to the Duke of Rutland to further the Whig cause in Leicestershire until Lord Grey, the future 4th Earl of Stamford, had challenged him successfully by being returned to the Commons for a brief spell as a Whig opposed to Walpole.

The 4th Earl's connections with Cheshire and Lancashire and his renewed interest in Staffordshire obliged him to take a keen interest in a wider political field. From 1754 the Cheshire seat in the Commons was monopolised by county gentlemen such as Samuel Egerton, Thomas Cholmondley and John Crewe. The seat for the borough of Chester was more or less the preserve of the Grosvenors whose service to, or rather control of, the borough over 159 years was almost unique, even by national standards. Lancashire, on the other hand, was of little interest to the Greys and in any case was dominated, as it had been for many years, by the Stanleys of Knowsley.

Stamford's best prospects lay in Staffordshire and in 1754 his uncle, John Grey, the second son of the third Earl, was elected for Bridgnorth.[8] A seat in the Commons provided a powerful opportunity to promote self interest as well as those of the community one represented. It was, after all, the county and borough members who saw in to law proposals for canals, turnpikes, enclosures and the like. Placing members of one's family in the Commons required skilful planning, considerable expense, the careful nurturing of the electorate between elections and, usually a powerful backer. Most of the seats in the Commons were in the "interest" of great landowners. Lord Lowther controlled no fewer than nine constituencies. Lord Grey, the 4th Earl's eldest son and future 5th Earl, was actually returned unopposed for the county of Stafford in 1761 as a result of the patronage of Lord Gower with whom the Greys had family connections.[9]

The cost of the expensive lifestyle and free spending of the 4th Earl were met from a variety of sources. Although deprived of lucrative grants and fees of offices of profit in the service of the crown, from which a man might accumulate vast sums, and while not being in the same league as the richest in the country, such as the Duke of Bedford who was worth £30,000 a year, Lord Stamford was certainly a wealthy man. He derived a very substantial income from the rents from his three main Estates of Groby, Enville and Dunham. The years following 1715 saw profits from agriculture rise sharply with Lord Stamford well placed to take advantage of improving circumstances. There was, too, the income from his woodlands, which extended across the parks at Dunham and Bradgate and covered large parts of his lands on the surrounding Charnwood Forest.

There is no evidence to suggest that the Grey family had any connection, direct or otherwise, with other ways in which it was possible to amass a large fortune in the early 18th century. There was no investment in the world of banking where men like Henry Hoare of Stourhead in Wiltshire grew very rich in the thriving money markets of London. Also, the Greys showed no entrepreneurial spirit by sinking venture capital in such groups as the East India Company and the South Sea Company which were pioneering trade with the developing empire. It is also clear there were no connections with the slave trade and with the slave plantations in the West Indies from which a man like William Beckford of Fonthill might return home with a huge fortune to buy land and seek a title.

With the first signs of the Industrial Revolution of the later 18th century, Lord Stamford's financial interests began to diversify. To the profits of the traditional milling along the river Bollin near Dunham were added incomes from local brickworks and saltworks and from the limeworks at Breedon in Leicestershire. The technical developments in mining enabled Stamford to expand production from his collieries in the north Midlands. The mines had come into the family during the time of the 2nd Earl and by 1748 were realising a rent of £1,600 a year. Lord Stamford granted them on leasehold rather than by providing investment capital which was the practice of the largest coal owners such as the Dukes of Northumberland, the Earls of Scarborough and the Lowther family. Towards the end of his life the 4th Earl had a gross income from his estates in Leicestershire, Staffordshire and Derbyshire alone of £6,858.[10] Less than 30 years previously, in the time of his father, the same properties had been worth only £4,866 per annum.

Lord Stamford died in 1768 at the age of 52 and was buried in Enville church. At about this time great changes were taking place both at home and abroad. By the Treaty of Paris (1763) Britain was recognised as having succeeded against the French in Europe, India and North America and was poised to expand the Empire to all corners of the globe. At home the Whigs' hold on government had been broken and the rapid march of industry was to bring change, the scale and nature of which most aristocrats could hardly foretell.

*George Harry Grey, 5th Earl of Stamford and Warrington as a young man (Anton Raphael Mengs)*

# Chapter 16

# *The Golden Years*

## George Harry Grey, 5th Earl of Stamford and Warrington (1737-1819)

George Harry was 30 years old when he succeeded as the 5th Earl of Stamford in May 1768. He was probably born at Bradgate since he was christened at the village church in Newtown Linford three weeks later. As a young boy he attended the town school at Leicester and rode daily from Bradgate and in the company of his younger brother, Booth. In the school room he rubbed shoulders with the sons of the leading members of the town and its corporation.[1] Later, like most sons of aristocrats, he went on to a university college, in his case Queens at Cambridge, where he collected his MA in 1758.

The following year he was sent on a tour of Europe where he encountered many other young English gentlemen of quality. The purpose of the Grand Tour was to enable the sons of aristocrats to gain a knowledge of the classical cultures of ancient Greece and Rome which were fashionable in 18th century England. The usual programme of study included art, music, architecture and theatre. A Tour also enabled a young man to polish up his Latin and Greek and to prepare himself for the place in society it was expected he would occupy. The wealthier tourists visited Geneva, Paris, Rome, Genoa and Venice over a period of two to three years (or even longer) and at considerable expense to his family. The more modest kind of Grand Tour, which George Harry travelling as "Lord Grey" undertook must nonetheless have cost his father between £2,000-3,000. Many noblemen took this once-in-a-lifetime opportunity of acquiring at first hand a collection of cultural items and works of art. Lord Dainlow bought pictures totalling £20,000 from the Duke of Orleans to furnish Cobham Hall.

In Rome, Lord Grey was in the company of Sir Henry Mainwaring and the two clearly enjoyed all the aspects of life which that city had to offer. Along with his formal portrait by Anton Raphael Mengs, which now hangs in Dunham Massey Hall, there is a delightful miniature by the same artist showing Lord Grey with Sir Henry enjoying the delights of the countryside. In a cartoon by Thomas Patch, a group of noblemen including Lord Grey and Sir Henry are shown at Pola. A second painting, also by Patch, is entitled *The Punch Party at Hadfields* and depicts a group of revellers boisterously spending time away from viewing the sights of Florence.

Shortly after his return to England Lord Grey was elected to the Commons as MP for Staffordshire. Sharing the benches with him was another young nobleman, William Henry Cavendish-Bentinck, the eldest son of the 2nd Duke of Portland and MP for Weobley. It was about this time that Grey met Bentinck's sister,

*Henrietta Cavendish-Bentinck, wife of the 5th Earl of Stamford*

Henrietta, whom he married and with whom he was to have 56 happy years. Here was a case of two young people in love, but of course there was much more to it than that. This connection with the Portlands was to have important benefits for the Greys.

The nub of the matter was that the Stamfords had married into one of the most wealthy, influential and cultured families in the country. Henrietta's father, who died a year before the wedding, was the grandson of the Bentinck who had accompanied William of Orange to England in 1688 and who had become an immensely rich and important man. The Whig credentials of the Cavendish-Bentincks were therefore impeccable. The bride's mother, Margaret Cavendish Harley, was the daughter and heir of Edward Harley and her mother was the daughter and heir of the 1st Duke of Newcastle, an important Whig in government. Harley himself was the custodian of a vast collection of books and manuscripts which has become known as the Harleian Collection and which is now housed in the British Library. The 2nd Duke of Portland's prominent social position meant that he would inevitably be marked for a career in politics at a high level. Clearly, the Greys had married upwards in a way that made Lord Grey's own Booth lineage, while certainly most honourable, appear lack-lustre in comparison. Apart from social prestige, Henrietta brought wealth to the marriage but no lands. Further, it was not until the death of his own mother in 1772, possibly of a stroke, that the Warrington inheritance passed to the 5th Earl. He and his wife foresook Enville and made Dunham their principal residence, thus re-establishing the Grey presence in Cheshire. Here they had aristocratic neighbours in abundance. The county, it was said, could boast of no fewer than fifty noblemen with incomes of between three and ten thousand pounds per year. Those at the pinnacle of county society, including the Grosvenors of Eaton Hall, the Egertons of Tatton, the Stanleys of Alderley Park and the Mainwarings of High Peover were among the wealthiest families in the entire north-west. The Stamfords' star was rising once again, at least in a social and cultural sense.

After the death of the 4th Earl, his widow Mary moved to Dunham Massey Hall. The building and its interior had remained substantially untouched since the death of her father, Lord Warrington. When Mary died there in December 1772 it was in need of repair and modernisation. The 5th Earl employed a relatively unknown man, John Hope, an architect and builder from nearby Millington. Hope is said to have designed several residences before he added a suite of rooms to Dunham which were to accommodate the 5th Earl's growing family. Hope's son, also John, later worked on several noble residences in the north and north-west. However, the improvements brought about by the Hopes did not impress everyone. In 1790 the itinerant Lord Torrington wrote in his diary that although the setting at Dunham was "very verdant and every kind of tree grows to wonderful stature ... I approached a modern red brick tasteless house which I had no wish to enter."[2] Evidently the earlier plantings in the park by Lord Warrington were approaching maturity.

Gradually over the years the principal rooms of Dunham were redecorated and refurbished; the dining room (now the saloon) in 1773; the grand staircase in 1778 and the great gallery in 1784. A light plasterwork ceiling decoration contributed a note of sophistication to Lord Warrington's plain interiors. To add to his souvenirs of his Grand Tour, the 5th Earl acquired some excellent pieces of late 18th century furniture, notably some handsome mahogany bedroom items and a fine pair of satinwood cabinets. The Earl's activities can be seen as an expression of the second phase of good taste at Dunham. The gardens adjacent to the hall were also improved and the Countess took a delight in keeping ducks and growing pineapples.[3]

Although not the Greys' principal residence, Enville Hall had also been improved and modernised with the help of John Hope senior. In 1801 Stebbing Shaw described the hall as "A handsome white structure,which although for the greatest part modern, carries with it the air of respectable antiquity, happily corresponding to the venerable aspects of the surrounding woods."[4] The 4th Earl's efforts at gardening were reaching maturity. That same year the greenhouses were supplied by James Bateman with a cast iron furnace.[5] This allowed the growing of some of the exotic species which were entering the country as a result of the expansion of maritime exploration.

The same Lord Torrington who wrote of Dunham also visited Bradgate in June 1790. In what was an equally casual observation he could only record the obvious: that the house "although a noble place ... with grounds very bold and diversified..." had long since burnt and that the local farmers "destroy wantonly" what remained of the ancient fabric.[6] What Torrington did not record was the fact that Lord Stamford was spending much on the improvement of his ancient and very beautiful park. Many miles of external and internal walls had been built and stables for horses and kennels for foxhounds had been constructed. An imposing folly known as "Old John", the design of which was based on that at Mow Cop in Staffordshire, was sited on a prominent hill in the park. Around the base of this a private racetrack was laid out. Some years later a floating meadow (adjacent to the river Lyn) was constructed at considerable expense to provide early spring grazing for the deer and the domestic stock with which they shared the park.

About the year 1782 the Stamfords rented a house in London. A home in the capital was important for Lord Stamford's visits to the House of Lords. It also allowed him to keep a close watch on the political scene and the fortunes of his financial affairs. The house concerned was 37 Charles Street in Mayfair and near the newly laid out Grosvenor Square, a development by his Cheshire neighbours. The Square was one of a series of lordly enterprises which included Hanover and Berkeley where many of the great families of the nation lived and entertained.

The rapid concentration of such wealth in the West End of London gave rise to "the Season", a round of social and cultural events enjoyed by the elite. The programme got underway in early summer and developed into an almost constant round of birthday celebrations, card parties, visits to the theatre and opera, soirées and particularly grand balls. Whatever other benefits it offered, the Season became the chief means by which parents of the upper class attempted to find suitable marriage partners for their offspring. Although lying away from the most prestigious locations, the houses of Charles Street could still command a rent of about £1,000 a year. Such residences appealed to families like the Greys who were clearly not in the top league of aristocrats but who could not afford to be away from the London scene, its scandals and its gossip.

At home on his country estates for much of the year, Lord Stamford pursued those interests and activities typical of a country gentleman. "One of the Englishman's great joys," wrote François de Rochefoucauld in the mid 18th century, "is field sports. They are all mad about it." The Frenchman's observation described Lord Stamford's interests perfectly. First among these was horse racing which he shared with his brother, Booth. Horses from the Dunham stables were raced at meetings at Knutsford and Chester. Those stabled at Enville which were run at Bridgnorth, Burford and Worcester were trained on a specially laid out track. This was sited near the hall and was screened from the outside world by carefully positioned plantings. Horses stabled at Bradgate and run at Leicester, Lichfield and Warwick were trained in the secrecy provided by the park. A presence at Newmarket, the leading racing venue, came some years later in the time of the 7th Earl.

Racing was clearly an expensive luxury for the Greys and required a large staff, from head trainer to the humblest of grooms. Nevertheless it was not until 1812, when Booth Grey had a colt in the Derby, that the family name became associated with top class blood stock.

Racing allowed the different social classes to mix and mingle, if only occasionally and for short periods. The Greys' other great love, foxhunting, demanded a high degree of exclusiveness. Stamford took to hunting at the same time that Hugo Meynell, founder of the Quorn Hunt, was breeding hounds in Leicestershire which had the speed and stamina to chase foxes over long distances. Almost as much time, effort and expense were devoted to the development of pedigrees and bloodlines in his hounds as were to the breeding of the horses which carried the hunters. The Enville Hunt, with kennels and stables at the hall, had been founded by 1790 and with the 5th Earl as its master. Over much of the two counties of Staffordshire and Leicestershire there were foxes in great abundance, and in the latter half of the 18th century there were still large unfenced areas of rolling countryside which offered gloriously long and uninterrupted runs.

The Greys enjoyed a lifestyle which grew ever more expensive. Their three houses, each with an army of servants, meant a heavy routine expenditure. To this was added the cost of the endless round of balls, parties and receptions together with unavoidable and more official duties, all of which formed part of the aristocrat's year. At the same time, the maintenance and improvement of the parks and gardens of the three main properties demanded a second army of estate workers. The interest in racing and hunting together with the provision of routine transport for each member of the family engaged a third group of employees. The social scene in London, as long as the family considered themselves part of it (which meant as long as they could afford it), was yet another costly expense. Then there were recurrent election expenses and, of course, the individual members of the family had to be provided for. The 5th Earl was to have ten children to feed, clothe and educate. Six of these were daughters of whom five were to demand dowries to take to their husbands. Even after his death, the estate was obliged to make provision for his wife during her years as a dowager. Yet at the close of 1788 Lord Stamford, from an income of about £19,000, was able to show a clear profit of about £3,500 with which he bought the Old Hays estate at Ratby adjoining his manor of Groby in Leicestershire.[7]

The Greys' substantial and rising income which made all this possible can be put down to a tide of national prosperity which the Greys rode with great skill and which swept them forwards and upwards into the next generation and beyond. The key, of course, was the rise of industry, a phenomenon later to be termed the Industrial Revolution. Central to this was the wide availability of coal from which large quantities of energy could be released to produce steam. It was the application of steam power to the advances in science and technology which enabled entrepreneurs to establish the Factory System. In the days of the 5th Earl the "wood and water" society of the 18th century was giving way to a "coal and iron" economy. This was accompanied by a considerable increase in the prosperity of the countryside. The Greys were blessed with many fertile acres and ample reserves of coal. It is hardly surprising the family prospered.

Lord Stamford was particularly fortunate in that production of coal from his mines in Derbyshire and Nottinghamshire increased steadily. The pits were leased to entrepreneurs who recognised – or thought they recognised – a good business opportunity when they saw one. By leaving the problems of flooding and firedamp for others to overcome, Lord Stamford was not obliged to risk his own venture capital. He approached the matter of finance with the attitude of any modern hard-nosed businessman. Leases of his

*Part of Burdett's map of Cheshire published in 1777 showing the course of the Bridgewater Canal passing close to the north of Dunham Hall*

pits near Oldham cost the lessees £1,200 a year "whether or not they get enough coal to make a profit."[8]

Transporting the coal and the necessary raw materials of industry and later the manufactured goods was at first achieved by water. The first major canal in Britain's industrial history was that cut by the Duke of Bridgewater to take coal from his mines at Worsley to the growing town of Manchester. An Act of 1762 gave rise to the development of the canal between Manchester and Runcorn. Burdett's map of Cheshire in 1777 shows the extension of this waterway passing through the peaceful acres of the Dunham estate north of the hall. Bridgewater had negotiated an agreement not with the 4th Lord Stamford but with his Countess, Lady Mary Booth. Payment to her was partly made in free coal which she used to heat Dunham Hall. More important was the fact that the presence of the canal increased enormously the value of her lands in terms of their potential for industrial development.

During the national "Canal Mania" of the 1790s, Lord Stamford found himself in opposition to Lord Huntingdon when a scheme was proposed to canalise the river Soar between Loughborough and Leicester. Stamford and others with coal and lime interests in the north-west of Leicestershire feared this scheme would simply allow Derbyshire coal to monopolise the Leicester markets and local products would be unable to compete on price. Eventually a compromise was reached, but this still did not accommodate Huntingdon's interests which were in the far west of the county. Such was Lord Huntingdon's influence in the Commons that the proposed legislation was at first defeated. It was only after much negotiation that his Lordship was persuaded to drop his opposition but with no love lost between himself and Stamford.

Where industry flourished the population grew. At Altrincham the Bridgewater Canal brought great prosperity after 1765 and a great rebuilding of the town in brick rather than wood. By 1819, when manufactures were booming, an observer noted "it contains many houses of very respectable appearance and has a general air of neatness and cleanliness".[9] Since Lord Stamford owned some three quarters of the town, he could hardly fail to benefit from the rise in trade. Similarly at Stalybridge, home of water power manufacturing and another Stamford property, the introduction of steam power after 1776 saw the settlement change from a hamlet to a bustling market town with a population of 14,000 in 1831.

It was at neighbouring Ashton-under-Lyne, on the north bank of the river Tame, that the most dramatic change in the landscape took place at the hands of the Greys. Ashton in 1750 was described as "four narrow dark streets formed by mean-looking dwellings ... of a rude construction, being low and thatched".[10] Thereafter, and especially between the years 1760-1790, the town grew very rapidly and with a reputation for radicalism and violence. The growth had been largely due to an expanding cotton spinning industry with its many power looms located in the town and in the suburbs along the bank of the river. At its height of production, Ashton had the benefit of no fewer than three canals and three railways as it served the developing areas of Stalybridge, Dukinfield and Hyde with goods and provisions.

Since there was no resident lord of the manor at Ashton, day-to-day running of the community was left to lesser men. Inevitably the ad hoc nature of the development of the town reflected the lack of leadership to accommodate change. At this point Lord Stamford, as the non-resident lord and principal landowner, stepped in. From 1790 onwards he planned and built what was in effect a new town westward from the original centre. In contrast to the twisting narrow streets of the ancient settlement, his innovative development included a system of broad streets laid out in grid formation. Tenants were obliged to construct proper drainage and comply with other stipulations laid down by Lord Stamford. The overall effect was a

*George Harry Grey, 5th Earl of Stamford, in middle age (George Romney)*

markedly cleaner and healthier environment and the design was noted as bearing a close likeness to the famous New Town in Edinburgh. As a token of his goodwill, Lord Stamford gave 63 acres for a public park to be known as Stamford Park. Street names of this new development: George Street, Grey Street and Henrietta Street also reflected the influence of the family. For much of the 19th century the old Tudor town and the 5th Earl's new town in effect existed side by side.

The rents and profits from his rapidly growing industrial base were what separated the Greys from those aristocratic families who continued to derive their income solely or largely from agricultural sources. The Greys were benefiting, too, from the tide of enclosures taking place in those parishes where they were the lord of the manor or at least a major landowner. The family also enjoyed an enhanced income from the rise in rents which advances in agricultural efficiency and output were producing. In Leicestershire, they were the chief beneficiaries of the enclosure of Charnwood Forest which surrounded their Park at Bradgate and adjoined their manor of Groby. The Charnwood Forest Enclosure Act of 1808 encompassed 12,000 acres of wild, barren bracken-covered waste where flocks of stunted and under-nourished sheep grazed but which, at the beginning of the 19th century, were deemed suitable for improvement. Of this huge enclosure, large even by national standards, the Greys were awarded about half and Lord Hastings a mere one sixth. As a result, the Greys' lands encircled their slate pits at Swithland which, together with those at Groby, produced a profit of more than £500 a year. Some of the new enclosures on Charnwood were planted with trees which were added to the valuable stocks in Bradgate Park, in the grounds at Enville Hall and of course, to those so lovingly planted at Dunham by Lord Warrington.

Lord Stamford was following the example of his grandfather Warrington in skilfully managing his resources. He had safeguarded and enhanced the family name and provided for its members most satisfactorily. He could claim many of the possessions of a Whig "Major Oak": two fine country houses, a respectable if not top class house in the capital, a lifestyle which was at once recognisable as that of prosperous aristocrat and a substantial and rising income to support it all. He lacked only a Parliamentary "Interest", the mark of a truly great man.

Underpinning Lord Stamford's privileged position in society was the nature and functioning of the Constitution. During the first three decades of his Earldom (1768-98) there were major shifts in government. Shortly before his marriage to Henrietta, the Duke of Portland's sister, the Whigs lost the election of 1760. This marked the end of what many looked back on as the golden days his father and grandfather had known, days when the aristocrats more or less ran the country in their own best interests. After that fateful election the Whigs split into two factions. As power began to move decisively from the Lords to the Commons, so the need to control the latter intensified. In 1765 thirty-one aristocratic families elected a quarter of the Commons. Lord Hardwicke alone had four sons there at one time or another.[11] As Lord Grey, George Harry the 5th Earl had owed his own seat in Staffordshire to the very considerable influence of Lord Gower. His election had been engineered while he was still on his Grand Tour and it is likely that polling was taking place while he was still abroad. At the same time his uncle, the Honourable John Grey, sat for the Cornish constituency of Tregorney where the outcome was similarly arranged.

Following the split in his party, George Harry, as 5th Earl, lent his support to the faction which became known as the Aristocratic Whigs. In outlook they were against an authoritarian monarchy, were zealous for parliamentary liberty and were devoted to the continuation of rule by members of the old Whig families. At the same time Lord Stamford could show an independent streak. In 1768 the revolutionary John Wilkes mounted a bold and lengthy campaign to enter Parliament in order to challenge the system of electing members. Many MPs found him outrageously disrespectful and even subversive; but Lord Stamford voted that he be allowed to take the seat from which he had been disqualified following two previous successes at the polls. In a similarly independent vein, Stamford cast his vote to bring the War of American Independence to an early end.[12] His marriage had also brought political problems and he asked his brother-in-law, the Duke, to excuse him from attending the Lords so that he could not be pressured to vote for legislation which might go against the Portland interest.

As we have seen, it had long been a tradition, not to say a necessity, for an aristocrat with an interest in Parliament to nurture the voters between elections. At election time the securing of even an unopposed contest could cost hundreds of pounds. An opposed one might cost very much more and in 1790 Lord Falmouth reckoned that his three Cornish seats cost him £9,000. Stamford's son and heir George Harry, had made it known in 1790 that he was prepared to pay as much as £4,500 for a place in the Commons and he was eventually returned for Aldburgh in Suffolk.[13] Booth Grey, son of Booth Grey who was the 5th Earl's brother, was returned for Petersfield in Hampshire as a result of the influence of his Portland cousins.[14]

Elections in the 18th century were usually fraught with difficulties for families like the Greys. Electors were required to record their votes orally and in public. They were also liable to change their minds at the last minute by intimidation and bribery. Freeholders at Nottingham had made a business of seeking an extra income by selling their votes to the highest bidder and had made it generally known that each man had a figure of £20 in mind.[15] Voting usually extended over a period of at least ten days and the outcome might depend on the honesty and efficiency of the officials in charge. The Countess of Stamford wrote to her brother, the Duke of Portland, in March 1768 and described the campaign at Leicester, a town known for its political violence at election times, as "A dreadful uphill battle". The polling she added, "began last Tuesday and they do not expect it to be over till Friday. Thank God as yet they have had no riots."[16]

The seat for the town of Leicester was one of several in the three counties of Leicestershire, Cheshire and Staffordshire where the Greys had a presence. The sleepy old-walled town presented no particular problem in the mid 18th century. Hitherto it had largely been confined within its medieval gates and crumbling perimeter walls and had not greatly altered since the days of Elizabeth I. After the brief excitement of the Civil Wars, it continued as a sleepy semi-rural market town and in 1700 had a population of some 7,000. During the first half of the 18th century, the economy began to grow. Then, in 1760, the first regular mail coach arrived. Three years later the first banking enterprise appeared and in 1771 the Infirmary was founded. Horse racing and cultural events came to the town and with the rise of stocking frame-knitting, the population had risen to 17,000 by 1801. The making of what was to become a great industrial city was underway, a city in the governance of which there was to be no place for later generations of the Greys.

Latent Jacobite sympathies on the part of members of the corporation of Leicester were driven underground as a result of the election of 1768 in which Booth Grey, the 5th Earl's brother, at great expense and with the Duke of Rutland's support, proved triumphant. Six years later he was returned unopposed with the backing of Lord Rockingham.[17] At the election of 1780, there was a fierce contest as Jacobite sympathies surfaced once more. About one third of the 2,500 voters lived outside the town, but heavy spending by Booth and Lord Stamford resulted in another victory for the Greys. In the county contest the Duke of Rutland

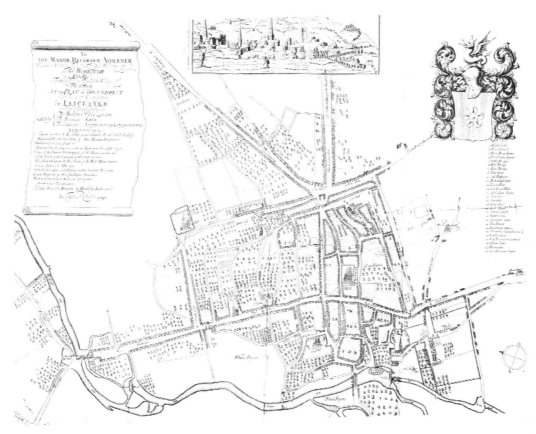

*Thomas Roberts' map of the town of Leicester, 1741, before the arrival of the Industrial Revolution*

returned one member and the independent gentry the other.[18] In retrospect one may discern that the government was using both Stamford and Rutland to monitor the political activities of the town council so as to be prepared for any possibility of the resurgence of political disturbances. The fat bucks which passed from the parks of both noblemen to the table of the town council were of more than just culinary significance.

In the county of Leicestershire where the Duke of Rutland reigned over the political and social scenes, the absence of the Greys as residents counted against them. In Cheshire, their recent return to Dunham meant they did not carry the gravitas which for so long had attached to the name Booth. Besides, the county seat, a Tory preserve, had not been contested since 1734. When the Greys did show an interest in 1796 the seat was won by a Cholmondeley who was second cousin to Prime Minister Pitt. Chester town was also Tory and had the name Grosvenor firmly fixed to it for a century and a half. In Staffordshire, representation by a Grey ended in 1768 and although Newcastle-under-Lyme was a Gower seat, it was never offered to the Greys. Stafford was becoming too open and too expensive and Tamworth presented similar problems.

The progress of the revolution which had broken out in France in 1789 sent shock waves throughout the British nation. In the early days, Stamford and the Whigs had welcomed the end of the rule of such an autocratic regime as a belated version of their own Glorious Revolution of the previous century. But, as the gutters in France ran red, the mood of the ruling classes in Britain changed abruptly and Lord Stamford's politics became markedly less liberal. The British elite feared the sentiments behind the forces unleashed in France would find root in their own country. There were already voices being raised advocating radical solutions to mounting social problems, such as poor housing, poverty, ill-health, inhuman working conditions and unemployment in the growing urban areas. The rich, including the Greys, were getting richer and the majority of the population was not sharing their good fortune. Radical reformers called for equality before the law, political freedom, electoral reform and more. Those who governed could see the prospect of their inherited privileged position in jeopardy along with that other unelected institution, the monarchy.

Suddenly Lord Stamford wanted little to do with the merchants, lawyers and others of the emerging middle classes in Leicester and even less with the lower orders such as the framework knitters whose cause he had hitherto espoused. The Revolution Club in Leicester, which had been founded after the election of 1768 as an intellectual and dining club and which had been supported by most of the local influential Whigs, did not meet again after 1792. In common with a good number of the other "Aristocratic Whigs", Stamford switched his support to the newly reformed Tories under Pitt, who were against Parliamentary reform and in favour of the war against Republican France.

It was his position as Lord Lieutenant for Cheshire that Lord Stamford faced his greatest challenge. This was a post he had coveted as early as 1770 but which he had landed only in 1783 through his Portland connection. One of the greatest of the many responsibilities of the post was the overseeing of the Royal Cheshire Militia. Such a force was the ultimate guarantee of law and order which the central government possessed at a county level. Following the French Revolution, Lord Stamford resigned his commission and saw the appointment in his place of his eldest son, George Harry, Lord Grey. Thereafter a body called the Stockport Volunteer Corps was raised with officers recommended by Lord Stamford. Its duty was "to overawe the democratic societies and suppress riots and tumults ... in the town or the neighbourhood from the prevalence of the levelling doctrines inculcated by these societies".[19] In common with another recently formed body, the Loyal Cheshire Rangers, membership was open to "gentlemen, yeomen and other substantial inhabitants".[20] With great speed the volunteers were organised, armed and drilled. In August of the following year, 1795, they were called upon to prevent outbreaks of violence on the streets of Stockport where men were bent on rioting.[21] The problem was not confined to Stockport; the simmering discontent was to be found in most towns across the nation.

There is a certain irony in the fact that, at this time of mounting unrest, violence and discontent with the failings of the rigid class system, Lord Stamford acquired an additional title. This was the Earldom of Warrington which his grandfather Booth had held but which had become extinct on the old man's death in 1758. Stamford was by no means the only favoured recipient of a second award; a great number of the many ennoblements of the late eighteenth century were made to existing peers. Also, having the Home Secretary of State, the Duke of Portland, as a brother-in-law to press one's case was a decided advantage.

After the year 1800 the 5th Earl of Stamford began to show signs of physical ageing but not the kind of mental deterioration which was troubling his monarch. As King George III's mental condition worsened his eldest son, the Prince Regent, was left to carry out the royal duties. At about the same time Stamford saw George Harry take a wife and dutifully produce grandchildren. Stamford also lost two brothers. The first was Henry who was drowned in a shipwreck off Barnstaple in Devon. The second was Booth who until 1784 had represented the town of Leicester in the Commons. The seat subsequently passed to nonentities backed by the Duke of Rutland who had made a complete about turn in his political thinking as a result of events at national level. His Grace also controlled one of the county seats. The only Grey in the Commons in 1807 was Booth Grey, son of Stamford's deceased brother who sat for Petersfield in Hampshire. His retirement in 1812 saw the end of three centuries of Greys in the Lower House.

Shortly after the outbreak of revolution in France in 1789, Francis Hastings, the 10th Earl of Huntingdon died while dining at the house of his nephew, Francis. Lord Huntingdon was the son of Countess Selina, the militant Methodist. He died unmarried, wary perhaps of encumbering himself with a wife of the likes his father had so nobly endured. The Huntingdon title now passed to a distant relative, although the 10th Earl had named his nephew Francis, heir to the Earldom of Moira, as his successor to his house and estates at Donington. This young man had carried the family name with honour during the war of American Independence. After his return to England he devoted much money from his inheritance to rebuilding Donington Hall and remodelling the grounds. In this he engaged the assistance of an up-and-coming landscape architect called Humphry Repton. In contrast to Stamford, who was content to sympathise with the unfortunate French aristocrats at a distance, Moira invited individual refugees to find temporary exile at Donington at his own cost. This was the beginning of a lifestyle of reckless expense which Moira was never able to control. During the troubled years of the early 19th century, he married Lady Flora Mure-Campbell, the Countess of Loudoun, and in so doing brought to his family titles and estates in Scotland. When in 1809, during the premiership of Stamford's brother-in-law the Duke of Portland, Moira entered the Lords under the ancient title of Baron Hastings, he was no nearer balancing his books.

As his own wealth increased Lord Stamford could observe Moira's finances slipping further and further into decline. The main concern was, as the diarist Farrington put it, that Moira "so conducted his affairs, so deranged his circumstances, that his dealings with jews, with brokers and people of all degrees, owing to his necessities, have destroyed the respect due to his character".[22] Moira's friendship with the dissolute Prince of Wales proved another handicap. In January 1812 it was rumoured that Moira might be made a Duke. Nothing came of this and the following month, in a fit of pique, he refused the Order of the Garter, only to change his mind four months later. At about the same time it was also rumoured that Moira would be asked to form an administration, which meant he would become Prime Minister. Eventually Lord Liverpool was appointed and Moira returned to the task of sorting out his financial affairs.

Moira now did for a second time a thing no Grey had ever done; he left his wife and family at home and sought restoration of his fortunes abroad. At length he emerged as Governor General of India and Commander-in-Chief of the British forces which, in February 1817, finally established British power. He was given the title Marquess of Hastings but solutions to his financial problems proved as elusive as ever. To escape his creditors he took the post of Governor of Malta in 1822 and died four years later. The once mighty House of Hastings was facing insolvency. The political influence of its members at national level was more or less at an end.

During the three decades following the French Revolution it was noticeable that the 5th Earl of Stamford increased the number of his charitable gifts in an effort to alleviate the rising tide of poverty among his tenants and neighbours. There were blankets for the poor at Groby and the *Leicester Journal* reported that £40 "was directed to be laid out in procuring for them (his tenants) such necessities as bread, coals, linen for shirts, sheets etc." There was money for relief in Dunham, Altrincham, Bowdon and Ashton. But philanthropy of this nature, even on a generous scale, was hardly a solution to the marked absence of social conscience on the part of the privileged towards those whose labours and sufferings were producing the wealth.

The long marriage of Lord Stamford and Henrietta was a happy one. The Countess could write to her brother in 1763 that "he indulges me in everything I ask, indeed he spoils me intolerably".[23] The little evidence from the few letters and other primary sources which survive show Stamford to have been a man with strong family values. Early in his marriage he and his wife began to refer to themselves as "Groby" and "Grobiana" and their fireside portraits strongly suggest a relationship in old age which today we might recognise under the title of "Darby and Joan". Lord Stamford's public image was quite clearcut. In *Tales and Sketches of Old Altrincham*, published in 1880, H. V. Leech recorded that "he lived in grand state and maintained the reputation of a fine old English gentleman." As such, "he dispensed liberal hospitality to all comers at the hall (Dunham) including visitors and servants".[24] But when he died in May 1819, aged 81, a great wind of change was blowing through the forest of the Great Oaks. Indeed, Britain was on the verge of revolution.

# Chapter 17

# *Unhappy Families*

## George Harry Grey, 6th Earl of Stamford and Warrington (1765-1845)

George Harry succeeded as 6th Earl in May 1819 and the following month was appointed Lord Lieutenant of Cheshire. Only eight weeks into the post he was involved in an event which was later to be known as the "Peterloo Massacre". Up and down the country in the early years of the 19th century the labouring poor and their middle class sympathisers were addressed at massed rallies by liberal politicians calling for reform of the parliamentary system. Petitions were organised, speeches made and marches led in support of demands.

In August 1819 Henry Hunt, a leading orator and politician, attempted to address a crowd in St Peter's Fields, Manchester. Before he took the platform a huge throng estimated at about 50,000 persons had already assembled, presenting a situation which might be seen as a serious crowd control problem for a modern, well-equipped police force. Before Hunt had an opportunity of addressing his audience, the magistrates who had been appointed by Lord Derby, the Lord Lieutenant for Lancashire, panicked and decided to take preventative action. The Yeomanry were called and when they attempted to arrest Hunt and disperse the assembly, unrest broke out and the cavalry drew their swords. In the violence which followed eleven people were killed and 400 injured.

This tragic affair was an unfortunate beginning for Stamford who had worked closely with Lord Derby in monitoring local discontent and mobilising the forces of law in order to contain it. The following year saw a further crisis, this time in London. The "Cato Street Conspiracy" involved a group of politicians in an attempt to assassinate members of the Cabinet, seize the Tower and proclaim a republic. The Government's response was to usher in a round of repressive legislation. Most of this gained Lord Stamford's support, although it did place even more responsibility for peace-keeping on his own shoulders and those of his fellow Lord Lieutenants. It also led him and most of his fellow Whigs to realise that some sort of fundamental political change which would alleviate the most deeply-rooted social problems was now inevitable.

George Harry was 53 when he became Earl. This was about the age at which both his grandfather and his great grandfather had died. He was a family man with two sons, George Harry aged 17, his heir, and Henry Booth aged 12. He also had three unmarried daughters: Henrietta Charlotte 21, Maria 19 and Jane 15. In 1797 and at the age of 32 he had married Henrietta Elizabeth Wemyss Charteris. She was ten years his junior and the daughter of Francis Charteris, Lord Elcho, later the Scottish Earl of Wemyss.

Why George Harry married so late is unknown. It is also difficult to understand why the heir to the wealthy, ancient and honourable Earldom of Stamford should choose a partner from the House of Wemyss. His wife's father, Francis Wemyss Charteris (1749-1808), carried to his dying day the stigma that he was the

*George Harry Booth Grey, Lord Grey of Groby and son of the 6th Earl of Stamford*
*(Sir William Charles Ross)*

nephew of the notorious David Wemyss. David, also known as Lord Elcho, had been a leading and active Jacobite and had fought for the Pretender, Charles Stuart (Bonnie Prince Charlie), at Culloden. For his treachery, he had been attainted and had forfeited the Wemyss Earldom. He fled abroad where he died in 1789.[1] The title then passed to David's brother, also Francis, to whom descended the enormous fortune of Colonel Francis Charteris of Amisfield (1675-1732). This out-and-out rogue and scoundrel had misappropriated army funds, gambled heavily and successfully, lent money at extortionate rates of interest, fought several duels and enjoyed the company of wealthy married noble ladies between the sheets.[2] If George Harry had ignored the political problems involved and married in the belief that he might inherit, via his wife, some of the Wemyss fortune, he was to be disappointed. In the event the money descended to his brother-in-law Francis, the 7th Lord Wemyss, who had a son and eight daughters.

Money and politics apart, it was a matter of only a few years after his marriage that a serious problem concerning George Harry's link to the Wemyss family began to show itself. His now wealthy brother-in-law, Francis, was given to "violent spasms" which were to remain with him all his long life. Eleanor, one of his eight daughters and Stamford's niece, was destined to die insane. Even worse, George Harry's own wife, Henrietta, was showing signs of an illness which was referred to at the time only as her "complaint". So sparse is the information about the malady that today its diagnosis can only remain a matter of speculation. When it is first mentioned in 1814 in the letters between her and her family it was causing Lady Henrietta considerable physical and mental suffering. Over the years it worsened and her behaviour caused George Harry and their children much unhappiness. At some point Henrietta moved or was moved out of the family home and for the following five years at least lived in a series of rented houses in London and on the south coast. At each she lived alone or with a female companion cum nurse, together with domestic help. By 1814 George Harry was no longer visiting his wife, although the children were encouraged to see her and from their lively company she derived much comfort and pleasure. The signs that their mother's condition was worsening were only too plain and their visits eventually ceased. After 1819 they were encouraged not to write to her on account of "her very nervous state".[3]

Thus personal communication between man and wife became by letter only. In June of 1814 Henrietta, in a distressed state, wrote to her husband that her physician, Sir Lucas Pepys (who had attended the King during his attacks of supposed insanity) "does not apprehend the present danger" and closed with the heartfelt cry of "God bless you my dearest Grey and believe me, your affectionate and faithful wife."[4] This touched her husband deeply but it was probably from that point that he gave up hope of ever seeing her again because, as he explained, "a meeting might be the means of creation of very painful and distressing sensations to both of us". He signed himself, "yours very affectionately, Grey".[5] During the following years and with the full agreement of Lord Wemyss, George Harry made his wife a generous allowance and paid all his wife's bills and medical expenses.

In a letter of 23rd July 1817 George Harry made it painfully clear to his wife that his father, the aged 5th Earl, was very sick. The old man feared his life was drawing to a close and he wanted his heir and the grandchildren to be resident at Dunham in readiness for the succession to the titles and estates. He died almost two years later in May 1819 at about the time the civil disturbances across the country were reaching their peak. Four months earlier George Harry had written to inform his wife that the pressure of "public duties" alone prevented him from seeing her.[6] Perhaps not surprisingly Henrietta's condition continued to

*Katherine Grey (née Charteris), Lady Grey of Groby and wife of Lord Grey of Groby*
*(Sir William Charles Ross)*

deteriorate further. In a letter to Lady Bromley, a friend of the family, Isabelle Ross, Henrietta's companion, wrote that Lady Stamford "is quite delirious" and reported that Dr Slater "thought it fit to confine her to her bed, not only for the safety of those about her but also for herself".[7]

Eventually Stamford bought Heath House on Hampstead Heath as a permanent home for his wife and it is possible this is where she died. In 1821 he begged to be excused attendance at the coronation at Westminster of William IV.[8] The gaze and gossip of peers and commoners alike, who knew of the Countess' condition, was more than he could bear.

It was about this time that Stamford decided to send his son on a Grand Tour. In the first week of February 1823 George Harry Booth Grey, Lord Grey, aged twenty-one, left Dunham for the family home in Hill Street. The capital at the beginning of the Season he found "rather dull".[9] He made his plans and wrote to his father that he intended to proceed through France to Rome with all speed. On 22nd February he had reached Paris where he met many English aristocrats. The City itself disappointed him. "This way of living does not quite suit me" he told his father "the rich dishes do not agree with me so well as the roast beef of Old England."[10] For no obvious reason he changed his itinerary and proposed to set off for Brussels, then make for Geneva in order to see Switzerland. Later he would move on to Naples and Rome. While in Paris he took dancing lessons, visited the Opera and the Louvre and even hosted a small party of his own.

He was still in Paris in late March, kicking his heels and waiting for his travelling companion, Cheslyn, to join him. Clearly Paris had already run short of ways of exciting his intellect. On 25th April he was en route for Brussels. There was nothing to interest him in the flat countryside but he was forced to admit that "the Cathedral at Lille was noteworthy."[11] From Brussels he spent a day riding to Amsterdam: "The weather was very cold, the journey extremely dull and the inns wretched."[12] From Rotterdam, "a vile dirty town", the two men proceeded to the Hague where he found "nothing worth viewing."[13] On 28th April he wrote to his father, "I never was so tired, having been shaken over near a thousand miles of the most uninteresting country to see dirt, filth and everything devoid of comfort and pleasure."[14] In his letters he showed much concern about family and friends, especially Lady Charlotte Charteris, and about news of the racing at Knutsford and Chester.

Eventually the boredom lifted a little. On 7th June they were in Dresden where, for reasons he did not explain, he had "five happy weeks". The 9th July saw him in Munich where he admitted to acquiring "some specimens for curiosity for every country" and felt that his carriage was well up to carrying home the whole collection. He had reached Geneva by steamer on 4th September 1823. At first the town was "enchanting" but later "rather dull" and he looked forward to Italy "all except the bed companions", by which, one assumes, he was referring to the insect life.[15]

In Italy he said goodbye to Cheslyn who returned home to attend to a family problem. Grey was not sorry to see him leave because, although the man had the best of manners, his lack of a title was proving something of an embarrassment to his lordship. In Milan during October, Grey went to the opera every night. Among the many English aristocrats he met was Robert Grosvenor, his immensely wealthy Cheshire neighbour. December found Grey in Naples which was "stupid" and "dull".[16] The time from November 1823 to the end of the following January was spent in Rome, where he enjoyed the hunting, but there were few parties and he found the city "dull as ditchwater". In March he was in Milan once more en route to Florence, Bologna and finally Venice. At the end of the same month he was home again. In a letter he thanked his father for all his help and kindness. Stamford, in turn, must have wondered just what lasting benefit this immature and self-centred young man could have gained from a tour which had cost well over £3,000.

Much of our knowledge of members of the Grey family during the first half of the 19th century comes from the diary of John Walsh, later 1st Lord Ormathwaite, who was born in 1798 and was the eldest son of a baronet of the same name. Walsh was a self-confessed social climber and came into contact with the Greys when he was attempting to court more than one of the Charteris girls. Eventually he married Jane Grey, Stamford's youngest daughter, and went on to make his name as a political commentator. He left behind a diary describing in detail the important events and people in his life.

Walsh left this description of Lord Grey. Although he could be a great bore in company, Grey was nonetheless a handsome man who attracted attention. He was "about 5 feet 10 inches in height. With an agreeable clear brown complexion, dark eyes, oval face, high forehead and well formed features." These, together with his strong fine black hair produced "a remarkably classical bustlike head." He was also a smart dresser. "His hats, his coats and his neck cloths all sat well upon him and his toilettes were the perfection of good taste." His manners, "though diffident and constrained with strangers, were exceedingly gentlemanlike." However, an initial and favourable appearance was off set by a "sheepish shy carriage and a silly laugh." Walsh discovered that his first impression of Grey as a "kind-hearted, goodnatured and unaffected young man with domestic tastes and habits ... with an absence of pride and rank" was quite ill-founded. The man was, in Walsh's later and considered opinion, jealous of his rank and position as the eldest son of a wealthy peer, was trusting of no one (least of all members of his family), and was interested in little but hunting, horse racing and studying his collection of rare plants.[17]

The first signs of the affliction which was to bring Lord Grey to an early death occurred at the beginning of his Grand Tour in Paris. Here he had what was described as a "fit". On his return to England he lost no time in seeking a wife and in 1824 began to court two daughters of Lord Wemyss. Although "dreadfully low in spirits" in that year, he managed to propose to Lady Katherine Charteris, when everybody had expected Lady Charlotte would be his choice. Katherine was the beauty and pet of the family, charming and possessing a feminine softness and delicacy. She was also, of course, Grey's first cousin. Both admitted to close friends that neither loved the other. The proposal of marriage by Grey had been made with no reference to his father. When Stamford was informed he was furious. With his wife gravely ill the thought of another link with the Charteris family appalled him; but he was able to delay the marriage for only twelve months.[18]

For the first few years of marriage nothing appears to have upset Lord and Lady Grey's attendance at an endless round of balls, parties, race meetings and musical events. Two children were born: George Harry in 1827 and Margaret two years later. In 1833 the fits returned, this time in a severe and shocking form. On one occasion, on a journey from Dunham to Enville, Lord Grey was taken ill near Newcastle and carried to the house of a local clergyman. An apothecary was called and leeches were applied to the unconscious man's head. Lady Grey reported that "it was the most dreadful sight to witness his delirium, his screams and endeavours to pluck them off ... his exclaiming constantly I am dying, I am dying." Over the following weeks the attacks grew worse as did his behaviour. Lady Grey, who nursed him throughout, took the brunt of his outbursts, but the anxiety, friction and unhappiness affected the whole family and particularly Lord Stamford, who was rude and ill-tempered to those around him.[19]

There was yet another powerful ingredient in the mix that came to make the ageing 6th Earl's life more unhappy than it might otherwise have been. This concerned his second son, Henry, who was born in 1776. Stamford had bought him a commission in the army, but Henry was not cut out for the life of a soldier, let alone that of an officer. Both John Walsh and John Wildman, the husband of Lady Margaret Charteris Wemyss and another brother-in-law of the wretched Lord Grey, agreed that Henry's problem was that he was weak and indolent in mind and body. He appears also to have exhibited something of his brother's temperament. He was conceited, self-opinionated, self-willed and ignorant. He did not enjoy the camaraderie of his fellow officers and became more and more a misfit. Such was his inadequacy in his cavalry regiment it was feared that Stamford would be obliged to withdraw him before he was dismissed.[20]

At the time of Lord Grey's illness in 1830, Henry was at home at Dunham, having given up soldiering. He was becoming "bewildered, odd and muddle-headed" and was also suffering from gout and rheumatism. His family noticed that he had at least reduced his drinking which Walsh thought "acted on an irritable nerve which made him obstinate and sullen and worked him into a state of almost morose insanity." Amazingly, Henry announced his intention of going abroad. He had bought a pair of carriage horses and planned to be away for three years. But it was not to be. During 1834 his mental condition deteriorated and in the July of the following year he was confined at an unknown location. Three months later Lord Grey, his brother, died. Henry was to remain in enforced custody by the family for a further 23 years before his death in 1857.[21]

In an effort to escape his cares and troubles, the 6th Earl of Stamford spent much time following the country pursuits his father had enjoyed. First among these was horse racing. His stables at Dunham produced runners for most of the important meetings, including those at Knutsford, Preston, Manchester and especially at Chester where the Earl subscribed £20 to the new grandstand. Stamford's horses from his Enville stables ran at Worcester where, by 1822, the Worcester Stakes had grown in importance and were noisy and colourful occasions and attracted much betting. Stamford's horse "Peter Lely" was the winner that year, beating his rival "Master Henry" and going on to win the Gold Cup.[22] Cricket, too, was an occasion when the Earl could meet his tenants and the members of the wider community. The game had been established in England in 1774 by the Earl of Tankerville and by 1821 had been taken up by many leading aristocrats. At Enville it was played by the Greys on a pitch laid out to the east of the hall.

As his family problems worsened and his public duties became more onerous, Stamford slowly reduced his public appearances in favour of shooting. This was an altogether more private pursuit, to be held away from crowds and enjoyed only with chosen relatives and friends. The records of his shoots, particularly in the 1820s, showed what fine sport was to be had on his Cheshire estates, including Dunham Park, Bowdon Downs, the Bollin and Dunham Field.[23] Carrington Moss, which the ornithologist TA Coward described as "a delightful low-lying moor ... one mass of purple ling ..." and which lay to the north of the hall, was known as one of the best grouse moors in the north of England and produced some of the largest bags of pheasant and partridge.

Yet it was the Leicestershire properties which produced the finest sport of all. Here the estate spread across more than 5,000 acres of countryside, much of it in Charnwood Forest. The extensive woodlands were managed with a keen eye for the hunting and shooting they could provide. In addition, there was Bradgate Park, 1,000 acres of bracken-covered wilderness, dotted with gnarled and ancient oaks and populated by generations of deer which had grazed in unbroken line since the early 13th century. In the open area known

*The Old Hall at Ashton-under-Lyne at the time of the 6th Earl of Stamford*

*Bradgate Park from the air showing the spinneys planted by the 6th and 7th Earls of Stamford*

as the High Park, the 6th Earl planted spinneys which were walled round from the deer and which sheltered the pheasants and partridge in great numbers. Such was the quality of the shooting which the Park provided that in his 73rd year Lord Stamford still travelled to Bradgate for his sport.

During the first quarter of the 19th century the wealth of the Grey family continued to increase. Their coal mines expanded production and by the mid 1850s there were 182 cotton factories belonging to various owners along the banks of the Tame at Ashton-under-Lyne. The Greys owned almost the whole of the parish and Lord Stamford, as lord of the manor, restored the Old Hall. This he used as an occasional residence and as a place for conducting the business of the ancient Court Leet. At the same time, he also purchased his London residence at 13 Hill Street from Lord Berkeley for £4,265. In 1796 the 5th Earl of Stamford was enjoying an income of about £40,000 which was the sum Lord Durham felt a man could comfortably "jog along" on.

It was at Dunham that the 6th Earl lavished most money and attention. The house was, after all, his main home and the centre of his social and political life away from the capital. In 1822 he employed a minor London architect called John Shaw, who had worked at Newstead Abbey, to create a neo-Classical dining room which remains today as the Saloon. Improvements apart, the costs of maintaining the Hall were considerable. In the last year of the 5th Earl's life, 1819, the housekeeping costs for himself and various resident members of the family totalled £8,322. In the following year, with his widow and daughter, the Lady Louisa, resident, the cost was £6,806. In 1822, the family stayed for only twenty-two weeks but the bills still totalled £5,792.[24] There was no shortage of money to maintain this well-managed household.

Try as he may to turn away from the politics of the day, Lord Stamford was unable to ignore the social and political changes taking place around him. As his income rose, his influence on local and national politics began to slip away. After 1820 the Whigs in London had produced a change of strategy. They were now bent on social reform before the tide of revolution which gripped the continent lapped against the shores of Britain. The lower orders were now beginning to mobilise. The Factory Acts limited the employment of young children in cotton mills and in 1824 trades unions were recognised as lawful organisations. Even worse to devout Anglican and defenders of the religious status quo like the Stamfords, Catholics were allowed into public offices after 1829.

Following the Peterloo affair the Whigs, once the undisputed rulers of England, were in disarray. Middle class reformers saw that treating the symptoms of the nation's problems was not enough; tackling the causes must take priority.

The prime target was the electoral system. Constituencies which sent members to the Commons had remained unchanged for two centuries and in many parts of England they no longer remotely reflected the great increase and redistribution of the population which was still taking place. "Pocket Boroughs", those constituencies controlled by aristocratic interests, were bad enough, but "Rotten Boroughs", such as Old Sarum in Wiltshire where a pile of earth, a heap of stones and seven voters returned two members, were seen as entirely indefensible. In 1821 a token move at reform had been made. The seat at Grampound in Cornwall, which a Grey had once represented, was re-allocated to Yorkshire. Liberals saw this as a crack in the dam holding back the pressure for reform. Eleven years later and on top of his own family troubles, Stamford could clearly see that the end of aristocratic government of the kind he supported could well be in sight.

The movement towards the Great Reform Act of 1832 was led by Earl Grey, who was not related to Stamford and who had a reputation for advocating reform. Although the passing of the Act swept away the rotten boroughs, redistributed seats, widened the franchise and increased the number of voters, the result was not the disaster Stamford had feared. The middle class gained the most, the radical trouble makers fared badly and the lower orders achieved nothing. Stamford and his fellow aristocrats, both Whig and Tory, were still in power to call the political tune, at least for the time being.

It was in January 1838 that Lady Stamford died. Her "complaint" had left her mental faculties unclouded for only a few brief intervals in her later years. Her funeral was held at Hampstead where she was laid to rest "in the common grave in a parish churchyard". Lord Stamford was not present. After the simplest of services, it was left to Walsh, his brother-in-law Wildman and six others to see the coffin, topped with a Countess' coronet, lowered into the ground.[25]

Lord Stamford celebrated his 73rd birthday on 31st October 1838. In the luxury and loneliness of Dunham Massey Hall he could reflect on the events leading to his family's distressed state. He had given up concerning himself too much with the important political, social and religious changes which were taking place around him, the sort of affairs he knew he ought to occupy his attention. He was an old man and it was becoming all too much for him.

The futures of his two grandchildren, George Harry and Margaret, were his most pressing problem. Both were resident with him and their mother at Dunham, but Lady Grey had little sense in the children's management and upbringing. Walsh wrote that "she ruined them by over indulgence and by utter blindness to the advantages of education." The result was that George Harry, "a fine, dashing and spirited boy, by wild and youthful vivacity, was perfectly ungovernable." His sister, a less excitable child, "seemed a fair way of being quite ruined and falling into a state of nervous depression for want of a fixed and regular occupation." All along Margaret's spoilt nature, ill humours and bad temper caused her mother much anxiety. Not least was the problem of introducing her, a half-educated and headstrong eighteen year-old, into polite society.[26]

Lord Stamford died in his 80th year in April 1845. Like his father before him he had presented two distinctly different images to the world. In public he was the typical kind-hearted, old-fashioned country gentleman who paid his needy tenants' doctors' bills and spoke to everyone with civility and politeness. He dispensed blankets to the poor during a flu epidemic and made available nutritious soup for the needy on his Leicestershire estates. For callers at Dunham, including tradesmen and servants, there was a permanent supply of ale and beef. At the same time he was careful to protect his station by declaring that he "didna dine with cotton lords". Perhaps he was only too aware that the rising wealth of the emerging industrialists and traders was now seriously challenging the pre-eminent position of many of the ancient aristocratic families.

Stamford's family was one with a pious tradition combined with philanthropy. He replaced the chapel at Ashton in 1827 and two years later gave the town its market place. In religion he was firmly Anglican and did all in his power to hinder the cause of Dissent by preventing Non-Conformists gaining property for their chapels and meeting houses on his estates. At Styal, Stamford rented some cottages to the overseers of the poor for use as a school, provided it was run on strictly Anglican lines.

In his diary John Walsh records what he saw as the good side of Stamford's character. The Earl was hospitable and gentleman-like in manner. He was plain and cordial and in most of his dealings he was honourable, unlike most of the members of his dysfunctional family who Walsh, the outsider, saw as "prying, gossiping and encroaching". In private, and among members of his family and close friends, Stamford was said by Walsh to display a less kindly side of his character. He records in his diary that, when he first met Stamford, the Earl struck him as a very good humoured old-country gentleman. After Walsh had married Stamford's daughter, Jane, that opinion changed. The Earl, Walsh believed, had made an early and determined effort to rid himself of his sick wife whose condition, had it been met with loving treatment, might have been very much less severe. He was able to detach himself emotionally from others and retreat into a private world. His wife and later his son, Henry, were never spoken of and the welfare of Jane and her husband (i.e. Walsh) hardly registered on the barometer of his emotions. The Earl was indolent in the sense that he could afford to attend to only those matters which he regarded as most pressing; he had little interest in matters unconnected to his own concerns. His estate and his position in society as the Earl of Stamford were the ruling springs of his actions.[27]

This was a harsh judgement indeed from a man who was barely able, or more likely was unwilling to understand the terrible burden of public duty and private sorrow which his father-in-law had been called upon to bear: his wife's long mental illness and their almost permanent separation; his eldest son's physical and mental illness and premature death; his second son's insanity and permanent confinement; the sharing of the tragedies of the Wemyss family; the taking over his aged father's responsibilities at a time of great and protracted crisis; accepting the responsibility of bringing up his two young grandchildren when he had turned 70 and, not least and for his daughter's sake, having to put up with the likes of the self-centred and self-seeking John Walsh.

*George Harry Grey, 7th Earl of Stamford*

# Chapter 18

# *The Playboy Earl*

## George Harry Grey, 7th Earl of Stamford and Warrington (1827-83)

From his early days George Harry, the headstrong grandson of the 6th Earl had received only such education as the immediate members of the family were able to provide. It was not until he was about eleven years-old that a tutor was found. The unenviable job fell to the medical man who had attended his father, Lord Grey, and who remained at Dunham until his charge could be sent to school. Evidently the poor man managed to inculcate at least some elements of learning and civilised behaviour, and in 1840 George Harry was sent to Eton College. After three years and at the age of sixteen, he left and was placed under the tutelage of a prominent academic, Dr Augustus Short, who succeeded in preparing the young man for entry to Cambridge University. It was during his leisure time, away from his studies with Short, that George Harry developed his love of athletics and sports, especially cricket.

The Grey family had an association with Cambridge University which reached back to the 15th century and the days of Elizabeth Woodville. While it surprised no one that the young Earl was sent to Trinity College, the University in 1845 was hardly the best place for many noblemen's sons, never mind those like George Harry. The entry examination for Trinity was no more demanding than those for other colleges and few applicants were ever turned away. At the end of a nobleman's stay the assessment for his degree, that is if he was actually called to take a final examination, was regarded as something of a joke.[1]

The change from the close restraint of the school room to the atmosphere of university was more than most students could cope with. An American undergraduate at Cambridge, C A Bristed, described how they were "suddenly thrown into a condition of almost entire freedom, in which they could go where they like, order what they wish and do almost anything they please." Only about two-and-a-half hours a day were required for study and students were expected to be in their rooms only between the hours of midnight and seven. Tradesmen would give them unlimited credit which enabled them "to fill their wardrobes with clothes and their cellars with wines and to engage in unrestricted smoking". Further, "they could gratify any greater vices they are so unfortunate to have, provided they do not outrage public decorum." Paradoxically, one problem was that after an undergraduate had been settled at Cambridge for some weeks he could nevertheless find life "was not a very diversified one" and the devil had little difficulty in finding work for the many idle hands.[2] This, then, was the environment into which the immature and headstrong young Lord Grey was launched, unattached, almost of age, and heir to one of the richest and most noble Earldoms in the country.

*Catherine Grey (née Cocks), second wife of the 7th Earl of Stamford*

By the time George Harry succeeded as 7th Earl in April 1845, the disaster everyone in the family feared was building. John Walsh, the young man's uncle, noted in his diary for 24th May 1846 that he and his brother-in-law, John Wildman, had become worried about reports of the behaviour of their nephew, Stamford.[3] At the end of September the full horror of the situation was revealed in a letter from Stamford to Wildman. In this he stated that it was his intention, on his coming of age (January 1848), to marry a woman with whom he had been living for some time. He left Walsh and Wildman to discover for themselves that the woman's name was Bessie Billage and that she was the daughter of Stamford's gyp, that is, servant, in the University. She was, as Walsh notes, "a well-known lady of pleasure". She had already been kept by several men and had probably had a child by one of them. She seemed to be about four years older than Stamford and it was clear she did not return the young man's affections to any great degree. At one point she kept a groom and two horses at Stamford's expense which she allowed some of her other admirers to use. The infatuated young man had also furnished a house for her, but she was given notice by the outraged landlord. The more Stamford spent on her the more she seemed to laugh at him, but always she managed to remain at the centre of the besotted young man's attentions.

Fearing that the family name and honour, to say nothing of the fortune, were at stake, Walsh and Wildman decided that decisive and urgent action was called for, although neither man could foresee the drama which would ensue. The first shock was to discover that the woman was also widely known as Mrs Newman. It seemed she was already married and that adultery was being added to Stamford's list of disgraces. On 15th October 1846 Wildman confronted Stamford in Cambridge and berated him to the point where the Earl swore an oath on the Bible that he would not marry the woman. The following day Walsh noted "I consider we are now safe against this particular danger."

During the following months Stamford was seen repeatedly in Mrs Newman's company and also with a woman of the same profession called Jenny Baker. On 14th February 1848, Wildman learnt that Stamford had applied for a special licence to marry which he, Wildman, managed to have cancelled. There followed several weeks of hurried journeys by coach between London and Cambridge as Stamford and Mrs Newman attempted to avoid their pursuers. At the same time during quiet moments in Stamford's absence, the woman was still enjoying the company of other men, particularly one Kennedy, a lawyer, with whom she slept. At the end of February 1848 Walsh and Wildman resolved to make terms with the woman in an effort to get rid of her. A sum of £500 a year was considered; but early in 1849 news reached Wildman that Stamford had married the woman and was living with her in Brighton.

For Stamford's family the game was lost. There was nothing for it but to pray that the reality of married life might bring the young fool to his senses. It has been said of this period of the Earl's life that Bessie, the new Countess, was out of place and ill at ease in social circles and in any case was never accepted by Victorian society. It is difficult to say whether or not she lived at, or even visited, Enville Hall and Dunham Massey. It has also been stated that the Earl soon tired of her and that he spent most of his time with his sporting friends and was actually in Scotland stalking deer when his wife died. Walsh's diary for September 1854 records otherwise, and that Lady Stamford "who has been in Brighton in a deplorable state of health" was dying. "She is quite insensible and is only kept alive by injections of broth etc as she cannot swallow." The apothecary in attendance had told him that not only was Stamford with her but that he (the apothecary) "never witnessed anything like the devotion of her husband and the affliction of her state". Walsh's son,

Arthur, called on Stamford "who received him very kindly but then wept like a child". Lady Stamford died on 22nd October 1854 and was buried at Kensal Green cemetery in London.

Great must have been the collective sigh of relief that was raised by the Greys in the understanding that the whole tragic episode was over and that some semblance of normality would return to the honour of the family. Fortunately the marriage had produced no children although, at the onset of her fatal illness, it was thought that the Countess might be pregnant. The Earl was now 27. It was time for a new start.

Those who looked to the revival of the family's fortunes were in for another grave disappointment. In January of the following year Walsh notes that Stamford "is always in the train of a pretty young actress and dancer at the Haymarket, Lydia Thompson, who passes for a maiden, a doubtful fact, but who is a good deal run after by the fast young men and who is reported to be laying herself out to be the second Countess of Stamford". But the danger from Lydia soon passed. It was not a lady of the stage who caught the Earl, but one from the stables.

Catherine "Kitty" Cocks was a woman with a past. Her father, Henry Cocks, appears to have been a farmhand at Sturminster Newton in Dorset. Her mother, an eccentric character, was said to be a gypsy. Catherine was born in 1826, the fifth child of a family of seven. At an early age she lost her father when the family cottage caught fire. Her eldest brother was already dead, the second was married and the third, Israel, was in Dorchester Prison for horse-stealing. The eldest girl was Tamar who produced three babies while in the workhouse and later found employment in service in Southampton. Eventually Catherine's mother moved to the workhouse from which she was sent to prison for "misbehaviour". Catherine was left to care for the two younger girls, Susan and Polly.[4]

Seeking their fortune in London the three sisters found their way to the stables of one Jem Mason who taught them how to break horses. They also learnt the art of bareback riding which they developed into an eye-catching circus act. With their raven-haired good looks and slim figures they quickly attracted aristocratic attention and Polly and Susan lived as kept women. Catherine took up with Percy Feilding, son of the Earl of Denbigh. She lived with Feilding on his estate in North Wales and by him had an illegitimate daughter, also named Catherine. In January 1855, six months after Feilding had left for the Crimean War, she met Stamford while performing at Mason's stables.[5]

For the Earl it was love, or rather infatuation, at first sight. In August of that year, less than twelve months after Bessie's death, he and Catherine were married. Walsh learnt of the event from the *Morning Post* of 31st August and wrote in his diary, "He is mad".[6]

Polite society was agog. More than one disappointed mother who had reckoned Stamford would not repeat his earlier mistake had marked him down as a suitable partner for her daughter. Optimists said that Catherine may well turn out to be just the sort of woman Stamford needed since opposites sometimes made a good pair. They recalled that Sir Harry Fetherstonehaugh of Uppark, at age 71, had married his twenty-year-old dairy maid and they had twenty happy years together.[7] Also, and nearer to the point, Sir Francis Boynton, the 8th Baronet of Burton Agnes Hall, married Sarah Bucktrout "a circus rider whose father kept the Black Swan in York" and they too had made a go of it.[8] But the majority view of the cynics prevailed. Although the number of rungs on the social ladder, which reached from the gutter to the pinnacles of Victorian society, was increasing, and movement up and down was quite possible, there were limits to what might reasonably be accomplished. A woman like Kitty with such squalid origins, who had risen so quickly,

*St Margaret's Church, Dunham Massey, erected by the 7th Earl of Stamford in memory of his sister Margaret*

could hardly expect to be welcomed with open arms by her class-conscious contemporaries of the establishment.

Stamford's response was to meet the challenge head on. His first move was to introduce his new Countess to his tenants and then to members of the county community. At Dunham affairs got off to a bad start. Shortly after his wedding the people of Bowdon deeply offended the couple when the wardens of the parish church refused to let the bells be rung in celebration. Stamford was equally unsuccessful with the Cheshire establishment: the Grosvenors, the Egertons and the Tollemaches and the others. Invitations were not received to balls and soirées; invitations to shoot with Lord Stamford were turned down with thanks and when election time came around Lord Stamford's views were not canvassed or even welcomed. They were making it clear to a wide audience that they no longer regarded his lordship as one of them. In response, Stamford moved the couple's residence to Enville where he and his wife were more kindly received and also to Leicestershire where they spent much time.

At the time of his marriage to Catherine, Lord Stamford hunted with the Albrighton Foxhounds in Shropshire. In the following year he was invited to accept the mastership of the even more prestigious Quorn. Despite the fact that he had agreed to underwrite the entire cost of the Hunt, there were problems

*The stables at Bradgate House*

*The conservatory erected by the 7th Earl of Stamford at Enville Hall, Staffordshire, in the 1850s*

from the start. Leading lady members such as Lady Blanche Egerton and the Countess of Wilton saw Countess Catherine as the interloper, a dark rank mare that had somehow sprung up in their patrician wheat field and who had "nobbled the best catch in the shires".[9] Competent horse women as they were, the two ladies could not match the prowess of Lady Stamford, who would chase for hours and take with ease hedges, ditches, gates and indeed anything else that appeared before her. Criticism or not, on the hunting field and elsewhere, Stamford was adamant; acceptance of himself meant acceptance of Lady Stamford.

No expense was spared in pursuit of this goal. Indeed, the cost of whatever the Earl did barely entered his head. On his coming of age in 1848 he had inherited an income of at least £40,000 a year, which was even greater than that of the Duke of Marlborough. Furthermore, the properties from which he drew his rents were unencumbered, that is he could do more or less what he liked with them and manage them as he thought fit. He had even purchased an additional estate of about 1,000 acres at Ulverscroft to adjoin his Bradgate properties.[10] After that he really opened his purse and embarked on what can only be described as a colossal spending spree which was to last for most of his life.

His first great expense followed the early death of his only sister, Margaret, in March 1852. The magnificent parish church at Dunham Massey erected in her memory, was paid for and endowed at the Earl's expense and at a total cost said to be about £22,000. In the early years it stood isolated and surrounded by fields and with no local congregation. Evidently Lord Stamford had been given, and more surprisingly had accepted, some good advice. The district, he was told, would inevitably be sought after as development land for housing by the wealthy middle classes of the growing town of Manchester. There was a fortune to be realised if the matter was handled skilfully.[11]

At about the time of his marriage to Bessie Billage, Stamford commissioned the firm of Dain and Parsons to build him a new house at Groby. As a young man he frequently visited the Leicestershire properties if only for the shooting, which was some of the best in the Midlands. Each visit meant taking over Steward's Hey, the very modest home of his agent. When he began mastership of the Quorn this arrangement proved entirely unsatisfactory for a man of his social position. The new house at Groby was not much less grand than his homes at Dunham and Enville, but they had been the work of others. Bradgate House would be entirely his own creation.

Building began in May 1855 and was completed the following year, a staggering achievement considering the scale of the task. The design followed the current fashion of making a new building appear to be much older than it really was. The Earl chose a pseudo-Jacobean style like that of Hughenden Manor in Buckinghamshire and Somerleyton Hall in Suffolk, both of which had been built a decade or so previously. Bradgate House contained sixteen main bedrooms, each with a dressing room, nine secondary bedrooms together with an additional 21 on the second floor for the indoor servants. In the dining room and elsewhere there was heavy oak panelling and no expense was spared with the remainder of the decoration. The palatial stable block to the north of the house was, by any manner of reckoning, a gross extravagance. It provided luxurious accommodation for 47 horses and contained a commodious coach house and quarters for the grooms. The cost of building Bradgate House is unknown but the stables alone were reckoned to have accounted for £30,000 of the final account.

The house, its stables and gardens were set in "widespread lawns and park-like pasture ... ornamented with many fine mature forest trees" which extended over 80 acres. Here on sunny days, guests could ramble through a landscape of bluebells and rhododendrons and perhaps roam as far as Newtown Linford and Bradgate Park a mile away. In winter the surrounding woods harboured huge numbers of pheasants for the delight of the more sporting-minded guests. Bradgate House was a grand home for a grand man, certainly one worthy of the undisputed master of the Quorn, England's leading hunt.[12]

As the new Bradgate House began to take shape, Lord Stamford was also spending huge sums on the gardens of his third residence, Enville Hall. The landscape there had remained little changed since the end of the 18th century and the days of the 5th Earl. Great advances in gardening had taken place in the 30 years since; it was now time for some catching up. The most important of the changes in fashion was the return to formality in design, which was to see the development in ribbon and carpet bedding and the reappearance of masses of colour from flowers and foliage. Stamford decided to leave the landscaped hills as he found them and it was the gardens to the north and north-west of the hall which were re-designed and much enlarged. Advances in the manufacture of glass and cast iron were employed in the manner Joseph Paxton had used in the creation of the conservatories at Chatsworth, and which he later employed in the construction of the Crystal Palace in London. A conservatory was the mark of a serious and wealthy gentleman gardener. That which Stamford erected at Enville was reckoned by many observers to stand second in size only  to the Crystal Palace. It was filled with a vast number of plants, including many newly-discovered species which plant hunters had brought home from the Empire and other distant places.

In addition to these amazing developments, the Earl also built at Enville a feature which once more challenged the leading landscape designers. Lord Stamford's fountain was in the form of a river horse. The massive centrally placed jet, which rivalled the Emperor Fountain at Chatsworth, was ornamented by a number of subsidiary jets set at different heights and angles. John Walsh records seeing the steam pump which raised water to a reservoir which fed the whole fountain by gravity. By manipulating valves, a boatman could produce two contrasting displays which in fine weather caused a splendid rainbow effect.[13] In all, the pleasure grounds at Enville extended over 100 acres, half of which could be illuminated at night with candle lights to produce a magical scene. Stamford was understandably proud of his achievements. For many years he opened the park and gardens to the local people and at one time drew crowds of 6,000 a week from Wolverhampton and around.[14]

If hunting and shooting were Stamford's joint first loves, his interest in cricket ran them a close third. His lordship was a strong, well-built and athletic man who had taken up the game while at Cambridge and who had been elected president of the MCC in 1852. The  arrival of a cricket pitch in the grounds of Enville Hall came as a surprise to no one. As the *Illustrated London News* pointed out in August 1857, the ground at Lords covered seven acres while that at Enville extended over eleven.Of these, six and a half were levelled for play and were "literally as smooth and as even as a billiard table". Such was the skill in its construction and the care in its maintenance that it was reckoned to be superior to the turf at Lords.

The same journal described a match on a bright sunny day, when a range of snowy tents was pitched on the ground. "The bright waving flags and the players in their cricket flannels, the scarlet and the blue dresses ... (seen against) ... the dark background of the wooded heights, relieved by the gleaming glass of the conservatory and the upward rush of the fountains sparkling far above the treetops" made a fabulous scene. Stamford was known as one of the fastest and most effective bowlers and hardest hitters among the gentlemen of England. Many important matches were played at Enville, including those involving all

England Elevens, and at the time when players of the calibre of Tinley and Jackson were at their peak. A three-day match in 1853 attracted a crowd of over 10,000 and in 1872 a team drawn from various counties played the MCC.[15] Lord Stamford's influence on and patronage of the game were immense.

Another major expense for Stamford was his London house in Hill Street which his grandfather had purchased in 1825 and which he now refurbished in the manner of his own times. The house provided a residence when Stamford visited the House of Lords. He was a declared Conservative and attended to vote against Gladstone's Bill to dis-establish the Irish Church in 1869; otherwise there is no evidence that he spent much time on the crimson benches.[16] He had consciously given up any real involvement in either local or national politics; he was too busy enjoying the life of a playboy. The home in Hill Street was more a place where the Earl and Countess stayed to make what they could of the Season. From here they would take the train to the rented grouse moor in Scotland or would set off on their travels abroad where the family, or at least their money, was more welcome.

It may reasonably be asked just how Lord Stamford could afford such expenditure on top of his regular outgoings as a landed gentleman. The short answer is that he did what so many other men in his position did: he raised prodigious sums by means of mortgages. Borrowing in this way by the aristocracy was an age old means of raising cash to meet dowries, jointures and debts, to improve, extend or rebuild the family seat or for a variety of other purposes. Throughout Stamford's life his income continued to rise. During the periods of rural prosperity, income from agricultural rents and timber sales rose steadily. More important, the returns from his industrial concerns: factories, coal mines, granite quarries and slate pits-together with controlled sales of land for housing development, made huge profits. The land he sold in Bradgate Park for the construction of Cropston Reservoir alone brought him £24,000. The new watery acres improved the fishing and introduced superb wildfowling at no cost to himself.

In May 1859 the Earl borrowed £100,000 together with a loan, two months later, of a further £200,000. These were followed up in September 1866 by a third loan, this time for £220,000 which was obtained on the strength of his Leicestershire and Lancashire estates.[17] At various periods the Manchester banker Cunliffe Brooks was reckoned to have loaned him no less than £950,000 at four percent interest on the Dunham and Ashton estates. If the Marquess of Bute was raising even larger loans in order to develop his docks at Cardiff and the Earl of Scarborough was pouring huge sums of borrowed money into laying out the town of Skegness, they were both investing for a future profit. The 7th Earl of Stamford was borrowing simply to enjoy himself.[18] With inflation near zero for much of the time, Lord Stamford could keep up interest payments and in the long term pay off the debt, that was so long as he structured his finances carefully and provided there were no unforeseen catastrophes.

It was in 1863 that he decided to resign his mastership of the Quorn. He had met the entire expenses of the hunt for the previous eight years and it was costing him a sum similar to the £2,000 a year which the Duke of Rutland was finding for his own hunt, the Belvoir. Fox hunting was enjoying enormous popularity, to the point where a family which failed to send at least one of its members on to the field lost face in the best circles. But the truth was that Stamford was no nearer achieving Lady Stamford's acceptance into the company of those who hunted the Midland shires.

Matters were not helped by the arrival, uninvited and unwanted on the hunting scene, of the notorious courtesan, Catherine Walters. She was better known to all the rakes of the royal court as "Skittles" and was described by Sir William Hardman as "a whore, sir, much sought after by fast young swells".[19] Like Lady Stamford, Miss Walters could also ride horses and seemed to take to the chase in order to annoy her Ladyship. The affair was viewed by the ladies of the Quorn as a battle of wills between two women of whom better could not perhaps be expected. Skittles would ride in front of the Countess, cut across her path and talk in a loud voice of horse-breakers. Eventually, the long suffering Stamford told Skittles she must mend her ways or leave. "Tell the bitch she was never first in the profession, so can't be first in the hunting field" was her parting shot as she left the field on the final occasion.

However, the matter did not rest there. In a fashionable London drinking saloon-cum-music hall, a burlesque play entitled "Skittles versus Lord Stamper and Warneroffe" was staged. The two leading roles of the Countess, and Kitty (as "the Strumpet") were played by male impersonators. The show was highly successful. It ran for eight weeks and drew an audience from the nobility and gentry. For Lord Stamford it was the final straw.[20]

Even before he instructed Tattersalls to auction his hunters, Stamford was already making a major change of direction, from the Field to the Turf. As early as 1859 he followed the sport which had been a keen interest to members of at least four generations of his family. At about the time of the Skittles problem, he established stables at Heath House on the Bury Road at Newmarket, the premier racing centre of England, where most of the leading trainers of the day were resident. His Lordship made himself unpopular with other owners by employing men to spy on their horses during training so that he might place his bets with more confidence. Stamford's own young horses were trained and exercised in secret on his private tracks at Enville and Bradgate. His horse "Diaphantes" won the 2,000 Guineas but later Stamford had a dispute with his trainer who took him to court and successfully sued him for the balance of an outstanding fee.[21]

*Bradgate House prior to demolition in the 1930s*

In the year of his departure from the Quorn, Stamford had success with his horse "Lady Augusta" which won the 1,000 Guineas and another of his horses put up a strong performance in the Derby. It was in the same year that the ancient rivalry between Grey and Hastings saw its bizarre and final episode played out, not on the field of battle, in the tumult of the hustings or in rivalry at Court, but on the green turf of the race courses of England.

In chapter 16 we saw how the political ambitions of the Hastings family had come to an end with the death of the 1st Marquess in 1826. His son George Augustus, dubbed the Foxhunting Squire, lacked almost all of his father's more sterling qualities and spent most of his life on his estates at Donington, while his wife toured the world. His son, the 3rd Marquess died at an early age and the next son, Harry, succeeded in 1851 while still a boy of nine.

At the age of 21 Harry Hastings married in secret a society beauty, Florence Paget, who was the daughter of the Marquess of Anglesey. There was just one problem; at the time of the wedding she was still betrothed to Harry's close friend, Harry Chaplin, a wealthy Lincolnshire squire. The shock, shame and delightful scandal of it all can well be imagined as society mamas doubled the chaperonage of their eligible daughters. There were echoes here of the disgrace that Lord Stamford had brought to his family with his marriages half a generation earlier.

Shortly after his wedding, the Marquess turned to the turf with a burning desire to beat the regime of racing and betting known as "The Ring". At the time of his coming of age in 1863 he had stables at Daresbury and soon after he became a member of the Jockey Club. Rivalry and conflict between him and the Earl of Stamford, a man with similarly inflated ambitions, was now inevitable.

Both Stamford and Hastings spent heavily on bloodstock. Stamford paid big prices for his horses and was generous when everything was going well, but looked for substantial returns for his investments. Hastings bought young horses at inflated prices from dealers who took advantage of his inexperience and arrogance. By 1864 he was drinking and gambling heavily and let it be known that his main aim in life was to win the Derby. At the same time he was ignoring his social duties and neglecting his wife.

Stamford gradually handed over control of the Enville bloodstock to his wife who was having some success in curbing the wilder flights of her husband's spending. Both Stamford and Hastings entered horses in the Derby of 1865 but neither saw their runners placed. A win in the 2000 Guineas the following year brought little respite to the Marquess' financial affairs, which were now in a parlous state. Foolishly he accepted the mastership of the Quorn, which only added to his problems. In desperation he turned to the money lenders to tide him over until the Derby of 1867. His misplaced confidence in his ability to back the winner ended in disaster. First past the winning post was the horse owned by Henry Chaplin; his own entry was unplaced and he lost a bet of £120,000.

Stamford's passion for success on the turf can be seen as much as anything as a vigorous attempt to re-enter a society that had so roundly rejected him and his wife. That he did not go the way of Lord Hastings can be attributed to the steadying hand of his Countess behind the scenes. Stamford was not a silly or wicked man and was certainly not suffering from the mental problems which had afflicted his father and grandmother. Countess Catherine's influence showed the same level of skill in controlling her man that she demonstrated with her horses. Indeed, Lady Stamford built up the Enville bloodstock into a profitable business and even after her husband's death could still pay £8,000 for the successful horse "Barcaldine".[22]

*The visit of the Prince of Wales to Bradgate House in 1882*

The Countess' role in the management of Enville and Bradgate involved many of the members of her own family. Her sister Polly's sons were both employed in the stables, one at each house. Her brother Israel, released from prison, became a coachman. Of her sister Tamar's children, one, Sarah Letitia lived at Enville and Robert, one of her two sons was the steward at Newmarket. Having in effect married a family and not just a wife from a disreputable background, it is perhaps not surprising that Lord Stamford's struggle for respectability was such an uphill one.

Stamford's racing career continued almost to his death and it was stated by the *Warrington Guardian* that he had spent half a million pounds on his horses and that his lack of success was as much as anything a matter of plain bad luck.[23] Success in the main events on the flat eluded him but in 1880 his horse "Geheimniss" won the Oaks. To the end, Lord Stamford was not popular with ordinary racegoers and there were boos rather than cheers for his colours – light blue, black and gold belt and black cap – from the crowds who thronged about the winner's enclosure.

In spite of his shortcomings Lord Stamford demonstrated many of the qualities expected of an aristocrat of his times. His obituary in the *Leicester Daily Mercury* in January 1883 noted that with his tenants he showed "a benevolent disposition, a genial temperament and a courteous approach". His obituary in *The Times* remarked that he was much beloved and respected by the inhabitants of Manchester and other large towns in the neighbourhood of Dunham Massey for the liberal use of his park, which he granted for festivals and gatherings. In this he was following the custom of his grandfather and of his great-grandfather, the 5th Earl. That he seemed to have lacked obvious intellectual and artistic talents was not important. He was popular with most ordinary people if not his peers.

In a letter to the Reverend Harry Grey, Henrietta Law, Stamford's aunt wrote of her young nephew that "his kindness of heart and natural amiability is very great ... Lady Stamford told me that Stamford daily reads the scripture lessons to her and that Bibles and prayer books are carefully referenced in the rooms they occupy." The Stamfords could be generous when they saw a need or when they wished to be so. The 7th Earl provided the expanding town of Altrincham with its first town hall, an act which recognised the inevitable change from seigneurial control to a new, more democratic form of local government. At Ashton, he gave five acres for the site of the Infirmary, land for the erection of baths and a Mechanics' Institute and land for the sites of several churches. Also at Ashton, he donated 35 acres for Stamford Park which was opened in July 1873. During the 1860s, when there was much unemployment in the cotton trade and when the Poor Law Guardians were overwhelmed with applications for assistance, Lord Stamford subscribed £1,000 to their funds. Lady Stamford herself gave money for the founding of schools at Enville, Amblecote and Groby.

August 1875 saw the Stamfords' 20th wedding anniversary, but the joy of the celebrations was tempered with the sadness that they were still childless and the prospects of producing an heir seemed remote. In the same year Stamford drew up his will with the particular aim of determining how his estates were to be partitioned after his death.

Towards the end of his life Lord Stamford was visited at Bradgate by the Prince of Wales. The Prince was received at Leicester railway station with great ceremony in January 1882 and was escorted through cheering crowds to Bradgate. Here the Earl's tenants provided a rousing welcome along the lantern-lit drive to the house. Rockets of white, red, blue and green, were sent up and bonfires lit. The following day a party of twelve guns, led by Lord Stamford and the Prince, set out to shoot over the park. By the time the light was failing at about four o'clock, the party had shot more than 2,000 birds.[24] In a letter dated 14th June 1882, the Prince thanked the Earl for his hospitality and wrote of "the excellent sport ... (which) ... far exceeded my expectation." Almost three decades had elapsed since the Earl's marriage to his second wife but the social recognition which the Stamfords had so craved appeared to be theirs at last.

Lord Stamford died the following year at Bradgate of pleuro-pneumonia accompanied by complications. He was 55. The *Warrington Guardian* of 13th January of that year records that his funeral procession wound its way through the beautiful grounds of Enville Hall and attracted throngs of people from the surrounding district. The mourners included civic dignitaries drawn from the various townships of the Dunham area, together with tenants from all his lordship's estates. The newspaper also noted that very few members of the aristocracy were present.

With his death the Earldom of Warrington and his Barony of Delamer became extinct. His widow, who had nursed him to the end, died at Bradgate 22 years later and was buried at Enville along with her husband.

# Chapter 19

# *The South African Connection*

**Harry Grey, 8th Earl of Stamford (1812-90)**

In spite of his many debts the 7th Earl of Stamford died a wealthy man. Bateman's survey of the great landowners of Great Britain and Ireland, which was published in 1879, listed his Lordship's estates as follows:

|  | acres | gross annual value in £ |
|---|---|---|
| Leicestershire | 9,012 | 12,876 |
| Cheshire | 8,612 | 16,000 |
| Staffordshire | 7,339 | 11,367 |
| Lancashire | 5,231 | 17,465 |
| Shropshire | 606 | 508 |
| Worcestershire | 68 | 130 |
| Yorkshire(W.Riding) | 93 | 46 |
| Warwickshire | 1 | 1 |
| *Total* | *30,962* | *£58,393* |

The survey revealed that the Earl's wealth placed him in the top 750 or so families and almost qualified him for the title of "territorial magnate".[1][2]

In his will the Earl left all his estates to his widow for life, subject to an annual charge of about half the annual value of the Dunham estates. This figure was income for his successor in the title, to whom the Cheshire estates descended in strict entail. The Leicestershire estates, including the park of Bradgate with the ruins of the great house of his ancestor Thomas, first Marquess of Dorset, passed to his niece Mrs Arthur Duncombe, who was the daughter of his much-loved late sister, Margaret. The Earl gave the Staffordshire lands to Catherine Sarah Lambert, the grand-niece of his widow and wife of Sir Henry Foley Lambert, Bt. Finally, the Lancashire estates were divided between Mrs Duncombe and Lady Lambert. For want of a legitimate male heir it seemed the Grey empire was being effectively dismembered.[3]

The truth was, of course, that the 7th Earl did have an entirely legitimate male heir. He lived in South Africa in such circumstances that members of the family in England avoided all mention of him. His name was the Reverend Harry Grey and he was the grandson of the Honourable John Grey (born 1743), who was the second brother of George Harry, the 5th Earl of Stamford. The 7th and 8th Earls were related only in that they had Harry the 4th Earl as a common great-grandfather. Harry, the 8th Earl was one of nine children born to yet another Harry Grey who was vicar of Knutsford in Cheshire.

Before he succeeded to the title at the age of sixty-nine, Harry had led what might best be described as an unorthodox life. He was born in Knutsford and entered St Edmund Hall, Oxford, where he graduated with a BA degree in 1836. During his days at university it is alleged that he was addicted to alcohol and that he had close associations with women of humble birth. Nevertheless, he was ordained into the Church of England and served as a curate in Devon. Here he met and married Susan Gaydon, of whom nothing is known except that she was unable to sign her own name and, as *The Times* of 4th May 1892 recorded, she had a "humble station in life". The marriage lasted only a few years, probably on account of Harry's drinking. There was no divorce and no children and Mrs Grey died in 1869.

Harry's behaviour was an embarrassment to his god-fearing family and particularly to the 7th Earl who was desperately attempting to persuade Victorian society to accept his own lowly-born wife. Under the circumstances it was decided to persuade Harry to leave the country. With a small allowance from the 7th Earl, Harry arrived in Cape Town in 1854, where his brother-in-law, the Reverend Henry Master White, was a canon at St George's Cathedral. Thereafter, and for the next seventeen years or so, Harry almost disappears from sight. In 1864 he was reported living at Wynberg, then a prosperous wine producing area but now a leafy and residential district of greater Cape Town. Later he was said to be working at the copper mines 800 miles to the north, in the dry and arid country which was opened up in the 19th century by advances in mining and the arrival of the railway.

At an unknown date Harry set off south to return to the place whence he started. At Wellington, forty miles north of Cape Town, impoverished and alcoholic, he fell ill and was given food and shelter and nursed back to health by a local woman named Martha Solomon. With her and her children by other men, he remained, working as a herdsman for a nearby farmer. Each month he would visit the post office to collect his meagre remittance from England.

Although the events of Harry's career become clearer after 1871, many of the details have been disputed and the substance of this chapter is based largely on the work of a South African writer, R R Langham Carter.[4] By 1871 Harry was back at Wynberg where he had an affair with a white woman, Carolina Christine Collins. By her he had a daughter, Emma, who was baptised as Emma Collins and who survived to adulthood. The relationship did nothing to help the even more difficult situation in which the 7th Earl in England found himself. With little prospect of a male heir, or indeed any legitimate children of his own, it now appeared probable that Harry, a man fifteen years his elder, would succeed to the Earldom of Stamford and the lands in Cheshire. For the family in England the affair took another turn for the worse when Harry married a European woman called Annie Macnamara, who was aged 34 and probably illiterate. Alas, Annie soon became sick and died less than two years after the marriage. The family in England sighed with relief. Since she and Harry had produced no children the situation had effectively returned to square one.

During her illness Annie had been nursed by none other than Martha Solomon together with her various children. Harry and Martha continued to live together at Wynberg and in October 1877 Martha bore him a son, who was baptised John Grey. In October 1879 a daughter, Frances, was born. The next year Harry and Martha were married and another daughter Mary arrived the following year. When the 7th Earl died at Bradgate in 1883, Harry in South Africa had four children; Emma aged about twelve, John five, Frances three and Mary about eighteen months. Frances died of smallpox the same year.

The social, legal and financial problems surrounding the succession to the Earldom which had been quietly developing over the previous two decades now came to the surface. The first was one of race. It is not known if Martha was negro or Hottentot but she was certainly black. The illegitimate children she had borne before she met Harry were probably all black, but both John and Mary were half-caste. Harry's other daughter, Emma, was of course white. Ripples of excitement, which developed into cries of indignation and finally horror and outrage, ran through the polite society of Victorian England. Those who had so soundly rejected Catherine Cocks, wife of the 7th Lord Stamford, now faced the prospect of an even greater embarrassment: a black dowager Countess and a half-caste 9th Earl resident at Dunham, presiding over a large slice of rural, high-Tory Cheshire.

The second problem concerning the Earldom was that, under the original grant to the 1st Earl of Stamford in 1628, only male heirs of the body lawfully begotten could succeed. The crucial point was quite plain. Was Harry's son, John, legitimate? In terms of the Dutch Law which prevailed in the British Colony of the Cape of Good Hope, marriage had the effect of legitimising children born out of wedlock. However, his son's status under English law was quite different. John was clearly illegitimate and had no legal claim to the Stamford title.

There was more to come. In August 1883 the Committee of Privileges in London summoned Harry to take the Oath of Allegiance and take his seat in the Lords. His failure to do this and his absence from England made it particularly difficult to settle the matter of his entitlement, said to be about £8,000 a year, from the Cheshire estates.

The matters of both succession and finance passed through the English law courts. Eventually a compromise was reached. Harry as 8th Earl would recognise his nephew William, who was the son of his brother also William, as his legitimate heir and successor as 9th Earl of Stamford. Harry himself would receive the revenues of the Cheshire estates for his life. John, his half-caste son, was to receive capital compensation which was to be paid to him by the 9th Earl. There was also an unwritten understanding that both John and his sister, Lady Mary Grey, would maintain a discreet distance between themselves and the public affairs of the 9th Earl and his family.

Harry never returned to England. A wealthy man in Cape Colony, he bought several landed properties which went some way to support the dignity of his title. At Muizenberg, on the coast near Simonstown, he built three small plain brick houses. They were named Stamford House, Stamford Lodge and Stamford Cottage. Harry occupied the house, his three children under a European governess lived in the lodge while Countess Martha had the cottage. But when visitors called at the house, Martha would open the door of Stamford House herself, only to fade into the background in such a way that at least one person mistook her for a servant. All three buildings were guarded by one simple gate, above which stood a large wooden notice, carved in England, displaying the Stamford coat of arms.

The Right Honourable Harry, 8th Earl of Stamford, died in June 1890 aged 78 and was buried in St John's Anglican cemetery in Wynberg. In his will this colourful and eccentric man left nothing to his wife because he had already provided for her during his lifetime. Of his and Martha's several children, only Emma, John and Mary are mentioned. Each received equal shares in the residue of his estate which totalled about £15,000. While Catherine Grey, the dowager Lady Stamford, resided in luxury at Bradgate, the black

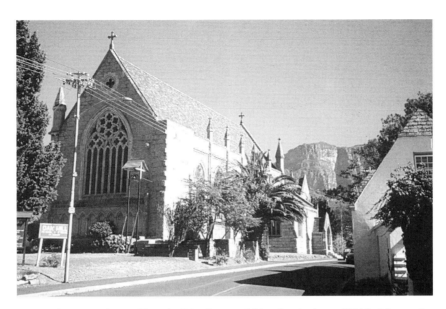

*St John's Anglican Church, Wynberg, within the shadow of Table Mountain.*
*The last resting place of the 8th Earl of Stamford*

Countess continued to wear the head scarf favoured by the local coloured women and asked to be known simply as "Aunt Martha". To the executors of her husband's will she was simply noted as "the widow Grey". On the occasions when the family were together, they could be seen driving around in their two horse landaulet, a mixed bag consisting of Harry who was white, Martha who was black, his illegitimate white daughter Emma and the couple's partly-coloured children: the illegitimate John and the wholly legitimate Mary.

Martha was married again two years later in 1882, this time to a local man called Piet Pieterse. She could both read and write and she pursued an interest in education for coloureds by endowing a school at Wynberg. She died in 1916 at the age of 77 and was buried in the cemetery beneath a simple headstone and next to her beloved Harry. In his later years Harry appears to have been drinking less and did not suffer the bouts of depression he had experienced as a young man. This improvement may perhaps be attributed to the love and care he received from Martha. Although he did not enter the social life of Cape Colony, he entertained members of the local clergy, four of whom were present at his funeral. Shortly before he died, and with the generosity which was typical of the Grey family through the ages, he gave a site near Stamford Lodge for the erection of an Anglican church.

The trustees of Harry's estate in South Africa sent both John and Mary Grey abroad for their education. John, as Mr John Grey, arrived in England to study law and became a solicitor. Mary, as Lady Mary Grey, spent some time at school in Switzerland before moving to England. She became a personal friend of the 9th Earl and his family who were living in Weybridge. She married Meredith Starr in 1917 and they had two sons who were fair skinned. Later, she was divorced and lived in London. She died in 1945. One of her sons, Gordon, was a friend of Roger Grey, the 10th Earl. Neither she nor her brother ever returned to the country of their birth.

*William Grey, 9th Earl of Stamford (English School late 19th century)*

# Chapter 20

# *A Loyal and Christian Gentleman*

## William Grey, 9th Earl of Stamford (1850-1910)

William Grey, the future 9th Earl of Stamford, was born in Newfoundland in 1850. This was about the time that George Harry, the 7th Earl, was embarking on his colossal spending spree in England and a little before Harry, the future 8th Earl, arrived in South Africa. William was the son of the Rev. William Grey, the principal of the College of St John's in Newfoundland and, like the 8th Earl, was the grandson of John Grey, brother of the 5th Earl. Young William's mother was the former Harriet White whose grandfather was both the vicar of Fulford in Hampshire and the youngest brother of the Rev. Gilbert White of Selborne (1720-93), the famous naturalist. On both sides of William's family there was a strong tradition of men in holy orders serving the Church of England. It was expected that William too might eventually follow the same path.

When he was three years of age William and his family left Newfoundland for England and his childhood was spent in Devon. He entered Bradfield College, a Church of England school, as a boarder in 1859. It was not long before his inherent ability showed itself. The Rev. E. Bayly wrote to William's father in 1862 that William was "by far the cleverest lad in the school ... his memory and powers of application are extraordinary".[1] The classics were the mainstay of the curriculum and William became known for the quality of his Latin verse. He was a shy boy but played games regularly, enjoying skating, swimming and particularly walking. It was noted by his teachers that he possessed the quiet sense of humour which was to remain with him all his life. The school was the choice of his father who saw no separation between education and religion. In later years, William maintained that he was thankful to have heard the scriptures read and the psalms recited daily and that he had been obliged to know the Psalter by heart, as they brought much comfort as a resource through life.

Eventually the young man won an open scholarship to Oxford. At Exeter College he gained a first class degree in Classics in 1873. Although never of robust health, he managed to pursue a wide range of interests. It was during the long walks in the Oxfordshire countryside that his tutor, the Rev W Jackson, formed this opinion of the young academic, "In his relations with all sorts and conditions of men he was what Chaucer would have called 'a very perfect gentle knight'." It was William's candour and obvious sincerity which gave him the ability, as Jackson explained, "to bring together all men of goodwill" and to get on with people.[2]

His degree of MA followed in 1875 after which he began to look for employment. His first post was a return to the world of education, as an assistant master at Mill Hill school. There he remained for two terms before

*Codrington College, Barbados, mid 19th century*

accepting a similar position at Harrison College in Barbados. Evidently the relaxed atmosphere and the sunny climate of the Caribbean agreed with his health and temperament, for after five terms he took up the post of professor of Classics at Codrington College, also in Barbados.

The College was situated on the south-east coast of the island, fourteen miles from Bridgetown. It was a peaceful centre of religious study and classical culture among all the busy machinery of the sugar estates. The long building, with broad flights of steps, arches and dormer windows, stood overlooking the sea against a background of the green hills of the island. Later, William was to say that the five years spent in this idyllic and tranquil outpost of academia were the happiest ones of his life. He was known by most people as a reserved and dignified young man, and – in the words of an anonymous writer – as "generous, kindly, courteous with a hatred of everything mean or bad ... A man of the highest aims ... A most delightful companion".[3]

What might easily have become exile for life was brought to an abrupt end in 1883 with the death of the 7th Earl at Bradgate. It was known that Harry, William's ageing uncle in South Africa, would inherit the Stamford title and probably a large portion of the family fortune. After Harry's death the earldom would probably pass to William. A return to England now appeared advisable.

For the next seven years or so William lived at Weybridge in Surrey and divided his time between social work and travelling in Europe and beyond. The summer of 1883 found him in Cape Town for a brief meeting with Harry, now the 8th Earl. Alas, all that is known of the interchange between these two men of such totally different temperaments and lifestyles is that, as William recorded, he had two "somewhat pleasing interviews". He stayed with his maternal uncle, Archdeacon White, and spent most of the remainder of his time in the Colony travelling.

The following year saw him touring Europe and in 1886 he visited Newfoundland to see his father's old friends. From there he set sail for Mauritius and then moved on to Australia. In New Zealand he met Sir

George Grey, a distant kinsman, who was the premier of the Colony at that time. Both Australia and New Zealand made lasting impressions on William. "The peace and tranquillity of the place" he wrote of New Zealand, "is something delightful" and the countryside provided superb opportunities for long walks. The return to England was via the USA where he met the publisher G. H. Putnam, President Cleveland and leading politicians and socialites. On his return he could reflect on the fact that only a century earlier his kinsman, the 6th Earl, had considered himself fortunate to be able to tour only part of Europe at great expense. Times had certainly changed when a man could now sail round the world in much greater style, in much less time and at a fraction of the cost.

In contrast to William's time spent travelling were the hours he put into social work. In the autumn of 1885 he was working as chairman of a local Sanitary Aid Committee in the East End of London. Out of doors he led volunteers on a programme of locating and repairing sanitary defects. Sir Cyril Jackson, one time chairman of the LCC explained that the work involved "visiting the worst slums, inspecting lidless dustbins in back yards, and examining sinks to see if drains were properly trapped and any bad smells were apparent".[4] The work required courage and tact and William was able to draw on his own particular strengths and qualities. He was not fond of committee work and was prepared always to be among people. He personally delivered pensions to those in receipt "bringing into their houses the human sympathy which was so fully his gift and winning their complete love and devotion." The strain of the winter of 1885-86 took a toll on his health and it was as much for recuperation as adventure that he set sail again for Newfoundland.

News of the death of his uncle in South Africa reached him by telegraph in June 1890. At the age of 40 William had become the 9th Earl of Stamford, but it was not to be for another fifteen years that he was able to take up his full inheritance. He was also unmarried and the desire for an heir, preferably male, now occupied more of his thoughts. His choice of wife was one of the heart. For him there was no appeal in a fling with an actress in the manner of the 7th Earl, just as there was no thought of a wealthy social-climbing daughter of an American tycoon such as Consuela Vanderbilt to whom the Duke of Marlborough was engaged. Least of all did he look for a woman from a newly-ennobled and very wealthy family such as the brewers Guinness, Allsopp and Bass, members of the so-called "beerage". The chosen lady was Penelope Theobald, third daughter of the Rev. Charles Theobald, the Rector of Lasham in Hampshire. Although some whispered that Stamford had married "down", he had nevertheless found a godly woman and one also of great strength of character and strong personality.

Eighteen months after their marriage a son was born, the first legitimate male heir for an Earl of Stamford for ninety years. He was named Roger, to recall a fourteenth century ancestor. A daughter, Jane, followed three years later. Roger's health like that of his father was never robust, although it was not to give cause for concern until his teenage years.

During the fifteen years before his return to Dunham in 1905, Stamford was involved in a quite extraordinary programme of social work and good deeds. His biography lists over 40 different organisations to which he was connected in various ways. These reflected his particularly wide interests in art, music, missionary work, wildlife, health, medicine and, of course, concern for the better welfare of the poor. For some, such as the Agricultural Organisation Society and the Commons and Footpaths Preservation Society, he was simply a subscribing member, turning up for meetings whenever other commitments allowed. For

*"Good Will". Spy cartoon of
William Grey, 9th Earl of Stamford*

others he was a vice president, performing the role which holders of that office have traditionally performed by lending his name to the headed notepaper and performing the occasional favour asked of him.

As a member of many of his societies Stamford played an active part. He was a member of the council of such diverse bodies as the National Association for Promoting the Welfare of the Feeble-minded and and also of the Midwives (Higher Training of) Group. Many commitments reflected his interest in the Church and with Social Reform. Some of his attachments were long-standing ones, such as the fourteen years with the Society for the Promotion of Christian Knowledge and the British and Foreign Bible Society. After his move to Dunham he became particularly sought after as a high profile patron. The thrust behind all he did was always to create the conditions by which the under-privileged were given an opportunity to help themselves.

As the 9th Earl, Lord Stamford attended regularly the work of the House of Lords. He was particularly active in such matters as legislation for the Newfoundland Fisheries, on matters concerning Trinidad and Dominica and other parts of the Empire he had visited. He was also able to assist in committee work with the Poor Law where, in contrast to virtually all his fellow peers, he was able to draw on first hand knowledge of the conditions of ordinary people. In 1897 he moved the second reading of the quaintly entitled "Verminous Persons Bill" which authorised local authorities to make available facilities for infested persons to de-louse themselves.

He was also active in promoting the reform of public morality. Lord Stamford made no permanent mark on the House of Lords. He was, according to *The Times* "A quiet, loyal and Christian gentleman ... Too nervous in manner to make a powerful speaker, yet the obvious earnestness with which he put his case ... carried people with him".[5] At the same time there is no reason to believe that in his efforts and desire to relieve the sufferings of the poor, Lord Stamford wished to see the end of the social system in which he occupied a prominent and privileged position. Estates with tenants and businesses with employees were still part of his scheme of things. He showed no leaning towards the socialism with which his son was to flirt.

After the death of the widow of the 7th Earl at Bradgate in 1905, the way was clear for the Greys to return to Dunham. The hall it will be remembered, had been vested in the name of the 7th Earl so as to guard against any possibility of Martha, the black wife of the 8th Earl, turning up with a gaggle of lawyers in tow. Many of the contents of Dunham had been moved to Enville by the 7th Earl and had been willed to his wife's niece, Lady Lambert, along with the remainder of the Staffordshire properties. Since the Dunham estate had been used as little more than a place for shooting and fox-hunting, the hall itself had stood empty or had been let to tenants for more than 50 years. One of these was T. A. Walker, the contractor for the construction of the Manchester Ship Canal. In common with many tenants, he had done the minimum required to maintain the place and there was an urgent need for a major refurbishment.

Improvements began in 1905 and constitute what can be seen as the third and final phase of good taste on the part of the owners of Dunham Massey Hall. To the exterior of the hall's south front, a bare and rather austere mass of red brickwork dating from the time of the 2nd Earl of Warrington, was added a stonework entrance. This was decorated above with a massive carving of the Stamford coat of arms, a feature which the writer of a recent souvenir guide book dismissed as "a fussy piece of historicism harking back to the 17th century".[6] Also, the line of the eaves was lowered to allow for dormer windows which add much to the attractive appearance of the south front. Perhaps the present and future generations should be grateful that Dunham escaped the massive remodelling which was then the fashion of the very rich. This saw improvements and the addition of Gothic wings to Eaton Hall, the home of the Grosvenors in Cheshire at a cost of £600,000 and the refashioning of the Duke of Rutland's Belvoir Castle which cost £400,000.[7]

The improvements to Dunham Hall were accompanied by alterations to the gardens. In the main courtyard a central pond was added and climbers were planted in beds so that they would cover the walls. Before the north front, the splendid parterre which remains today was laid out to replace a raised circular flower bed. Along the banks of the stream flowing through the grounds and feeding the moat, a water garden was created.

Inside the hall several of the rooms were reassessed so that the best of contemporary taste could be introduced. The Stamfords were fortunate in that the Countess' cousin was Percy Macquoid, the fashionable designer and pioneer furniture historian. He was also a partner in the firm of Morant and Co. who were decorators to King Edward VII. He combined his different interests to produce "a series of rich and comfortable interiors". This was achieved by selecting individual pieces of furniture from the collection at Dunham, including the 2nd Earl of Warrington's chairs and the 5th Earl of Stamford's satinwood cabinets, noted in an earlier chapter. The room in which each piece was placed was then redesigned round it, by what one writer described as "the intermixing of historical fabrics and the inspired use of colour'.[8] The Great Hall, a plain room of the 1690s, was transformed by the addition of heavy plaster decoration to elaborate the very plain panelling. Furniture, upholstered with textiles of a subtle range of colours, was also introduced. In 1907 a billiard room was formed from a bedroom, a closet and a dressing room. When the 9th Earl died in 1910 the work was still incomplete.

The move to Dunham marked the beginning of Lord Stamford's brief career as a great landowner. On 8th August 1906 the Earl and Countess, together with their young son and daughter, travelled in an open carriage through the streets of Altrincham and Bowdon to the cheers of the local people. At Dunham they were greeted by their tenants from Dunham, Bowdon, Altrincham, Hale, Little Bollington and Carrington, the oldest of whom explained that what lay behind the hearty welcome was "their satisfaction at their (the Stamfords') decision to dwell among them". In specially erected marquees, speeches of welcome were made, gifts presented, loyal toasts proposed and glasses raised. Outside on the lawns a band played and at the end of the afternoon the entire assembly sat down to tea. The *Altrincham Guardian* remarked that Lord Stamford was a landlord who was evidently set on encouraging those movements which "might be set on

*The 9th Earl of Stamford and his family return to Dunham Massey, August 1906*

foot for the moral and social welfare of the district" and one who, by implication, expected the active cooperation of those he was trying to help. Feudal ties were now being replaced by a spirit of partnership.

Triumphant though it had appeared, the return to Dunham by Lord Stamford as a country gentleman was much at odds with the wider world, which was now increasingly shaped by the forces of international politics and finance. Since the death of the 7th Earl in 1883, little more than twenty years previously, great changes had been taking place in the British nation. The sudden and widespread collapse of the agriculturally-based European economy had been brought about in the 1880s by the influx of cheap meat, grain and dairy products from Canada, Australia, New Zealand and other parts of the Empire. Agricultural rents fell to the point where land, for centuries the basis of wealth and power, became a liability as the wealthy looked for safer and more lucrative ways of investing. A second reform of the franchise in 1867 followed by a third less than twenty years later saw landowners finally lose control of the Commons. Everywhere the reform of local government was at hand. In 1888 county councils were established, charged with organising and administering the police, transport and other local matters. Whereas ancestors of families like Lord Stamford's had monopolised the appointment of JPs, their descendants now sat as appointees of an elected body, the county council, which was not an extension of county society.

Reforms were opening up posts in public life which had hitherto been filled by the aristocrats and their relatives. A man no longer bought a commission in the army or could expect to be gently eased into a post in the Civil Service, Foreign Office or even the Church. An expanding population was creating a society of increasing complexity and one which required large numbers of skilled people. The widened franchise had seen the appearance of political parties and the strikes and riots of socialist agitators. At the same time, many of the ancient families had gone quietly bankrupt. As Lord Delamere of Vale Royal near Nantwich swapped his heavily encumbered 6,000 Cheshire acres for 100,000 in the Kenyan bush, more than one parvenu industrialist, seeking respectability for his new wealth, hovered to occupy a place in county society. The final blow was Lloyd George's bill of 1909 which took away the power of the Lords to kill a finance bill. At the time the Stamfords were returning to the ancestral seat, many aristocrats were moving out of theirs.

During the final years of the 19th century the age-old problem of Irish Home Rule surfaced yet again. In 1893 the second Home Rule Bill, which proposed a measure of detachment of Ireland from the rest of Great Britain, reached the Lords. In voting for its defeat Lord Stamford's politics changed abruptly. In siding with the Unionists he was effectively turning his back on the liberal element of his family's Whig ancestry. The Whigs, the Duke of Westminster had once told Gladstone, were "in advance of the people ... leading them gently and wisely along the path of reform'. By 1900, after two centuries since its emergence in the days of the 1st Earl of Stamford, Whiggism was dead and buried. The people were now taking control of their destiny.

Although set against a background of rapidly declining aristocratic power and influence, the years at Dunham provided happy times for the Stamfords. There was, however, one perennial worry for the Earl. This was the discovery of a loophole in the will of the 7th Earl which enabled the half-caste John Grey, son of the 8th Earl, to mount a legal challenge to his exclusion from the revenues of the Cheshire estates. This resulted in the 9th Earl settling with the young man out of court by means of a single payment, said to be in the region of £125,000. The money was found partly by the sale of sections of the Dunham Estate and partly by a mortgage, not repaid until 1935, raised on other lands.

When not supervising the improvements to Dunham and running the estate, Stamford and his Countess found time to entertain with the house parties so typical of the Edwardian years. These would be seen as the Indian summer of the Victorian aristocracy. For many families it was a lifestyle which was to disappear completely in the aftermath of the Great War.

*Roger Grey, 10th and last Earl of Stamford*

# Chapter 21

# *The Last of the Line*

## Roger Grey, 10th Earl of Stamford (1896-1976)

When the 9th Earl died in May 1910 his son and heir Roger was aged thirteen. It was unfortunate that the boy was recovering from an appendix operation and was unable to attend the funeral. The absence of a father and the long and dominating presence of a strong-willed mother were to exert powerful influences on him from childhood to middle age. Lady Stamford, it will be recalled, was the daughter of a clergyman and she was the only one of her family to marry into the aristocracy. When her husband died, she was left with two young children and a large house and estate to run. Since her own family lived in the south of England and most of her husband's relatives were dead, there was no one to whom she could readily turn. The welfare of her family and the survival of Dunham were in her hands.

The young Lord Stamford was a bright boy but had the rather delicate constitution of his father. He left Eton before completing his secondary education and went to Italy with a private tutor. There he visited Rome, Naples and Florence and was resident in the country long enough to master the language. It was almost the Grand Tour which several of his ancestors had made. Also, Lady Stamford took her son and daughter on trips to the Continent. On one occasion they visited Count Zeppelin at Metz. It was just one of the many visits Stamford was to make to Germany which were to give him a close knowledge of the country, the language, the people and their politics.

One man who was an influence over the young Earl was a clergyman called Hewlett Johnson, who later gained international notoriety as the "Red Dean" of Canterbury. An engineer by training, he later took holy orders in the Church of England and was appointed by the 9th Earl of Stamford as curate of St Margaret's, the church built by George Harry, the 7th Earl. Hewlett Johnson was the man who became an outspoken advocate of Russian Communism, a friend of the Chinese leader Cho En-lai, an uncompromising critic of the American military involvement in the Korean War and an advocate of the overthrow of capitalism. He became a leading figure in the post World War Two Peace Movement and died in 1966.

At the outbreak of the First World War, Stamford endeavoured to enlist in the Army, but was turned down on medical grounds. He spent the war in uniform in London where he inhabited a ministerial office. Dunham Hall was meantime turned into a hospital for wounded soldiers of all ranks. Lady Stamford tackled the challenge this presented with her usual energy and determination. The stone floor at the bottom of the Grand Staircase made a good site for an operating theatre. Here the Countess and her young daughter, Lady

Jane, acted as nurses and general assistants during operations. It was the two ladies' proud claim that there were no deaths at Dunham in spite of such makeshift facilities. The recovery and convalescence of the injured was also organised and overseen by Lady Stamford. She wrote frequently to her son in London telling him about life at the hall, how difficult it was to find sufficient beds and naming the visitors who had called.[1]

On Christmas Day 1917 Lady Stamford managed to give the patients turkey and Christmas pudding while she and Lady Jane had pheasant from the estate. In the evening carols were sung by Lady Stamford and the staff around a Christmas tree which stood in a large tub at the end of the Great Hall. Soldiers who were mobile joined hands with the staff and danced round the tree, "cheering and shouting and it was so merry". Lady Stamford's letters would close with the advice to her son to take milk or soup at night, keep warm and look after himself. She addressed him as "dearest boy" and closed "your truly loving mother, Penelope Stamford".[2] Roger Stamford was now almost 21; he must have been very relieved to escape from his mother's stifling and over-protective company, if only for a few months.

In the aftermath of the War, one response by the international community to the horrors of the conflict was the establishment of the League of Nations. This organisation was dedicated to the prevention of future military aggression between member states. The foremost advocate of the League was the American President, Woodrow Wilson, and its headquarters were established in Geneva. It was to Bern that Lord Stamford was posted on behalf of the British Government. The Foreign Office was perhaps the final area of administration where an aristocrat like Stamford could expect to gain a place on the strength of his inherited social standing. It was as a result of his family background and all that went with it – confidence, poise, savoir-faire and an ability with languages – which saw Stamford appointed as honorary attaché. It was said of him later that, had he not inherited the responsibilities of Dunham, he might well have found a career in the diplomatic field. In Geneva he also met many important personnel of the League and there he developed a strong admiration for its aims and ideals. These sentiments were to remain with him until 1945 when the League was dissolved and replaced by the United Nations.

World War One was won, it was said, because the entire resources of the country had been mobilised to that end. The introduction of conscription of men into the armed forces meant that every level of society could claim to have fought for "King and Country" and could therefore claim their rewards in the post-war years. This "Peoples' War" hastened the end of the barriers which had separated the social classes in 1914 and enabled socialism to gain a hold on the political system. During 1920 Lord Stamford spent a year at New College, Oxford to follow a one-year course in economics and political science. Here for the first time he was exposed to the radical ideas of the forces of the Left, and where he found the received wisdom and traditional values of his family were challenged and often rejected. Oxford was in a ferment of ideas and values new to Stamford, a political, social and philosophical adventure playground. The young, unworldly and earnest 10th Earl of the ancient line of Stamford was ripe for conversion.

At Dunham, Lady Stamford looked around and reflected on the fortunate position in which the Greys found themselves after four years of destruction and devastation in Europe. The hall and estate had suffered little damage and no immediate relatives had been killed or injured, although it was said that Stamford never got over the loss of the lives of so many of his friends. The family's finances had emerged relatively undamaged from the years of austerity and, apart from the need to repay the mortgage on the payment made by his father to John Grey, no major crisis threatened. The future of the Greys of Dunham appeared secure, as far as it was possible to forecast in such turbulent times.

The Greys were indeed fortunate for all around them post-war Britain was in social and economic turmoil. The value of land plummeted and its ownership was even more of a liability than it had been in the 1890s. If a noble residence was not supported by a family with a strong and varied portfolio of financial interests, then the broad acres surrounding it would often have to be reduced in number as part of a retrenchment. Alternatively, they would have to be given over to a new-style working estate, at odds with the show place atmosphere of the Edwardian years. For many families with a large house, fixed charges, declining incomes and the demands of the taxman, the conditions of the post-war years spelt disaster. Country houses by the score became in effect redundant as homes and turned instead into expensive white elephants. Many were sold as residences to the rising industrialists and successful entrepreneurs, whose places of work were elsewhere, or the buildings were converted into public institutions such as hospitals and schools. Many were demolished. Between 1920 and 1939 no fewer than 221 mansions which today would well merit the title "listed building" were reduced to piles of rubble by their impoverished owners. Such was the volume of sales in the early 1920s that in total more land changed hands than had done so since the days of the Norman Conquest or the Dissolution of the Monasteries. It has also been remarked that the level of loss of young aristocratic heirs to landed estates had not been so great since the Wars of the Roses of the fifteenth century.[3]

At Enville, which descended to the step niece of the 7th Earl, the estate was held together; but many valuable items of art, including pictures and silver ware, which had been removed from Dunham in 1870, were sold at auction in the 1920s. Over the years, the 10th Earl devoted much time and money to acquiring many such items, especially the silver, which had not gone abroad and to returning them to Dunham, the place he felt they belonged.

It was a different matter in Leicestershire where the nationwide malaise was reflected among the Greys' aristocratic landowning neighbours. Lord Howe sold his Gopsall estate, Lord Ferrers left Staunton Harold Hall and the Duke of Rutland parted with about half the 30,000 acres he owned in the county. Mrs Katherine Grey, too, was obliged to sell the five thousand acre estate centred on Groby that the Greys had held since the middle of the 15th century. Many of the purchasers of the individual farms were her own tenants, some of whose families had farmed the land for generations. Excepted from the sale was Bradgate Park which her daughter sold a year later. It was bought privately by a local industrialist, at what is believed to be a bargain price, for the express purpose of conveyance to a trust who would administer it as an open space for the benefit of the local populace.

Even before 1914 the Hastings family in Leicestershire became bankrupt. After the death in 1868 of the 4th Marquess of Hastings, who squandered a large part of the family fortune on the turf, the Loudoun title and what remained of the estate passed through the female line. The 11th Countess was Edith Maude, the late Marquess' sister. After her death in 1874, her husband obtained the title of Baron Donington; but not even his wealth could prevent the sale of Donington Hall and estate around the turn of the century. They were eventually bought by the family of the Hastings long serving agents. A further disaster for the Hastings was the death of both of the first Baron's sons who were killed in action in 1915. The Loudoun title, devoid of any of the great wealth it had known for many centuries, passed once more through the female line.

To the local people of Cheshire, Lord Stamford was seen as returning home to occupy the position of country gentleman, even if the role would be somewhat different from that his father had known. The Duke of Westminster had described his own similar circumstances as changing from leisure, during which time he saw it as his time-honoured duty to serve his community, to pleasure, where he was no longer needed, or even wanted, by those same people. Henceforth he would please himself.[4] Apart from being a good landlord, Stamford, too, had little direct influence on the politics of the communities in the vicinities of his estates. The new democracy meant that the political parties were wooing the tenants rather than the landlords. In Cheshire, the professional and entrepreneurial middle classes had been in control of the most important positions in county administration since 1889 and in Parliament few local men sat for the county.

Throughout 1914-18 the dowager Lady Stamford ran the house with the same vigour and sense of purpose that she had shown in the pre-war years when her husband was alive. She had risen from humble origins to embrace the values and lifestyle of an aristocrat. Her husband's politics may have been liberal, but she cherished the class system and had a firm idea as to what she wanted for Dunham and how this would be achieved. To the servants she was formidable and she did not suffer fools gladly. In recognition of her wartime efforts she was awarded the OBE in 1920 which added to her sense of purpose. It was her desire to create at Dunham a lifestyle and ambience which in effect would be an extension of the Edwardian country house years, most of which she and her husband together had been denied by his early death. In this she was supported by the strong element of the Romanticism perpetuated in the pages of such magazines as *Country Life*. Among her achievements, Lady Stamford rescued Dunham from the decline and decay of many country houses which had survived the war, and she was also able to produce a measure of improvement.

The scene was now set for the inevitable social and personal conflict between mother and son. On the one hand was the young rebellious Earl, unattached and very soon to be the owner of a large house and estate, who had embraced left wing politics during his days at Oxford with a certain pride. Sharing the same roof was a mother who was the archetypal die-hard Tory with an iron will, who felt the need to protect her wayward and feckless offspring. She loved him dearly but at the same time saw him as inadequate to play the role she expected of him. Their love-hate relationship of the inter-war years was gradually to mellow and develop to the point where mother and son could tease each other without offence being given or taken.

Politics apart, it was unfortunate that Stamford found little in common with his aristocratic neighbours such as the Grosvenors and the Tollemaches. He did not like riding, hunting and other field sports and he did not shoot. His delight in the open air was to walk in the Peak District, on Kinder Scout, Mam Tor and a dozen other wild places. He also enjoyed playing cricket. It was his uncle Ridley Theobald, his mother's brother, who acted as host at the sporting occasions which Lady Stamford made a point of arranging as part of her vision of the Dunham scene. Stamford's major interests lay indoors: reading, book collecting, architecture, opera, drama and, of course, international affairs.

January 1924 saw the election of the first Labour Government under Ramsay MacDonald. Stamford was pleased, since MacDonald had worked to make the Party a plausible and governing force, especially in the field of foreign affairs. The names in the visitors' book for the 1920s show the dual role which Dunham played in the life of its inhabitants. The signatures of Stamford's guests: Arthur and Hugh Gaitskell with Philip and Irene Noel Baker, contrast clearly with Lady Stamford's choice of guests: Percy and Theresa Macquoid, Mrs Katherine Grey, the Bishop of London and other family members and friends. In return for his hospitality, Stamford was invited to Chequers during MacDonald's period in office as Prime Minister (1929-35). Here he met MacDonald's daughter, Ishbel, and for a time his name was linked romantically with hers, but the couple became no more than friends. It was as a result of contacts at this level that Stamford widened his circle into a group influential in the politics of the times.

One of Lord Stamford's friends from the 20s, about whom his mother raised no objections, was Sir Patrick Abercrombie, a man some seventeen years older than the Earl and who was born near Dunham at Ashton-upon-Mersey. Abercrombie distinguished himself as an architect and rose to become professor of Civic Design at Liverpool University. Although he had a keen interest in urban development, he is best known to a wider public as the man who was responsible for the foundation of the Council for the Preservation of Rural England, of which he was honorary secretary and executive chairman. Lord Stamford had a deep interest in the preservation of rural life and a strong civic pride which his family had nurtured since the beginning of the great expansion of Manchester and the growth of the Cheshire towns in the years of the 5th Earl. In Abercrombie he found a link between his essentially amateur interest and the activities of the rising numbers of professional planners. The 10th Earl kept an eagle eye on developments in and around his Dunham estate. Over the years he became something of a one-man civic society, embarrassing the planners at Altrincham and Chester with his knowledge of planning laws and the wiles and shortcomings of those appointed to administer them.[5]

Lady Stamford's influence on the household extended to her daughter, Jane. As a young girl, Jane had enjoyed a happy and conventional childhood in Surrey, but when the family moved to live permanently at Dunham after her father's death in 1910, her life changed abruptly and she came to hate the place. It was a very large and empty house, there was no sense of the family life she had known at Weybridge, there were no friends to play with and she saw very little of the few cousins she had. She was taught by a governess in the school room on the top floor and there were no children to share the lessons. Much of her life was spent looking forward to visits away from Dunham: to London, to distant relatives, abroad, anywhere! As time passed, she was very aware that her mother was losing no opportunity to find a suitable marriage partner for her. But Jane had other ideas. During voluntary social work in Bermondsey which provided an opportunity to escape from Dunham for a time, Jane met first hand the sufferings and privations of the working classes. In 1927 this rebellious girl, who so wanted to live in an ordinary house and raise an ordinary family, married Peveril Turnbull, a humble clergyman she had first met when he was the curate at St Margaret's at Altrincham.[6] When Lady Stamford failed to conceal her disappointment at her daughter's choice, it was gently pointed out to her by friends and family that she too was the daughter of a cleric.

All through the 1930s the Stamfords continued to enjoy a life style which they shared with fewer and fewer other aristocrats. The financial problems which had characterised the 1920s returned to wreak havoc on many noble lives. Even the Duchess of Rutland was obliged to sell her town house in London in 1934 and some aristocrats had tackled their financial problems by moving abroad or embarking on what turned out to be a lifetime world tour. Otherwise, peers were setting up businesses, becoming directors of companies, joining the boards of institutions such as banks and accepting all manner of paid employment.

The uneasy dual role also continued at Dunham into the 1930s with Lord Stamford in residence if not altogether in control of his inheritance. The guest lists for sherry parties contained names of family and friends, military men, churchmen, journalists and politicians. Here the Earl and Countess of Crawford and

Harold and Lady Dorothy Macmillan rubbed shoulders with the Noel Bakers and the Craigies. Alternatively, one week would see the Halifaxes resident, another the MacDonalds when the company would sing the Red Flag in the Great Hall. Such parties were important to Stamford's guests. Left wing peers provided a genteel tone to the essentially cloth cap image of MacDonald's inter-war administrations. Stamford was not alone in his supposed guilt about his past. There was a trend developing in genteel defections to the left, with Frank Packenham (Lord Longford), Stafford Cripps and Stamford's Cheshire neighbour, Christopher Isherwood. Many of these original "champagne socialists" added much social glitter but little substance to the movements they joined. Stamford, too, may have become just an ornamental local figurehead when he became Charter Mayor of Altrincham in 1937 were it not for the depth of his civic pride and his involvement in town and country planning.

It was during these same years that Lord Stamford visited Switzerland and Germany, especially the Saarland, and witnessed at first hand the move toward re-armament which was being so wilfully ignored by the politicians in Britain. In 1935 he played host at Dunham to the distinguished polymath Albert Schweitzer and was on the platform of the meeting in the Free Trade Hall in Manchester when Mr Winston Churchill warned the nation of the danger posed by German rearmament. Three years later the Italians demonstrated the impotence of the League of Nations by invading Ethiopia. Disgusted at the British Government's neglect of the deposed Emperor, Haile Selassie, Stamford made a point of inviting him to visit Dunham.

At the outbreak of World War Two, Stamford was too old for military service and was appointed Deputy Chief Air Raid Warden for Cheshire. It gave him no consolation to know that the fires he was called to put out in the industrial areas of the county were the result of the British Government's misguided policy of appeasement towards Hitler. Fortunately for the Stamfords, Dunham Hall suffered no damage from the Luftwaffe. The New Park was turned over to the army and was later the site of a hutted POW camp. Parts of the Old Deer Park and Hall garden were given over to growing potatoes for the war effort. At one time it was proposed to close the park entirely but the scheme was abandoned after a local outcry in the *Manchester Evening News* from those many workers who valued it as a vital place of relaxation.

The Second World War delivered the final crushing blow to the class system which had maintained aristocratic pre-eminence for so many centuries. Country houses had been ruined, many at the hand of the British army. Parks had been damaged and the economies of estates disrupted. Impoverished owners were now desperate to rid themselves of homes which had become economic monsters; land was sold to raise ready cash and family treasures were sent to auction. In post-1945 Britain the government had little time or thought for the conservation of the remains of the nation's heritage and had even less money with which to finance any proposals. Not least was the problem of the psychological effect on the owners; they had lost faith in their class, in themselves, in their purpose and in their future.

Seen against this depressing background, the survival of the Dunham estate was all the more remarkable. The hall was undamaged and the park had escaped the enormities which many other historic landscapes had suffered. Both facts were no doubt due in some measure to the watchful eye of the indomitable Countess Penelope. Although the Stamfords made some land sales during the post war years and reduced the number of servants, they did not find it necessary to open the estate to what Lady Stamford regarded as outrageous money-raising measures such as the Duke of Bedford's safari park at Woburn Abbey and the funfair at Alton

*Dunham Massey Hall, 2002*

Towers. There was no thought of opening the house at all since the public already enjoyed free access to part of the park. None of the valuable contents of Dunham Hall reached the sale rooms and Lord Stamford was never obliged to seek salaried employment. Yet in spite of this apparent affluence, there was a firm belief among local people that the Greys were poor.

Amid the austere conditions of 1945 the election of the Labour Government cheered Lord Stamford who probably knew many of those who then found themselves in high office. Stamford's adherence to his left wing views distressed, confounded and enraged his family. In letters to the Earl, his uncle, Ridley Theobald, kept up a running battle of words with his nephew. "Victoria would never have accepted Bevan or Shinwell as ministers," he declared in 1949. At one time he had been a member of the royal household and took a dim view of Stamford's references to "dear" Bevan and "old" Dean Hewlett Johnson. The names of both men struck a violent discord with uncle Rid. The Dean of Canterbury was "a nasty, mischievous old dog (and) a swine and a scoundrel." Bevan, Ridley thundered , was "a fearful blackguard". In response to the bait of Stamford's gentle taunting, Ridley responded tersely, "Don't send me the *Daily Worker*, it only disgusts me." His letters were addressed to the Earl, then in his fifties, as "Young Roger". It seems he shared the Countess' opinion regarding Stamford's developmental progress.[7]

The strained relations between mother and son continued through the 1940s and 50s but slowly mellowed. Gatherings at Dunham followed the pattern of the inter-war years. One week it was Stamford's friends, such as the Attlees who attended; the next saw people such as the Edens as the guests of Lady Stamford. There

175

were times when the Earl felt the need to escape the claustrophobic atmosphere of Dunham and took extended weekends in Buxton, returning home once a week to attend to important matters. Lady Stamford told friends that she would not move out because she was needed to run the place properly. She might also have feared that her son might have done something really silly such as marry one of the maids. Such behaviour after all was not without precedence in the family.

During the 1930s Stamford had been linked romantically, mostly by his mother, to various prominent women, including the Princess Royal. When Lady Stamford died in 1959, after 49 years of widowhood, her son was aged 63 and still unmarried, but hardly the eligible bachelor he had been at the end of the Second World War. After the distress of his mother's passing and in spite of the changed circumstances which followed, Stamford felt himself too old and unsuited to setting out along the path of matrimony with a view to producing an heir to his title. The extended periods of dark depression from which he suffered deterred even the more mature would-be partners who might otherwise accept and adapt to his bachelor ways and approach to women. Instead, Stamford devoted his declining years to conserving and improving the Dunham estate, safeguarding the treasures of his ancestors and delivering a service of interest and care to his tenants and staff.

During the 1970s the downturn in land prices, except for building development, and the fall in the returns from agricultural rents caused Stamford to re-examine his financial situation. As inflation soared he found himself in the same position the country had experienced in the 1920s. Since none of his few close relatives, the children of his sister Jane, was prepared to shoulder the responsibilities of the hall and estate after his death, Stamford entered negotiations with the National Trust which became the eventual beneficiary in 1976.

The last Lord Stamford continued throughout his life the spirit of paternal benefaction which had been a characteristic of his family for two centuries. He gave land for building in Altrincham in 1917 and more for a similar development in the same town three years later. Within Dunham Park a permanent training ground was laid out in the early days of the Scouting Movement and for a time this was second only to Gilwell in leadership training. There were, too, many other modest benefactions including the restoration of the window of the north transept of the parish church of Selborne in Hampshire in memory of his great-great uncle and naturalist, the Reverend Gilbert White. Stamford also gave freely of his time. He was president of the Ancient Monuments Society before its move to London; he sat as a trustee both on the Board of the John Rylands Library in Manchester and the Brontë museum at Haworth, and he was a governor of the grammar schools at Manchester and Altrincham.

In religion Stamford followed his family's Anglican traditions and in the 1930s held daily prayers in the chapel in Dunham which all the servants were expected to attend. His sister, Jane, was more interested in the Ecumenical Movement, from seeds sown in early childhood when, on trips abroad, her mother had insisted that the family worship in the church of the host country.

To the end Lord Stamford was a supporter of the left, although he had sat in the House of Lords on the Liberal benches and at no time was a member of a political party. He supported the joint Anglo-French invasion of Suez in 1956 and as he grew older the early flush of redness in his cheeks mellowed to a gentle shade of pink. There was in him more than a small remnant of underlying Whiggism. The hall and estate of his ancestors were very dear to him and he could not bear to see the house taken for an hotel or conference centre and the park broken up by some speculative developer offering even very up-market housing. These sentiments harked back to the 1890s when the Whigs were faced with the choice of liberalism or landlordism and when most of them decided on the latter. For Lord Stamford, historic Dunham proudly occupied a prominent and important part in the nation's heritage. One wonders what his lordship would have made of the policies of the Thatcher years.

Lord Stamford was an intelligent, generous and courteous man with a sense of humour and a deep interest in the welfare of those around him. At the same time, and although far from being a recluse, he was also seen as a lonely man who kept much of his private life to himself. He died much respected, a sentiment which was shared by a wide range of people including his political opponents. When the National Trust raised the rents of their Dunham properties in 1999 there was much feeling among the tenants that Lord Stamford might have seen the matter differently.[8]

Roger Grey, 10th and last Earl of Stamford, Baron Grey of Groby, could trace his certain descent along an unbroken male line of Greys through at least 22 generations

*The final resting place of the last Earl of Stamford*

to the 13th century Henry Grey of Codnor. He died on 18th August 1976 and lies buried in the churchyard of the Parish Church of Dunham Massey, where he is surrounded by generations of his family's former servants and tenants. It is perhaps appropriate that his memorial is a little larger than the others, as befits the final resting place of the last Great Oak of what, indeed, had been a long and noble line.

# The Greys: a long and noble line

# *Postscript*

Readers interested in following the trail of the Greys could make no better start than by visiting Dunham Massey Hall, which lies two miles west of the town of Altrincham in Cheshire. Dunham Hall is the ancient home of the Booth family and was re-fashioned in the Georgian period by the Greys. It was reworked in the early 20th century by the ninth Earl of Stamford. It contains family portraits additional to those reproduced in this book, an exceptional collection of walnut furniture and the Earl of Warrington's magnificent Huguenot silver. There is a richly planted garden containing extensive borders and a very fine orangery. The surrounding deer park has woodlands showing the planting schemes of the second Earl of Warrington in the 18th century. Dunham Hall and Park, (and not least the excellent tearoom and restaurant), is maintained by the National Trust to the highest standards.

The 800 acre Bradgate Park lies four miles north-west of Leicester and adjoins the village of Newtown Linford. It contains some spectacularly beautiful scenery and the romantic ruins of the magnificent house built over many years by the Marquesses of Dorset in the first half of the 16th century. Visitors are advised that the ruins were heavily and insensitively restored at various times during the 20th century and that they should consult the guide book for further details.[1] The rugged, bracken-covered slopes of the Park are dotted with ancient oaks, some of which reach back to the time of Lady Jane Grey. There is also a herd of 300-400 red and fallow deer. Bradgate is administered as a country park by the Bradgate Park Trust and there is free admission all year round. The ruins of the House and the remains of the early Tudor garden are also open at certains times in the week and at weekends.

The third of the Grey houses is Enville Hall in Staffordshire, a few miles west of the Birmingham conurbation. It remains very much a family house and is closed to the public at all times.

In addition to the three Houses, there are memorials, items of stained glass, effigies, monuments and the like in houses, churches and manors widely scattered across England, where the Greys held property. Early homes long lost to the family include Shute Barton in Devon (National Trust) and Astley Castle (in the care of English Heritage and under renovation in Warwickshire).

For serious researchers, Manchester University's John Rylands Library holds the vast archive which was moved from Dunham Massey Hall after the death of the tenth Earl. The material, which is thoroughly catalogued, relates mostly to the Cheshire Estates and includes both Booth and Grey papers.

The Record Office for Leicestershire, Leicester and Rutland at Wigston Magna on the outskirts of Leicester has a smaller but very useful collection of documents for the Leicestershire Estates. The Public Record Office at Kew houses most if not all the official documents of State in which the Greys are mentioned.

And what of the Hastings? Their line, longer even than that of the Greys, continues in the person of Barbara Abney-Hastings, 14th Countess of Loudoun, who lives quietly in a house in the grounds of Ashby Castle, which her ancestor, William Lord Hastings built in the 15th century. The castle, now a magnificent ruin, is maintained by English Heritage and is open to the public. Donington Hall, on the banks of the river Trent, is now the busy headquarters of British Midland Airways and there is no public access. Kirby Muxloe Castle, begun but never finished by William Lord Hastings, is situated in the village of Kirby Muxloe, four miles west of Leicester. It, too, is an English Heritage property.

*As this book goes to press the death has been announced of Barbara, Countess of Loudoun. She is succeeded in the Earldom by her son, Michael.*

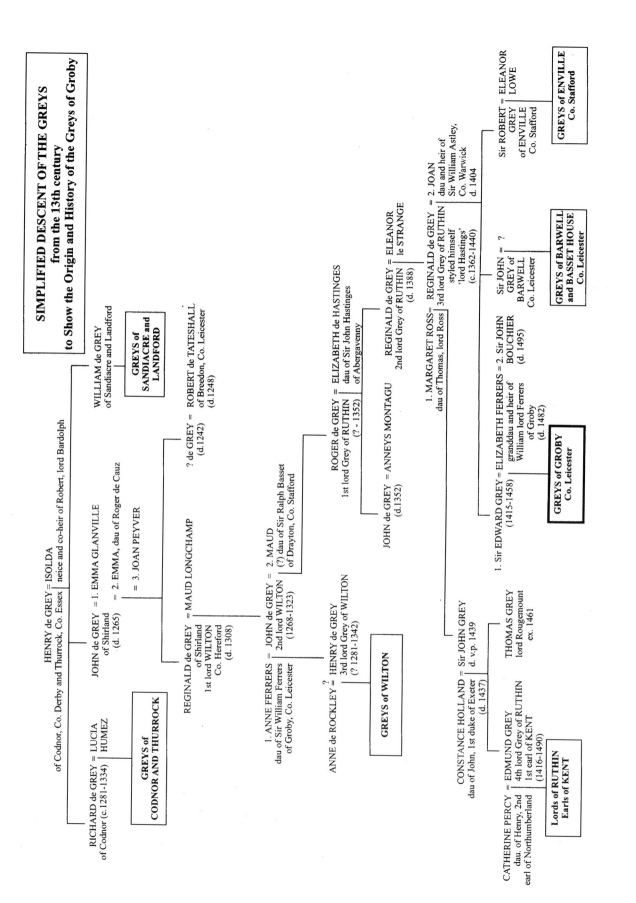

# SIMPLIFIED DESCENT OF THE GREYS
## from the 13th century
### to Show the Origin and History of the Greys of Groby

HENRY de GREY = ISOLDA
of Codnor, Co. Derby and Thurrock, Co. Essex | neice and co-heir of Robert, lord Bardolph

RICHARD de GREY = LUCIA HUMEZ
of Codnor (c.1281-1334)

**GREYS of CODNOR AND THURROCK**

JOHN de GREY = 1. EMMA GLANVILLE
of Shirland (d. 1265)
= 2. EMMA, dau of Roger de Cauz
= 3. JOAN PEYVER

WILLIAM de GREY
of Sandiacre and Landford

**GREYS of SANDIACRE and LANDFORD**

? de GREY = ROBERT de TATESHALL
(d.1242) of Breedon, Co. Leicester
(d.1248)

REGINALD de GREY = MAUD LONGCHAMP
of Shirland
1st lord WILTON
Co. Hereford
(d. 1308)

1. ANNE FERRERS = JOHN de GREY = 2. MAUD
dau of Sir William Ferrers | 2nd lord WILTON | (?) dau of Sir Ralph Basset
of Groby, Co. Leicester | (1268-1323) | of Drayton, Co. Stafford

ANNE de ROCKLEY ? = HENRY de GREY
3rd lord Grey of WILTON
(? 1281-1342)

**GREYS of WILTON**

ROGER de GREY = ELIZABETH de HASTINGES
1st lord Grey of RUTHIN | dau of Sir John Hastinges
(? - 1352) | of Abergavenny

JOHN de GREY = ANNEYS MONTAGU
(d.1352)

REGINALD de GREY = ELEANOR
2nd lord Grey of RUTHIN | le STRANGE
(d. 1388)

1. MARGARET ROSS= REGINALD de GREY = 2. JOAN
dau of Thomas, lord Ross | 3rd lord Grey of RUTHIN | dau and heir of
| styled himself | Sir William Astley,
| 'lord Hastings' | Co. Warwick
| (c.1362-1440) | d. 1404

CATHERINE PERCY = EDMUND GREY
dau. of Henry, 2nd | 4th lord Grey of RUTHIN
earl of Northumberland | 1st earl of KENT
| (1416-1490)

**Lords of RUTHIN Earls of KENT**

CONSTANCE HOLLAND = Sir JOHN GREY
dau of John, 1st duke of Exeter | d. v.p. 1439
(d. 1437)

THOMAS GREY
lord Rougemount
ex. 1461

1. Sir EDWARD GREY = ELIZABETH FERRERS = 2. Sir JOHN
(1415-1458) | granddau and heir of | BOUCHIER
| William lord Ferrers | (d. 1495)
| of Groby
| (d. 1482)

**GREYS of GROBY Co. Leicester**

Sir JOHN = ?
GREY of
BARWELL
Co. Leicester

**GREYS of BARWELL and BASSET HOUSE Co. Leicester**

Sir ROBERT = ELEANOR
GREY | LOWE
of ENVILLE
Co. Stafford

**GREYS of ENVILLE Co. Stafford**

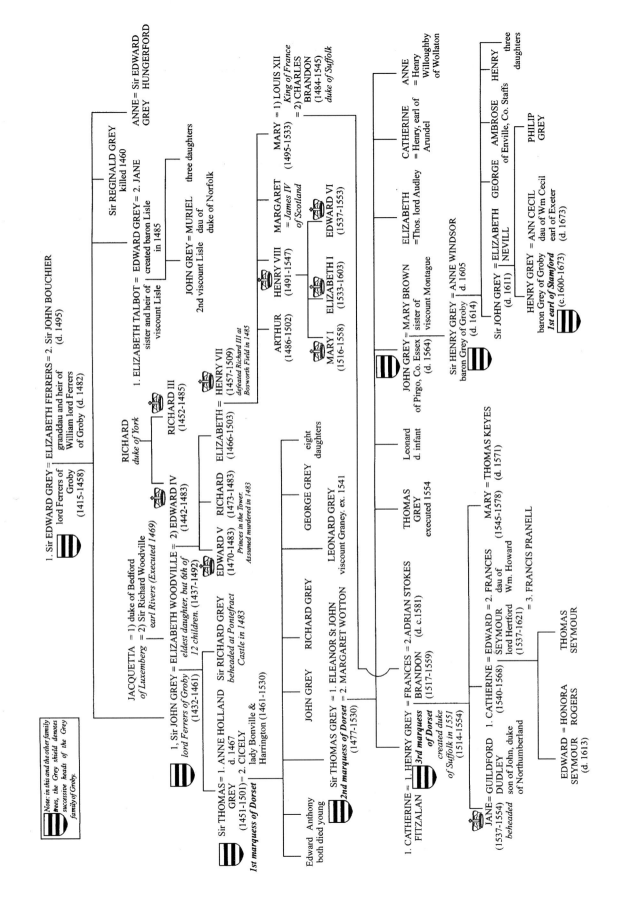

Note: in this and the other family trees, the Grey shield denotes successive heads of the Grey family of Groby.

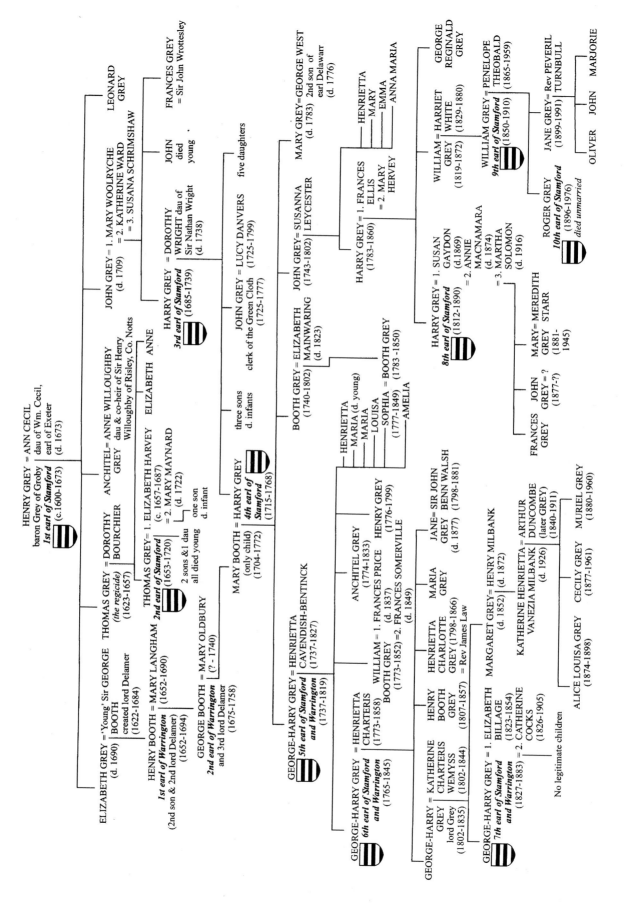

HENRY GREY = ANN CECIL
baron Grey of Groby, dau of Wm. Cecil,
**1st earl of Stamford** earl of Exeter
(c.1600-1673) (d. 1673)

ELIZABETH GREY = 'Young' Sir GEORGE BOOTH  THOMAS GREY *(the regicide)* (1623-1657) = DOROTHY BOURCHIER
(d. 1690)  created lord Delamer (1622-1684)

ANCHITEL GREY = ANNE WILLOUGHBY  ELIZABETH ANNE
dau & co-heir of Sir Henry Willoughby of Risley, Co. Notts

JOHN GREY = 1. MARY WOOLRYCHE (d. 1709) = 2. KATHERINE WARD = 3. SUSANA SCHRIMSHAW

LEONARD GREY

HENRY BOOTH = MARY LANGHAM
**1st earl of Warrington**  (1652-1690)
(2nd son & 2nd lord Delamer) (1652-1694)

THOMAS GREY **2nd earl of Stamford** (1653-1720) = 1. ELIZABETH HARVEY (c. 1657-1687) = 2. MARY MAYNARD (d. 1722)
2 sons & 1 dau all died young
one son d. infant

HARRY GREY **3rd earl of Stamford** (1685-1739) = DOROTHY WRIGHT dau of Sir Nathan Wright (d. 1738)

JOHN died young

FRANCES GREY = Sir John Wrottesley

GEORGE BOOTH = MARY OLDBURY
**2nd earl of Warrington** (? - 1740)
and 3rd lord Delamer (1675-1758)

JOHN GREY = LUCY DANVERS clerk of the Green Cloth (1725-1777) (1725-1799)

five daughters

MARY BOOTH = HARRY GREY **4th earl of Stamford** (only child) (1715-1768)
(1704-1772)

three sons d. infants

BOOTH GREY = ELIZABETH MAINWARING (1740-1802) (d. 1823)

JOHN GREY = SUSANNA LEYCESTER (1743-1802)

MARY GREY = GEORGE WEST (d. 1783) 2nd son of earl Delawarr (d. 1776)

HARRY GREY = 1. FRANCES ELLIS = 2. MARY HERVEY (1783-1860)

HENRIETTA  MARY  EMMA  ANNA MARIA

HENRIETTA  MARIA (d. young)  MARIA  LOUISA  SOPHIA = BOOTH GREY (1777-1849) (1783-1850)  AMELIA

GEORGE-HARRY GREY = HENRIETTA CAVENDISH-BENTINCK
**5th earl of Stamford and Warrington** (1737-1827)
(1737-1819)

ANCHITEL GREY (1774-1833)  HENRY GREY = 1. FRANCES PRICE (d. 1837) = 2. FRANCES SOMERVILLE (1776-1799) (d. 1849)

JANE = Sir JOHN GREY BENN WALSH (d. 1877) (1798-1881)

WILLIAM = 1. FRANCES ELLIS ...

WILLIAM = HARRIET WHITE GREY (1829-1880) (1819-1872)

WILLIAM GREY **9th earl of Stamford** (1850-1910) = PENELOPE THEOBALD (1865-1959)

GEORGE REGINALD GREY

JANE GREY = Rev PEVERIL (1899-1991) TURNBULL

ROGER GREY **10th earl of Stamford** (1896-1976) *died unmarried*

OLIVER  JOHN  MARJORIE

GEORGE-HARRY GREY **6th earl of Stamford and Warrington** (1765-1845) = HENRIETTA CHARTERIS (1773-1858)

WILLIAM = 1. FRANCES PRICE BOOTH GREY (1773-1852) = 2. Rev James Law

HENRY BOOTH GREY (1807-1857)

HENRIETTA CHARLOTTE GREY (1798-1866) = Rev James Law

MARIA GREY

GEORGE-HARRY GREY = KATHERINE CHARTERIS WEMYSS (1802-1835) (1802-1844)
lord Grey

MARGARET GREY = HENRY MILBANK (d. 1852) (d. 1872)

KATHERINE HENRIETTA = ARTHUR VANEZIA MILBANK DUNCOMBE (later GREY) (d. 1926) (1840-1911)

GEORGE-HARRY GREY **7th earl of Stamford and Warrington** (1827-1883) = 1. ELIZABETH BILLAGE (1823-1854) = 2. CATHERINE COCKS (1826-1905)

No legitimate children

ALICE LOUISA GREY (1874-1898)  CECILY GREY (1877-1961)  MURIEL GREY (1880-1960)

HARRY GREY **8th earl of Stamford** (1812-1890) = 1. SUSAN GAYDON (d. 1869) = 2. ANNIE MACNAMARA (d. 1874) = 3. MARTHA SOLOMON (d. 1916)

FRANCES GREY  JOHN GREY = ? (1877-?)  MARY = MEREDITH GREY STARR (1881-1945)

# *Bibliography*

*Only titles mentioned in the references have been listed. The place of publication is London unless given otherwise.*

**Anon.** Guide Book to Burton Agnes Hall. Burton Agnes Hall and Jarrold Publishing. 1990

**Anon.** William Earl of Stamford. Christophers, London. no date. (Printed for private circulation)

**Anon.** Uppark Exhibition. National Trust. 1998

**Andrews, C Bruyn.** The Torrington Diaries. A Selection From The Tours of the Honourable John Bing. Eyre and Spottiswode. 2 vols 1935

**Anglo, Sydney.** Spectacle, Pageantry and Early Tudor Policy Making. Clarendon Press, Oxford. Second Edition 1997

**Armstrong, CAJ.** The usurpation of Richard The Third. Clarendon Press, Oxford. 1969

**Bagley, JJ.** The Earls of Derby 1485-1985. Sidgwick and Jackson 1985

**Bamford, Frank.** Mansions and Men of Dunham Massey. Local History Magazine, Lenton, Nottingham. no 31 July 1991

**Bateman, John.** The Great Landowners of Great Britain and Ireland. Harrison. 1879

**Bayliss, Don. (ed).** Altrincham, A History. Willow Publishing. Altrincham. 1992

**Beckett, JV.** The Aristocracy in England 1660-1914. Basil Blackwell, Oxford. 1986

**Beckett, JV and Jones, Clyve.** "Financial Improvidence and Political Independence in the Early Eighteenth Century: George Booth, 2nd Earl of Warrington (1675-1758)". In Bulletin of John Rylands Library, University of Manchester. vol 65 1982

**Bennett, Edwin.** Enville Parish and Church: a Short History. Mark and Moody Ltd. Stourbridge 1905

**Bowman, Winifred M.** England in Ashton-under-Lyne. Sherratt for Ashton-under-Lyne Corporation. Altrincham. 1960

**Bristed, CA.** Five Years in an English university. 3rd edition 1873

**Brewer, Clifford.** The Death of Kings. Abson Books, 2000

**Burdett, PP.** A Survey of the County Palatine of Chester 1777. Reprinted in Facsimile with an introduction by JB Harley and P Laxton. The Historical Society of Lancashire and Cheshire Occasional Papers vol 1. Lund Humphrey. 1974

**Burke, John and Burke, Sir Bernard.** Burke's Peerage, Baronetage and Knightage. Ed LG Pine. 100th edition (1953)

**Burton, William.** The Description of Leicestershire. 1622

**Calendar of Close Rolls. Public Record Office.** HMSO 1485-1500 (1955); 1500-09 (1963)

**Calendar of Patent Rolls. Public Record Office.** HMSO. 1476-85 (1901); 1485-94 (1914); 1494-1507 (1916); 1550-63 8 vols (1936-48). 1580-82 (1986)

**Calendar of State Papers Domestic. 1629-31 Public Record Office.** HMSO. 1860

**Cannadine, David.** The Decline and Fall of the British Aristocracy. Yale 1990. Revised edition by Picador. Papermac 1996

**Cave, K (ed.).** The Diary of Joseph Farington. Newhaven, Yale University Press. 1982

**Chandler, John,(ed.).** John Leyland's Itinerary: Travels In Tudor England. Alan Sutton. 1993

**Cousens, Belinda.** Dunham Massey, An Illustrated Souvenir. National Trust. 1990

**Davey, Richard.** The Sisters of Lady Jane Grey. Chapman Hall Ltd. London. 1911

**Dictionary of National Biography.** Edited by Leslie Stephen and Sir Sidney Lee. 63 main volumes. Smith Elder. 1885-1901

**Elliott, Brent.** Victorian Gardens. Batsford. 1983

**Ellis, Henry.** Original Letters Illustrative of English History. vol 2. Second Series. Harding and Lepard. 1827

**Ellis, Sir Henry.** Three Books of Polidore Vergil's English History. Camden Society. (1844)

**Elton, Arthur; Harrison, Brett and Wark, Keith.** Researching the Country House; A Guide For Local Historians. Batsford. 1992

**Enville Hall Archives,** Staffordshire.

**Falkus, Gila.** The Life and Times of Edward IV. Weidenfeld and Nicolson. 1981

**Familiar Magazine.** Cape Town, South Africa. vol XI No 1 April 1974; vol XI No 3 September 1974; vol XII No 1 March 1976

**Fleming P, Gross A, and Lander JR.** Regionalism and Revision. Hambledon Press.

**GEC (GE Cockayne).** The Complete Peerage of England, Scotland and Ireland, Great Britain and the United Kingdom. Edited by the Honourable Vicary Gibbs and others. 13 vols. 1910-99. Alan Sutton reprint. Gloucester 1982

**Hammond, PW.** The Date of the Death of the Marquess of Dorset. The Ricardian. Vol IV No. 63 December 1978

**Hammond, PW and Sutton, Anne.** Richard III: The Road to Bosworth Field. Constable. 1985

**Hay, Denys.** The Anglia Historia of Polydore Vergil AD 1485-1537. Camden Series Volume LXXIV. Royal Historical Society. 1950

**Haynes, Sandy.** "A History of the 18th Century Gardens at Enville Hall" in The Ferme Ornee: Working With Nature. Staffordshire Gardens Trust. 1998

**Heeley, Joseph.** Letters on the Beauties of Hagley, Envil and the Leasowes. R Baldwin. 1977

**Hicks, MA.** The Changing Role of the Wydvilles in Yorkist Politics to 1483. in Ross, Charles (ed.). Patronage, Pedigree and Power 1979

**Higson, PJ.** The Nobility of England 1453-1558. MA Thesis University of Liverpool. 1959

**History of the House of Commons:**
1558-1603 vol 2. ed. PW Hasler. HMSO 1981
1660-90 vols 1 and 2. ed RD Henning. Secker and Warburg. 1983

1715-54 vol 1. ed. Romney Sedgwick. HMSO 1968

1754-90 vol 2. ed. Sir Lewis B Napier and John Brooke. HMSO. 1968

1790-1820 vol 4. ed. RG Thorne. Secker and Warburg. 1986

**Hoskins, WG.** Heritage of Leicestershire. City of Leicester Publicity Department. 1950

**Howard, Maurice.** The Early Tudor Country House: Architecture and politics 1490-1550. George Philip. 1987

**Ingham, Alfred.** A History of Altrincham and Bowdon. Cartwright and Rattray. Manchester. 2nd edition 1879

**Jerdan, William.** Rutland Papers. Camden Society. (1842)

**Jones, C and Jones, DL. (eds).** Peers, Politics and Power: The House of Lords 1603-1911. Hambledon. 1986

**Kendal, Paul Murray.** Richard III. George Allen and Unwin. 1955. 7th impression 1973

**Kendal, Paul Murray.** Warwick the Kingmaker. George Allen and Unwin. 1957. 2nd impression 1963

**Lacey, Robert.** The Life and Times of Henry VII. Weidenfeld and Nicolson. 1972

**Lander, JR.** Council, Administration and Councillors 1461-85. Bulletin of the Institute of Historical Research. vol XXXII. 1959

**Lander, JR.** Marriage and Politics in the Fifteenth Century: the Nevilles and the Wydvilles. Bulletin of the Institute of Historical Research. vol XXXVI. 1963.

**Lander, JR.** Crown and Nobility 1450-1509. Edward Arnold. 1976

**Lander, JR.** Government and Community: England 1450-1509. Edward Arnold. 1980

**Lander, JR.** The Wars of the Roses. Alan Sutton. 1990

**Leech HJ.** Tales and Sketches of Old Altrincham and Bowdon. Altrincham. 1880

**Letters and Papers of Henry VIII.** Public Record Office. HMSO September 1540-December 1541. 1898

**Loades, David (ed).** Chronicle of the Tudor Kings. Garamond Ltd. 1990

**Lockyer, Roger.** Tudor and Stuart Britain 1471-1714. Longman. 2nd edition 1985

**Lodge's Peerage,** Baronetage, Knightage and Companionage of the British Empire for 1912. 81st edition

**MacAndrew, Donald.** Equestrienne. The Saturday Book edited by John Heathfield. Hutchinson. 1960

**MacGibbon, David.** Elizabeth Woodville. Arthur Barker Ltd. 1938

**Miller, Helen.** Subsidy Assessment of the Peerage in the 16th Century. Bulletin of the Institute of Historical Research. vol XXVIII. 1955

**Mingay, GE.** English Landed Society in the 18th Century. Routledge and Kegan Paul. 1963

**Morris, Christopher (ed).** The Illustrated Journeys of Celia Fiennes 1685-c1712. Webb and Bower. 1982

**National Trust.** Dunham Massey, An Illustrated Souvenir. 1990

**Nichols, John.** The History and Antiquities of the County of Leicester. 4 vols. 1795-1811. S and R Publishers, East Ardley, Wakefield. 1971

**Nichols, John Gough (ed).** The Chronicle of Calais. Camden Society. (1846)

**Nichols, John Gough (ed).** The Chronicle of Queen Jane. Camden Society. (1850)

**O'Harrow, PDG.** The Country House Architecture of Henry VII and the Nobility. PhD thesis Cambridge University 1997

**Onslow, Richard.** A History of Newmarket and its Racing Headquarters. Great Ouse Press, Cambridge. 1983

**Parker, LA.** The Tudor Inclosure Movement in Leicestershire 1485-1607. PhD thesis London University 1947

**Paul, John D.** Bradgate House and the Greys of Groby. J and T Spencer. Leicester. 1899

**Pearson, John.** Stags and Serpents. Macmillan. 1983

**Plowden, Alison.** Lady Jane Grey and the House of Suffolk. Sidgwick and Jackson. 1985

**Pugh, TB.** "Henry VII and the English Nobility" in Bernard,GW (ed) Tudor

Nobility. Manchester University Press. 1992

**Ramsey, David.** Groby and its Railways. TEE Publishing,Hinckley, Leics. 1982

**Ramsey, David.** Was There a Village Called Bradgate? Published by the author, Groby, Leicestershire. 1998

**Richards, Jeff.** Aristocrat and Regicide: The Life and Times of Thomas, Lord Grey of Groby. New Millennium Press. London. 2000

**Riley, Henry T.** Ingulph's Chronicle of the Abbey of Croyland. Henry H Bohun. (1854)

**Robinson, John Martin.** The Dukes of Norfolk. Oxford University Press. 1982

**Ross, Charles.** Edward IV. Eyre Methuen. 1974

**Ross, Charles.** Patronage, Pedigree and Power in Later Medieval England. Alan Sutton, Gloucester. 1979

**Seward, Desmond.** Richard III, England's Black Legend. Country Life Books. 1983

**Seward, Desmond.** The Wars of the Roses. Constable. 1995

**Simon, Brian.** Education In Leicestershire 1540-1940. Leicester University Press. 1968

**Simons, Eric.** The Reign of Edward IV. Frederick Muller. 1966

**Skillington, SH.** Star Chamber Proceedings. Transactions of the Leicestershire Archaeological Society. Vol XII. 1921

**Stamford Shooting Records** for the 19th Century. Ledgers in private hands.

**Starkey, David (ed).** Rivals In Power. Macmillan. 1990

**Stebbing Shaw, The Rev.** The History and Antiquities of Staffordshire. 2 vols. J. Nichols, London. 1801. EP Publishing. 1976

**Stevenson, Joan, and Squires, Anthony.** Bradgate Park, The Childhood Home of Lady Jane Grey. Kairos Press, Newtown Linford, Leics. Second edition 1999

**Stoate, TL.** A Survey of West Country Manors 1525: the Lands of Cicely Marchioness of Dorset. Published by T Stoate,Bristol 1979

**Sylvester, Richard S (ed).** St Thomas More: The History of King Richard III. Yale University Press. 1976

**Throsby, John.** Select Views in Leicestershire. 2 vols. Printed for the author by J Nichols,London. (1790)

**Turberville, AS.** The House of Lords in the 18th Century. Greenwood Press, Connecticut. 1927

**Valentine, Alan.** The British Establishment 1760-1784. vol 1. University of Oklahoma Press: Norman. 1970

**Victoria County Histories:**

Essex vol 7. ed. WR Powell.Oxford University Press. 1978

Leicestershire vol 2. ed.WG Hoskins. Oxford University Press. 1954

Northants Families (genealogical volume). Constable. 1906

Warwickshire vol 4. ed LF Salzman. Oxford University Press. 1947

Worcestershire vol 2. ed JW Willis-Bund and William Page Dawson (Folkestone) 1971

**Walker, Sir Edmund.** Historical Discourses Upon Several Occasions. 1705

**Walsh, Sir John Benn.** The Diaries of Sir John Benn Walsh, (1st Lord Ormathwaite),1798-1881. Manuscript in the National Library of Wales, Aberystwyth.

**Waterson, Merlin.** Dunham Massey Guide Book. National Trust. 1981

**Webb, John.** Memorials of the Civil War Between King Charles I and the Parliament of England as it Affected Hereford and Adjacent Counties. Longmans Green and Co. 2 vols. 1879

**Wedgwood, CV.** The Trial of Charles I. Fontana 1967

**Witham, John A.** The Church of St Mary of Ottery in the County of Devon. British Publications Co Ltd,Gloucester. 1971

**Yass, Marion.** The English Aristocracy. Wayland Publishers. 1974

# *References*

## Abbreviations

*For details see Bibliography*

| | |
|---|---|
| **Cal Close R.** | Calendar of Close Rolls. |
| **Cal Pat R.** | Calendar of Patent Rolls. |
| **Commons History R.** | The History of the House of Commons. |
| **CP** | Complete Peerage, GEC (ed.). |
| **DNB** | Dictionary of National Biography. |
| **Enville Hall** | Archives of Enville Hall, Staffordshire. |
| **LLRO** | Record Office of Leicestershire, Leicester and Rutland. Wigston, Leicester. |
| **L and P** | Letters and Papers. |
| **Nichols Leics.** | John Nichols' History of Leicestershire. |
| **Portland Papers** | Manuscripts of the Portland Family, University of Nottingham Library. |
| **Rylands Library** | John Rylands Library, University of Manchester. |
| **TLAS** | Transactions of the Leicestershire Archaeological Society. |
| **VCH** | Victoria County History. |
| **Walsh Diaries** | Diaries of Sir John Walsh. |

### Introduction
1. Robinson 1982; Bagley 1985

### Chapter 1
1. CP VI p133
2. Ibid.
3. CP VI pp171-72
4. Ibid. pp151-58
5. Ibid. 151-58
6. CP IV pp190-191
7. Ibid. pp341-42
8. Ibid. pp342-61
9. Starkey 1990 p8

### Chapter 2
1. MacGibbon 1938 pp32-33
2. Simmons 1966 p113
3. Falkus 1981 p76
4. Riley 1854 p484
5. Armstrong 1969 p61
6. Lander 1990 pp104-05
7. MacGibbon 1939 pp30-31
   *Ralph subsequently had seven daughters*
8. MacGibbon 1938 pp30-31
9. Falkus 1981 p91
10. Lander 1980 p136
11. Kendall 1955 p146
12. Lander 1963 p136 1
13. Lander 1980 p51
14. Kendall 1955 p61

### Chapter 3
1. CP VI pp637-54
2. Ross 1974 p86

3. Seward 1995 p125
4. Sylvester 1976 p50
5. Stoate 1979
6. Lander 1976 p214
7. Cal Pat R. 1478-85 p139
8. see Postscript p179
9. Brewer 2000 p98
10. Ibid.

### Chapter 4
1. Seward 1983 p91
2. Ibid. p95
3. Sylvester 1976 p50
4. Seward 1983 p104
5. Hammond and Sutton 1985 p146

### Chapter 5
1. VCH Lancs vol. 8 pp132 and 247
2. Lander 1976 p286
3. Pugh 1992 p102
4. Ibid. p104
5. Cal Close R. 1485-94 pp180-81
6. Cal Pat R. 1485-94; 1494-1507
7. Cal Pat R. 1485-94 pp490-91; 1495-1507 pp 646-47
8. Witham 1979 pp9-11
9. Lander 1976 p228 and Pugh 1992
10. VCH Wars. 4 p179
11. Parker 1947 p202
12. Chandler 1993 p123
13. Ibid. pp 80, 124 and 272
14. Parker 1947 p202
15. Hammond 1978 pp37-38
16. Nichols' Leics. vol 3 part 2 p663

### Chapter 6
1. Nichols' Leics. vol 3 part 2 p572
2. Ibid.
3. Higson 1959 p291
4. Cal Close R. 1500-09 pp163-66
5. Nichols' 1846 p6
6. Burke's peerage 1953 p22. Lodge 1912 makes no mention
7. CP VII pp232-34
8. CP IV p240
9. Loades 1990 p112
10. Paul 1899 pp33-34
11. Sylvester 1976 pp56-57
12. Jerdan 1842 pp29-32
13. CP VII p234
14. LLRO 28D64 no. 1
15. L and P Henry VIII vol 13 p48
16. Chandler 1993 p279
17. Hoskins 1950 p60
18. Howard 1987 p202
19. Stevenson and Squires 1999 pp27-34
20. TLAS vol XII 1921-22 p130
21. Higson 1959 p269
22. Nichols' Leics. vol 3 part 2 p665
23. Burton 1622 pp51-52

### Chapter 7
1. Miller 1955 p29
2. CP VII p236
3. Lacey 1972 p157
4. Nichols' Leics. vol 3 part 2 p666
5. L and P Foreign and Domestic Hen VIII Sept 1540-Dec 1541 p234
6. Plowden 1985 p70

7. Paul 1899 p47
8. Plowden 1985 p50

**Chapter 8**
1. Plowden 1985 opposite p1
2. Nichols 1850 p127
3. DNB: Lord John Grey
4. Cal Pat R. 1553-55
5. CP VI p184
6. Cal Pat R. 1580-82 p183

**Chapter 9**
1. Nichols' Leics vol 3 part 2 p674
2. Cal Pat R. 1553-55 six vols
   Also Nichols' Leics vol 3 part 2 p674
3. VCH Essex vol 7 p16
   Also Nichols' Leics vol 3 part 2 p673
4. Davey 1911 p181
5. Ibid. p176
6. CP VI p506
7. Davey 1911 pp 200-01
8. CP VI p506
9. Plowden 1985 p168
10. Ibid. pp168-69

**Chapter 10**
1. This section is based on Cust R in
   Fleming et al 1998 pp145-162
2. CP X p225
3. Cal. State Papers Domestic 1629-31
   p491 and 1631-32 p54
4. CP XII/I p219
5. DNB: Henry Grey (1600-1673)

**Chapter 11**
1. Nichols' Leics vol 3 part 2 (Appendix p19)
2. Ibid. p23
3. Ibid. p30
4. Webb 1879 pp160-61
5. Ibid. pp176-77
6. Ibid. p179
7. House of Lords Journal vol 6 p346
8. Ibid. vol VIII p32
9. Walker 1705 p128

**Chapter 12**
1. Nichols' Leics vol 3 part 2 p612
2. Wedgwood 1967 p96
3. Lockyer 1985 p288
4. Throsby 1790 vol 2 (Excursions) p90
5. Lockyer 1985 p289
6. Nichols' Leics vol 3 part 2 p678
7. Ibid. p679
8. Ibid. p679
9. Brewer 2000 p171

**Chapter 13**
1. Commons History 1660-90 vol 2 p14
2. Ibid. vol 1 (Members C-L) p304
3. Ibid. p504
4. CP XII/I p223
5. Nichols' Leics vol 3 part 2 p679
6. Commons History 1660-90 vol 2
   (Members A-B) pp14-16
7. Ibid. p442
8. Cousens 1990 p6
9. DNB XII pp221-22
10. VCH Northants genealogical vol (1906)
    p216

**Chapter 14**
1. DNB: Henry Booth (1652-94)
2. CP VI pp659-60
3. VCH Leics vol 2 p119
4. Commons History 1660-90 vol 1 p295
5. DNB: Henry Booth p382

6. Ibid.
7. Cousens 1990 p4
8. Ibid.
9. Waterson 1981 p48
10. Stevenson and Squires 1999 ch. 3 and 6
11. VCH Leics vol 2 p121
12. Ibid.
13. CP VI p660
14. Gregg, Edward and Jones, Clyve in Jones,
    C and Jones DL 1986 pp177 and 179
15. CP XII/11 p356
16. Beckett and Jones 1982 pp19-20
17. Ibid. p21
18. CP XII/11 p356
19. Ibid.
20. Leech 1880 p13
21. Morris 1982 p184
22. Waterson 1981 p41

**Chapter 15**
1. CP XX/I p223
2. Ibid.
3. Stebbing Shaw 1976 ed. p270
4. Yass 1974 p73
5. Bennett 1905 p4
6. Heeley 1777
7. Stebbing Shaw 1976 ed. p270
   see also Haynes, Sandy 1998
8. Commons History 1715-54 vol 1 p275
9. Ibid. 1754-90 vol 2 p553
10. Rylands Library EGR 3/7/1/4/27

**Chapter 16**
1. Simon 1968 p107
2. Andrews 1935 p205
3. Portland Papers PWF 4619
4. Stebbing Shaw 1976 ed p270
5. Rylands Library EGR 4/1/6/2/2
6. Andrews 1935 vol 2 pp157-58
7. Enville Hall 5th Earl of Stamford's Day
   Books for 1788 and 1789
8. Rylands Library 13th Feb. 1799
9. Bayliss 1992 p465
10. Bowman 1960 p637
11. Turberville 1927 p465
12. Valentine 1970 pp393-94
13. Commons History 1790-1820 vol 4
    (Members G-P) p11
14. Ibid. pp98-99
15. Turberville 1927 p465
16. Portland Papers PWF 4559
17. Commons History 1754-90 p322
18. Ibid. pp322-23
19. Rylands Library EGR 4/1/2/1/7
20. Ibid. EGR 4/1/2/5/26-27
21. Ibid. EGR 4/1/2/7/30
22. Cave 1982 vol IX p346 23-24 May
    1809 and ed.
23. Portland Papers PWF 4154(b)
24. Leech 1880 p11

**Chapter 17**
1. DNB: David Wemyss (1721-1787)
2. DNB: Francis Charteris (1675-1732)
3. Enville Hall G2/3/1/17
4. Ibid. G 2/2/1/22
5. Ibid. G 2/2/1/24
6. Ibid. G 2/2/1/22-24
7. Ibid. G 2/2/3/1/8
8. Peter Lee in pers.com.
9. Rylands Library EGR 4/2/11/7/2
10. Ibid. EGR 4/2/11/7/3
11. Ibid. EGR 4/2/11/7/6
12. Ibid. EGR 4/2/11/7/7
13. Ibid.
14. Ibid.

15. Ibid. EGR 4/2/11/7/11
16. Ibid. EGR 4/2/11/7/22-23
17. Walsh Diaries Oct. 1835
18. Ibid. May 1824
19. Ibid. Nov. 1833
20. Ibid. Feb. and April 1830
21. Ibid. July 1835
22. VCH Worcs. vol 2 p235
23. Rylands Library EGR 4/2/7/21.
    Also ledgers in private hands.
24. Dunham Housekeeping Book,
    Manchester Central Reference Library
25. Walsh Diaries Jan. 1838
26. Ibid. Jan. 1844
27. Ibid. April 1845

**Chapter 18**
1. Mingay 1963 p137
2. Bristed 1873 pp26-29; 58-59
3. Walsh Diaries
4. MacAndrew 1960 pp94-95
5. Ibid.
6. Walsh Diaries 31st August 1835
7. Anon 1998
8. Anon 1990 p4
9. MacAndrew 1960 p101
10. Rylands Library EGR 4/6/1/5/2 6th Oct.
    1852
11. Bamford 1991 pp9-11
12. Sale catalogue Bradgate House 1925
    see also LLRO DE 1032/8
13. Elliott 1984 p82
14. Illustrated London News 1st Aug. 1857
15. Ibid.
16. Ingham 1899 p111
17. Crane and Walton Solicitors, Leicester
18. Peter Lee in pers.com.
19. Pearson 1893 p163
20. MacAndrew 1960 pp102-03
21. Onslow 1983 p84
22. Ibid. p149
23. Warrington Guardian 13th Jan. 1883
24. Illustrated London News 21st Jan. 1882

**Chapter 19**
1. Bateman 1879 p412
2. Cannadine 1996 p10
3. CP XII/I p228
4. Familiar Magazine (see Bibliography)

**Chapter 20**
1. Anon (no date) p3
2. Ibid. p7
3. Ibid. pp14-15
4. Ibid pp27-28
5. CP XII/I p228
6. Cousens 1990 p20
7. Yass 1970 p94
8. Cousens 1990 p14

**Chapter 21**
1. Lady Jane Turnbull (née Grey) in pers.
   com.
2. Rylands Libary
3. Cannadine 1996 p89
4. Ibid. p386
5. Peter Lee in pers. com.
6. Lady Jane Turnbull in pers. com.
7. Rylands Library
8. Peter Lee in pers. com.

**Postscript**
1. Stevenson and Squires 1999

# Index